Corruption and Governance in Asia

Corruption and Governance in Asia

Edited by

John B. Kidd

and

Frank-Jürgen Richter

Individual chapters © contributors 2003

All rights reserved. No reproduction, copy or transmission of this publication may be made without written permission.

No paragraph of this publication may be reproduced, copied or transmitted save with written permission or in accordance with the provisions of the Copyright, Designs and Patents Act 1988, or under the terms of any licence permitting limited copying issued by the Copyright Licensing Agency, 90 Tottenham Court Road, London W1T 4LP.

Any person who does any unauthorised act in relation to this publication may be liable to criminal prosecution and civil claims for damages.

The authors have asserted their rights to be identified as the authors of this work in accordance with the Copyright, Designs and Patents Act 1988.

First published 2003 by
PALGRAVE MACMILLAN
Houndmills, Basingstoke, Hampshire, England RC21 6XS and
175 Fifth Avenue, New York, N.Y. 10010
Companies and representatives throughout the world

PALGRAVE MACMILLAN is the global academic imprint of the Palgrave Macmillan division of St. Martin's Press, LLC and of Palgrave Macmillan Ltd. Macmillan® is a registered trademark in the United States, United Kingdom and other countries. Palgrave is a registered trademark in the European Union and other countries.

ISBN 1–4039–0560–6 hardback

This book is printed on paper suitable for recycling and made from fully managed and sustained forest sources.

A catalogue record for this book is available from the British Library.

Library of Congress Cataloging-in-Publication Data

Corruption and governance in Asia / edited by John Kidd & Frank-Jürgen Richter.
    p. cm.
Includes bibliographical references and index.
ISBN 1–4039–0560–6
    1. Corporate governance – Asia. 2. Business enterprises – Asia – Corrupt practices. I. Kidd, John. II. Richter, Frank-Jürgen.
HD2741 .C785 2002
338.095–dc21   2002027075

10 9 8 7 6 5 4 3 2 1
12 11 10 09 08 07 06 05 04 03

Printed and bound in Great Britain by
Antony Rowe Ltd, Chippenham and Eastbourne

Contents

Preface		vii
About the Authors		viii
1	The 'Oppression' of Governance? John B. Kidd and Frank-Jürgen Richter	1
2	The Challenge to Corruption and the International Business Environment Stephen Dearden	27
3	Poor Corporate Governance, Market Discipline and Cronyism in the 1997 Asian Crisis Christopher Gan	43
4	A Two-Stage Model of Cronyism in Organizations: A Cultural View of Governance Naresh Khatri, James P. Johnson and Zafar U. Ahmed	61
5	Understanding the Mind of the Chinese: A Historical Perspective Sui Pheng Low	86
6	The Competitive Advantage with Chinese Characteristics – The Sophisticated Choreography of Gift-Giving Matti Nojonen	107
7	The Economics of Corruption and Cronyism – An Institutional Approach to the Reform of Governance Barbara Krug and Hans Hendrischke	131
8	Taming the *Sokaiya*: Can Economic and Corporate Reform Eliminate Extortion in Japan? Teri Jane Ursacki	149
9	Fighting against Corruption: The Japanese Approach to Reform Corporate Governance Maiko Miyake, Kathryn Gordon and Iwao Taka	166

10 Singapore's Anti-Corruption Strategy: Is this Form
    of Governance Transferable to Other Asian Countries?   180
    Jon S. T. Quah

11 A Human Resource Development Program to Foster
    Individual Moral Development in Indian Corporations:
    Aligning Corporate Governance with Natural Law   198
    Dennis Heaton, Thomas Carlisle and Ian Brown

12 Corruption in Asia – A Bottom-up Approach to
    its Resolution   210
    Paul Robins

13 Doing the Right Thing – Incorporating the Ethical
    Imperative into the Sustainable Development Process   225
    Hock-Beng Cheah and Melanie Cheah

Index   251

Preface

Corruption and Governance in Asia provides a stark reminder of what unaccountable and irresponsible business behaviour, often bordering on the criminal, could do to the supposedly unassailable dragon and tiger economies. If Asia is to profit from the lessons of the crisis that effectively wiped many of our countries off the economic radar screen, we must embrace the fact that the unbridled excesses that underpinned our bubble economies were really no substitute for good corporate governance.

One of the most pressing contemporary issues facing management in much of Asia is business ethics, or not to put too fine a point on it, corruption in business transactions which puts an unnecessary burden and cost on investors. It is a subject that is receiving a great deal of international attention because of heightened awareness that bad governance contributes directly to corruption.

John B. Kidd and Frank-Jürgen Richter deserve our admiration and gratitude for putting together a highly relevant and readable volume. It sends a clear message, a wake-up call, to those with business involvement in Asia that no change or improvement in the way they manage their business operations is possible if their attitude to good governance is out of kilter with contemporary global trends.

It is important for us to remember that where good governance is firmly in place, there will be less of a problem with corruption. Also worth noting is the fact that good governance is not incompatible with a healthy balance sheet. Business whether in Asia or elsewhere is not just about making sound investment decisions, taking and managing risks, and coping with economic uncertainties. Today, it is also about social responsibility, putting all our actions under public scrutiny and responding to the concerns of those among whom we conduct business. Clearly, Asia has to reinvent itself if it is to avoid another devastation which bad governance is guaranteed to trigger.

In conclusion, let me just say that good governance is no longer the luxury of the ethically correct businessmen and women; it has indeed become a global business necessity in the fight against corruption.

TUNKU ABDUL AZIZ
Vice-Chairman,
Transparency International
Berlin

About the Authors

Zafar U. Ahmed is a Full Professor of Marketing and International Business at the Texas A&M University – Commerce, Texas, USA. He has over 10-year industry experience earned across Africa, and 15 years of academic experience to his credit accumulated at the State University of New York at Fredonia; Minot State University, North Dakota; Nanyang Technological University, Singapore; Sacred Heart University, Connecticut; Fort Hays State University, Kansas and Texas A&M University – Commerce, Texas. He has been an advisor and consultant to numerous governmental organizations across Africa and Asia. He has more than 100 scholarly publications to his credit, serves as the Editor-in-Chief of the *Journal of International Business and Entrepreneurship*, and is listed in the 'Harvard Directory of International Business and Management Academics and Researchers'.

Ian Brown is Professor of Vedic Management at Maharishi Institute of Management in Chennai, India, and a consultant with the Maharishi Corporate Development Programme in Chennai. He is a frequent contributor to management seminars and periodicals in India.

Thomas Carlisle has 19 years experience consulting to corporations on the implementation and evaluation of stress management programmes for human resource and organizational development. He has served as U.S. Regional Director, National Research Coordinator, and International Director in India and in Indonesia for the Maharishi Corporate Development Programme. He has researched and conducted courses for MCDP in large US firms such as General Motors and Entergy, and such Indian firms as Bhoruka Power and HMT. In addition to his doctorate in administration, he holds a PhD in psychology and has taught both management and developmental psychology courses at university level. He is the author of two books and is currently writing a third under the working title of *Management Beyond Ego*.

He is presently residing in Chennai, India, where he is Director of the Maharishi University of Management distance education MBA programme covering five sites in India.

Hock-Beng Cheah researches and teaches at the School of Economics and Management, University College, University of New South Wales.

In Economics, his research interests are focused on sustainable development and political economy in the Asia-Pacific region. In the Management field, his teaching and research interests include Human Resource Management, Organizational Development, and Entrepreneurship. He was a visiting Research Fellow at the Snider Entrepreneurial Center, University of Pennsylvania, where he proposed a new perspective of the entrepreneurial process. He has also undertaken research at the Entrepreneurship Development Centre, Nanyang Technological University, Singapore; Economics Research Center at Nagoya University, Japan; and the Institute of Southeast Asian Studies, Singapore.

His work has been published in a variety of monographs and journals including: *Creativity and Innovation Management, Journal of Business Venturing, Journal of Enterprising Culture, Manchester Papers on Development*, and *Labour & Industry*.

Melanie Cheah (Xie Yu Lin) is presently undertaking studies at the Foreign Affairs College, Beijing, China. She was a corporate lawyer at Allen, Allen and Hemsley in Sydney. She received a Japanese Government Monbusho scholarship to undertake studies at the Graduate Institute of Policy Studies in Tokyo, Japan, from which she has recently been awarded a Master of Public Policy. She previously worked as an intern at the Capacity Building Unit (Africa Region) at the World Bank, Washington DC.

She has a keen interest in management, entrepreneurship and development issues, with a particular focus on sustainable development. She is a Director in Development Options, a new entrepreneurial venture that is seeking to promote sustainable solutions for communities in developing countries in Asia.

Stephen Dearden is a Lecturer in Economics at Manchester Metropolitan University. He is Convenor of the Development Studies Associations' European Development Policy Study Group and has published a number of articles in the area. He is Joint Editor of European Economic Integration (Longman) and editor of a forthcoming book which examines the European Unions' economic relations with the Commonwealth Caribbean.

Christopher Gan is a senior lecturer in Lincoln University, New Zealand. He teaches financial markets, institutions and policy, advanced microeconomic, international finance, postgraduate commercial banking, applied research methods and international finance to graduate students. He is also a consultant with the Mekong Institute in Thailand conducting economics and financial training courses for middle level management from the Greater Mekong Sub Region Countries. He obtained a PhD in Agriculture Economics from Louisiana State University and an MS in International Economics from the Indiana State University, before moving to New Zealand.

Christopher has published in several areas including resource and environmental economics, non-market valuation techniques, international trade, eco-tourism and Asian financial crisis. His research interests include resource and environmental economics, development economics, applied microeconomic, international trade and financial issues in Asia.

Dennis Heaton is Chair of the Department of Management and Public Affairs at Maharishi University of Management, Fairfield, Iowa, USA. He has a doctorate degree in Educational Leadership from Boston University. His teaching activities include delivering MBA courses by distance education at five locations in India, in conjunction with the Maharishi Institutes of Management in Bangalore, Chennai, Hyderabad, Lucknow, and New Delhi. He has authored presentations and publications concerning Maharishi Vedic Management in the Academy of Management, the Organizational Behavior Teaching Society, the *Business Research Yearbook*, and *Chinmaya Management Review*.

He is co-author of the chapter 'Awakening creative intelligence for peak performance: Reviving an Asian tradition', in J. Kidd, Xue Li, and F.-J. Richter (eds.), *Human Intelligence Deployment in Asian business: The Sixth Generation project*. London and New York: Palgrave (2001).

Hans Hendrischke As an associate professor he is Head of the Department of Chinese and Indonesian Studies, and also Director of the UNSW-UTS Center for Research on Provincial China at the University of New South Wales in Sydney. He publishes on economic and political reforms in China and has co-edited *The Political Economy of China's Provinces: Comparative and Competitive Advantage*, Routledge, 1999. He is presently involved in a joint project on 'Entrepreneurship and the emergence of the private business sector in China'.

Kathryn Gordon works on investment issues at the Organization for Economic Co-operation and Development (OECD). Her most recent responsibilities include research relating to the fight against corruption and, more generally, the management by international companies of compliance with law and regulation and unwritten societal expectations on business conduct. She also participated in negotiations that resulted in the revised OECD Guidelines for Multinational Enterprises (non-binding recommendations by governments to multinational enterprises covering nine areas of business conduct). In earlier positions at the OECD, she co-ordinated the microeconomic content of the OECD surveys of member economies. This covers a wide range of fields including taxation, human capital, competition policy and financial markets.

Prior to moving to the OECD, Kathryn was a professor at a French business school (the Ecole Superieure des Sciences Economiques et Commerciales). Although she is a citizen of the United States, Kathryn has been a resident of France for nearly twenty years. She obtained a PhD and an MBA in Finance from the University of California, Berkeley before moving to France.

James P. Johnson is Associate Professor of International Business at the Crummer Graduate School of Business, Rollins College, Winter Park, Florida. His research interests include managing international joint ventures, strategic decision-making processes in multinational corporations, and strategic change in companies in emerging economies; he has published in *Management International Review*, *Journal of Business Research*, *International Marketing Review*, and the *Journal of World Business*. A member of the Academy of Management, the Academy of International Business, and the Ibero-American Academy of Management, he has previously lived and worked in Britain, Spain, Finland, Yugoslavia, and Mexico.

Naresh Khatri is Assistant Professor of Strategic Human Resource Management and Transformational Leadership in the Department of Health Management and Informatics, School of Medicine, University of Missouri at Columbia. He holds a PhD degree from the State University of New York, Buffalo and an MBA from the Indian Institute of Management, Ahmedabad.

Dr Khatri's research and teaching interests focus on understanding behavioural issues at the organizational apex. Specifically, in view of the critical role of people in the success of modern organizations, Dr Khatri is interested in examining the proactive role of managing people dimension in achieving competitive advantage. Further, only a few organizations fully understand the impact of behavioural issues on organizational performance; most focus on financial outcomes alone to find to their dismay constant erosion in their competitiveness as a consequence. Dr Khatri advocates ways that unleash the potential of people in organizations. He has published numerous articles on the above issues in refereed journals, such as *Academy of Management Best Papers Proceedings*, *Human Relations*, *Human Resource Management Journal*, *International Journal of Human Resource Management*, *Asia Pacific Journal of Management*,

Decision, International Journal of Cross Cultural Management, Personnel Review, and *International Journal of Manpower,* among others. Currently, he is working on a book project entitled 'Critical Issues in Managing Human Capital'.

John B. Kidd was educated in the UK and worked for several major UK organizations before returning to University scholarship. In the Universities of Birmingham and now Aston Business School his research focused on the development of IT use in SMEs; the management of projects; and the softer management issues that concern multi-national joint ventures. He has held visiting professorships in several European Universities, and in the China Europe International Business School, Shanghai.

His recent books on Asian matters, co-edited with Li Xue and Frank-Jürgen Richter, are *Maximising Human Intelligence Deployment In Asia: The 6th Generation Project* and also *Advances in Human Resource Management in Asia,* London & New York: Palgrave (both 2001).

Barbara Krug received her PhD in Economics from the University of Saarland, Saarbruecken; to be followed by the Habilitation Doctorate in Economics (venia legendi in economics), University of Saarland, Saarbruecken, Germany. She was Guest Professor Economics Faculty, National Taiwan University, Taipei, Taiwan, 1983–84; Visiting Fellow, St. Antony's College, Oxford University, 1988–89; Guest Lecturer, Economics Faculty, Justus-Liebig Universitaet Giessen, 1990–91; Visiting Member, School of Social Science, Institute For Advanced Study, Princeton, 1993–94; ETH Zuerich, Switzerland 1995–96, and is presently Head of Department Organisation Theory and Human Resource Management, Rotterdam School of Management where she holds a chair for Economics of Governance.

Her publications include *Chinas Weg zur Marktwirtschaft*; *Blood, sweat or cheating: politics and the transformation of socialist economies in China, the USSR and Eastern Europe',* Studies in Comparative Communism; *On custom in economics: the case of humanism and trade regimes',* Journal of Institutional and Theoretical Economics.

She is presently working on 'Entrepreneurship and the Emergence of a Private Business Sector in China' in collaboration with Hans Hendrischke, University of New South Wales, and Yao Xianguo, Zhejiang University, Hangzhou.

Sui Pheng Low is Associate Professor and Vice-Dean (Research) at the School of Design and Environment, National University of Singapore.

A Fellow of the Chartered Institute of Building, he holds a BSc (Building) (Hons) degree from the National University of Singapore and an MSc (Eng) degree from the University of Birmingham. He also holds a PhD from the University of London specializing in international construction marketing.

He has a special interest in how cross-cultural behaviour can influence international project management, especially in the context of China. Dr Low has conducted extensive studies on how international cultural differences can affect quality management systems in the construction industry. He is acknowledged internationally as an authority on the study of ancient Chinese philosophies and strategies for modern day business. His latest book *Asian Wisdom for Effective Management* was published in June 2001 by Pelanduk Publishers, a publishing house based in Kuala Lumpur, Malaysia which specializes in Chinese and Asian titles.

Maiko Miyake is a research officer at Multilateral Investment Guarantee Agency (MIGA), World Bank Group where she researches on foreign direct investment, investment insurance, risk management and various economic developments. Previously, she held a position of project officer in the International Finance Corporation (IFC), World Bank Group providing advisory services for companies on human resources management strategies and corporate governance. Prior to joining the World Bank Group, she worked at the Organization for Economic Co-operation and Development (OECD), where she dealt with a wide range of subjects related to investment and multinational enterprises, such as Mergers & Acquisitions (M&As), financial crisis, development, corruption and corporate social responsibility.

Maiko, a Japanese national, has studied and/or worked in Japan, USA, Argentina, UK, Switzerland, Brazil, Mexico, France, Guatemala and Nigeria. She has a PhD in International Business from the University of Bradford and an MA in Development Studies from the University of East Anglia.

Matti Nojonen is a Sinologist and a graduate of the Department of East Asian Studies at the Stockholm University. At the moment he is a Research Fellow in the Department of Management at the Helsinki School of Economics and Business Administration, Finland.

Currently, he is finalizing his PhD thesis on '*Guanxi* in three different Chinese cities; Beijing, Shanghai and Qingdao'. In developing his thesis Nojonen conducted ethnographic fieldwork over a two-year period (1996–98) in these cities. Nojonen also has a more general research interest in contemporary social and economic issues in China, medieval Chinese economic history and thought, and Chinese idea history.

Jon S.T. Quah is Professor of Political Science at the National University of Singapore (NUS), Co-editor of the *Asian Journal of Political Science*, and is a member of Transparency International's Governance Research Council. He has published widely on corruption, civil service reform, and public personnel management in Asian countries. His publications include nine books and monographs, and 136 journal articles, book chapters, and conference papers. As the lead consultant for the United Nations Development Programme's Mission to Mongolia from September to November 1998, he formulated the National Anti-Corruption Plan for the Government of Mongolia. He completed an evaluation of the personnel management of Macau's Civil Service from September 2000 to May 2001 at the invitation of the Government of Macau SAR. He teaches a module on Corruption and Governance in Asian Countries at NUS and frequently participates in workshops on corruption issues organized by the ADB, OECD, UNDP, and the World Bank.

Paul Robins is a lecturer in the Aston Business School at Aston University. He graduated as a Botanist, specializing in ecology, at Imperial College, London University and spent many years as a research scientist investigating a variety of broadly environmental topics, including the water use of forest trees, the micrometeorology of dry prairie grasslands and the use of technical information to support decision making of local and national governments.

His serious concern for ethical issues arose while investigating possible mechanisms for making technical information available to support essentially political decision-making. He has continued to be concerned with all aspects of the process of creating and presenting advice in a variety of contexts. This concern caused him to support the study of Buddhist ethics, which has provided the foundation for his contribution.

Frank-Jürgen Richter is the Director-in-charge of Asia at the World Economic Forum, Geneva. He was educated in Germany, France, Mexico and Japan. At one time he was based in Beijing for several years where he managed the operations of a European multi-national enterprise: there he developed naturally a keen interest in Asian business practices. As a scholar–practitioner, he has written several books about Asian business, international management and global competition. His most recent books include *The East Asian Development Model* (Macmillan, 2000).

Iwao Taka teaches business ethics at Reitaku University in Japan. From 1991 through 1994, he studied at the Wharton School as a Fisher-Smith visiting scholar, and later he joined the Project for Global Business Ethics Principles initiated by the Conference Board. In 1999 he organized the ECS2000 project to issue 'the Ethics Compliance Management System Standard 2000'. In early 2001, he launched a new initiative, so as to make and release R-BEC001, an ethics-compliance oriented SRI framework.

Now, he is a member of the National Council for Consumer Policy of the Japanese Government, an executive committee member of ISBEE, and senior director of the Business Ethics and Compliance Research Center at Reitaku. He has given lectures and advice upon business ethics to a number of institutions, such as the Cabinet Office, Keidanren, Japan's Banking Association, Japan's Securities Exchange Association, and Japan's Corporate Auditors Association.

His recent interests are anti-corruption, SRI, CSR, and pension fund reform. His publications includes *The ECS2000: A New Business Ethics Standard* (with Scott Davis, 2000), *Contextualism in Business and Ethical Issues in Japan* (1998), and *Business Ethics: A Japanese View* (1998).

Teri Jane Ursacki has interests in Japan dating back to 1980, when she began studying Japanese. After receiving her MBA and completing a work exchange programme in Japan, she was employed in trade finance studies by a major Canadian bank for several years. She received her PhD in international business from the University of British Columbia in 1991. She is currently an associate professor at the University of Calgary in Alberta, Canada, where she teaches international business and courses on 'doing business' with Japan.

She has written extensively on a variety of aspects of Japanese business, including foreign banking operations, international trade, executive succession practices, ethical issues, diversity, and women in management.

1
The 'Oppression' of Governance?
John B. Kidd and Frank-Jürgen Richter

Introduction

This book is focused upon the governance of firms in Asia. It is a concept that must be extended to include all forms of 'venturing' since co-joining firms seem to create conflicts between 'us and them' even if operating in one's home nation, and more so if co-joining with a firm from abroad. However, we must say that we use the term 'governance' in this book to reflect those values developed 'at home' by governments that will be cascaded to their indigenous firms and institutions. We do not take a limiting view of 'governance' being entirely a function of corporations – though the interface between the public who lose much through poor 'corporate' governance has focused attention more on this aspect in recent months. We note various drivers over recent years, such as 'globalization' that has been a theme on the tongues of many managers. This is emphasized by the World Trade Organization (WTO) which stresses the transition from a national to a global economy in many Asian countries, most notably in China. Thus, it is prudent and timely to consider the nature of 'governance' – and its good and bad aspects – to aid our understanding of what may constitute 'better' joint governance in multinational firms.

We have inclined to use the word 'oppression' in the title of this chapter since there is often a feeling within the middle and lower manager levels that their bosses, to a great extent, exploit their abilities. Of course, without these good middle and lower level staff there would be problems: the quality of output would be poor, and thus the firm would soon lose its foothold in its marketplace. Who in this age wishes to buy shoddy goods, even if they come cheap? So the senior staff must somehow inculcate quality consciousness and the drive to produce goods to meet time and quality specifications. In this instance, we understand it is not just 'working according to the letter of the Standard' but being thoughtful about one's individual work and how that meshes with the work of others. In other words, the senior managers must support learning societies who think about their own task, wherein its members must talk with others to exchange ideas and mental models. In many western societies where there is much stress on the 'me', 'I' and individualism, the Senior's instructions to share knowledge with ones peers is often met with derision. But even in these firms, friends will share their tips and hints upon better ways of working – since they jointly wish to have an easier working life – and we trust our friends not to pass this new knowledge to those we don't like. Further, our Senior managers trust us implicitly not to pass this knowledge to our competitors – who may thus gain, and acquire our business.

It is imperative that we concern ourselves more about the role of Intellectual Capital in the firm. In these modern times of exchangeable material goods ('when it is broken, swap in a new unit') we see a tendency in building a new system to use a set of 'black boxes' ('don't design from the basics'). Thus, the advantage of a firm usually lies in its Intellectual Capital (its knowledge of how to build with 'black boxes') that is seen as complementary to the needs of an acquiring firm. At the heart of any analysis of competitive advantage lies the concept of knowledge imitability (Spender and Grant, 1996). Thus, the two firms forming an alliance (as discussed in more detail below) will need to exchange their unique organizational learning (OL) and have to engage quickly in inter-organization knowledge management (KM) initiatives. The promotion of these concepts will depend heavily on the human resources management in each firm so as to persuade all their respective staff to work for the (new) common good. This is not easy since it is often the case that following a major merger, there are many redundancies: so the staff work in a fundamental state of fright until the dust settles, waiting anxiously to find if they are still employable. We suggest the perceptions of 'us and them' lower down the organizational hierarchy will also determine the quality of OL (Kidd and Edwards, 2000) as the 'blue collar' workers grapple with their perception of the 'truths' being discussed by their leaders. This may be strongly felt by the lower staff when these individuals look across national boundaries, and wonder why their firm is being led into new forms of 'governance', and why therefore their CEOs are 'oppressing' them yet again.

In this short introduction, we have already raised many issues that seem insoluble. These encompass, most visibly, the creation of trust linked to the exchange of knowledge at both a task level as well at the macroeconomics level relating to the firm's place in the value and product chain. There are questions about maintaining standards – both for quality assurance as well as having set rules for performing tasks in the firm itself – such as maintaining audit trails, being transparent with respect to accounting, and so on. There is also the broad issue of organizational capacity – the ability to learn. This may be more apparent in a large organization where they have specialist staff (able to keep up with new technology) and maybe some 'spare' staff able to undertake research into new forms of governance enabled perhaps by new technology. However, the vast majority of firms in all countries are small and medium sized firms (SMEs) having below 250 employees, and often as few as four or even less staff. It is the SMEs who often operate as feeder firms in the product chain and in these we see little absorptive capacity: that is, an ability to investigate and absorb innovation (Cohen and Leventhal, 1990).

In the UK, in 2000, there were 99 per cent of firms defined as 'small', but they created 38 per cent of the nation's turnover (DTI Statistical News Release – P/2000/561 – 7 August 2000). There are probably grave problems in these firms, where, in the worst case, they may be grappling with legacy hardware, legacy software and legacy mental-ware (the knowledge base of the managers) and so are not able to integrate in digitally mediated commerce (COST, 1998; Chaston *et al.*, 1999; Hally and Guilhon, 1997). There is nothing in our view to suggest this is not the case throughout the world. Note for instance Ghani reporting on a meeting of the Malaysian Association of SMEs – he says that the nation's adoption of information and communications technology (ICT) is very low (Ghani, 2000).

Inevitably, the quality of the 'leadership' in firms is an important driver: it is these chief executives (CEOs) who help shape the 'culture' of their firm, as well as manage the perceptions held by their staff of 'us and them' in their alliances. There are clear differences in the ways in which UK and Japanese firms, and the managers therein, manage their day-to-day business (Kidd and Kanda, 2000). In parallel, the GLOBE studies are revealing very interesting differences between leaders in the 61 different countries that have been studied (the studies are based on a common analytic model: see their host Web site http://mgmt3.ucalgary.ca/web/globe.nsf/index; and Kennedy and Mansor, 2000). It is not implausible to suggest that the management team of a firm, which is approached to join an alliance, is likely to be drawn from the local population, while the acquiring firm's managers may have an international composition. This will result in divergent leadership perceptions. Once more it is the 'us and them' that will have very important consequences for KM and OL in the alliance.

The 'corporate' aspect of governance

Rather often 'governance' is taken to mean some formal approach to 'financial rules, accountancy, and transparency'. Of course this is in many ways correct. There are firms that have operated with impropriety (even under their local rules) that is associated often with embezzlement in some form or another sometimes aided by auditors who have bent the rules to allow the firms to practice money laundering, or tax evasion. When caught, those at fault have been judged against local laws – and often through the use of adept lawyers allowed to roam free. To counteract this tendency, at least in the US, President George W. Bush is 'sabre rattling' promising to double the gaol sentence of those found guilty of corporate malfeasance. Here, we see an instance of the 'sense of governance' we wish to support through this book: with governments leading the way, teaching, as it were, their institutions and organizations how their members should behave. Latterly, some forms of digitally mediated electronic-commerce conducted over the Internet have evaded local laws, and as a consequence much international research has been undertaken to review the limits of jurisdiction of local laws in these nebulous cases; and conversely, the limits to which supra-national laws may be applied locally. Naturally, there is some confusion within the European Union in these cases, as disintermediation may or may not apply when considering the 'ruling of the European Parliament' vs. local (European) governments.

If this is the case in the almost homogenous EU what might we expect when considering the case for a multi-national operation? Consider for instance allowable overheads – how can they be described as 'allowable allocations' against the tax of the 'business overheads' given that they may also be described as bribes? At least this was so prior to the country becoming a signatory to the international convention on Bribery and Corruption (OECD, 2000). Thus, to some extent in parallel with the OECD discussions, we find that corruption, related to financial impropriety, has been a driver for the deeper study of corporate governance.

Asians deploy opaque accounting practices, they keep the data 'in the family', and they also practice 'gift giving' (within their system of *guanxi*, which is discussed later) on a scale that seems to an American nothing short of bribery. To combat this effect, the firms in the US, and elsewhere in the West, press their Eastern firms (many of whom may already be venture partners) to conform to GAAP (Generally Acceptable Accounting Principles) although this methodology is not the only contender for a global standard (see the International Accounting Standards Committee, IASC). This is quite a vexing issue and it concerns ministers in the G7 and G8 committees as they attempt to provide a balanced view on accounting standards – their baseline viewpoint is the Basel Committee Review (see http://www.bis.org/publ/bcbs70.htm). Therefore, we must consider the meaning of '…generally acceptable' since it has been shown that accounting disclosure, at least historically, is strongly correlated with cultural measures (Gray, 1996; Salter and Niswander, 1995; Zarzeski, 1996). These authors state generally that the Oriental cultures are biased towards secrecy and thus non-transparency. Yet, it seems quite reasonable to elaborate international inter-company reports so higher managers may judge and decide on macro- as well as micro-policy changes. It has been found however that the accounting methods of Asian firms were not compatible with those created in their European or US branches – or, at least, they were too divergent to illuminate the global decision-making process. For instance, it was a surprise to UK managers to find that their Japanese senior managers in a UK joint venture, especially in a wholly owned subsidiary, derived their profit figure as a given – '…let's say 7% this year'! A local senior Japanese manager may have quoted this figure, whereas the professional expectation in the UK is that the profit is the final figure derived from a set of (transparent) calculations (Kidd and Teramoto, 1995).

Ultimately, one may question if different regularity practices and more open markets in these regions will force firms to be more transparent (in a GAAP sense). But perhaps it will just evince token gestures in the short term given that many Asian countries have been unable for years to disentangle their opaque systems from those resting on bribery and extortion. If that is so, we must attempt to create a broader system of trust to help develop co-operative transparency rather than press unwilling partners into 'compliance' through oppressive governance systems.

Trust between individuals

The initiation and maintenance of trust between individuals is fundamental to our very existence, not just to knowledge management that is the keystone in the process of innovation upon which all companies survive. However, it is a complex process, fraught with the possibility of error. We have only five senses (seeing, touching, smelling, hearing and tasting): we use them to create models of our environment. We use these models, sometimes unconsciously, to make predictions and to 'sense' our future. If that model yields good results we are happy, but if the results are in conflict with our belief we may be more or less disturbed and have recourse to rebuilding our models. Festinger and Carlsmith (1959) gave us the concept of 'cognitive dissonance' to explain our unease at finding our mental predictions at odds with our sensual perception – either because our model is wrong, or because we have a poor perception of reality – as in a distorting 'hall of mirrors'. The sensing of an 'error' can lead us to trust better – either in our own abilities to model the environment that is unique to ourselves, but more especially when in a shared space. Thus, we come to understand another person (and his or her environment) as they interact with us.

Naturally, there are many variations on this theme, and we must accept we are multidimensional, even when focused on one issue. Note that our children often say, at length, 'I did not do it, I was not there!' yet we find our feeling of trust in them still strong: we love our kids, despite their words. It should be emphasized that 'trust' is not an immutable construct: it is derived from snapshots of the situation at a particular point in time. 'Trust' can and will change over the lifetime of an alliance, especially in the early relationship-building stages.

The important role of HRM

In Figure 1.1 we illustrate that the CEOs will have had many talks with the target firm upon the raison d'être of the alliance: we can say this might take place in any pair-wise link in the supply chain. Furthermore, the aides of the CEOs will have performed due diligence. In the case where the alliance interface is between similar firms there can be many discussions on the relative merits of meaningful aspects of their work: herein the workers can quickly benefit. If the interface is between different sectors – such as a manufacturer and a logistics provider – then organizational learning has some difficulty in commencing (Ring and Van de Ven, 1994). Further, in the case of alliances between firms having different national origins we find the cognitive modeling processes of the individuals who ought to have conversations (in order to co-develop their organizational learning) are often alien to each other (Linstone and Zhu, 2000).

Often, the more active CEOs (in the KM sense) are the ones who also enter alliances, but they forget that their lower staff have not had access to the high-level inter-firm conversations which have led to the strategic alliance: these lower staff remain ignorant and fearful. Within

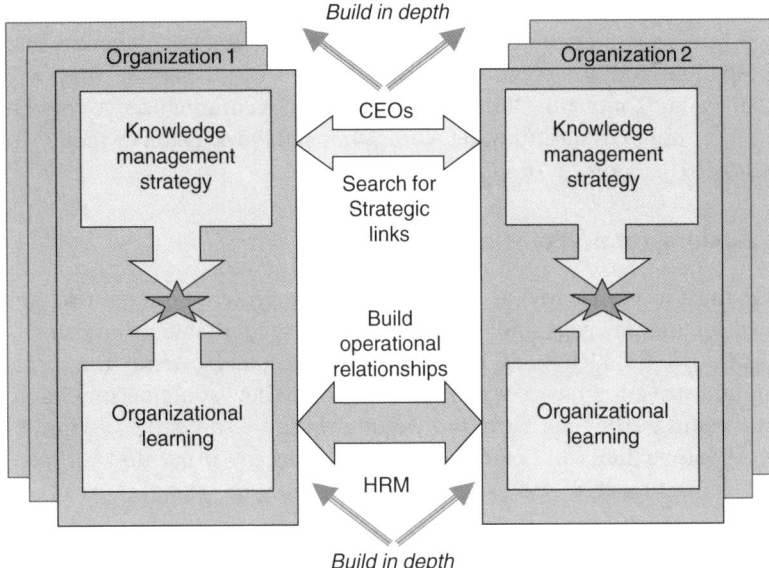

Figure 1.1 Role-play by the CEO and the HRM functions

quickly negotiated alliances (such as those supporting e-commerce) a deep understanding of joint business needs is not necessarily presented to the lower level staff. They may not have been given much information about the need for the alliance, nor will they have been told of how it may affect them. Since it is these people, once called 'blue collar workers', who are responsible for the outputs from the manufacturing process in their respective organizations, their 'happiness' is a vital ingredient in the continuance of firms. They engage in their own initiatives in OL – but these may be in conflict with mandates of senior managers who look to the maintenance of standard procedures, since under standardization the codification of data becomes relatively easy (Huber, 1991). We consider 'manufacturing' to include the service industries – as all complex processes contain considerable knowledge, there is the need to share this knowledge in an alliance.

It is vital in a learning organization that individuals volunteer their information although Huber has recently suggested that individuals have become unwilling to this – for several reasons, not least being their fear of being 'sucked dry of information' and made redundant. Thus, information elicitation may be described as a 'sticky process' (Huber, 2000); Szulanski (1996) also suggests this in a different context; and

Fruin (1997) repeatedly stressed 'stickiness' with respect to the Toyota workers' exchange of 'knowledge' in Japan. We suggest therefore that individuals cannot be conscripts in this process; otherwise they will deliver data for codification that is wrong or not comprehensive enough to be of use to others. In other words, they retain the detail of their own knowledge as a form of job protection.

Searching for a 'win–win'

We must recognize that an alliance is an arrangement between two parties for mutual gain and that these are not charitable arrangements (Burton, 1995; Richter, 2000). In these circumstances, we say that firms should strive for a 'win–win' situation where they would become more successful in the long term, but we find there are sometimes asymmetrical gains where one party essentially 'milks the other dry' (Inkpen, 1996; Khanna *et al.*, 1998).

The dynamics of learning in alliances

Larson *et al.* have proposed a model of the dynamic framework for learning in strategic alliances (Larsson *et al.*, 1998). They offer five categories or modes that a firm may use to develop knowledge jointly noting the dynamics (of learning) which may take place when two firms come together, ostensibly to collaborate and thus to learn strategically.

An alliance within one's culture

We note that the best situation is when both firms decide to collaborate (Simonin, 1997) as illustrated in Figure 1.2 when both firms decide to collaborate (the cell in the top right-hand corner). In this mode there is a strong transfer of knowledge reciprocally from A to B and from B to A; in addition, there is the potential for strong new knowledge creation available jointly to both firms. The next-best modes are when one firm wishes to collaborate while the other accepts to compromise its aims (for the joint good). There are, in fact, three such cases in the matrix (when one admits the compromise – compromise intersection) wherein there is a one-way transfer of knowledge from A to B or vice versa, and some generation of new knowledge, but this is weaker than when firms fully collaborate. In these latter cases, there is also an asymmetric knowledge exchange when A or B gains at the expense of the other. Finally, there is one modal form where no learning appears to take place: when both firms attempt to accommodate the other. Simonin points out that there are many alliance failures – herein there may be collaborative experience,

		Learning strategy of Firm A				
		Avoidance	Accommodation	Compromise	Competition	Collaboration
Learning strategy of Firm B	Collaboration		B > A +c > a	a > b, b > a +c > a, b	A > B +c > b	A > B B > A +C > A, B
	Competition		B > A +c > a	b > a	Co-opetition	B > A +c > a
	Compromise		b > a	a > b, b > a +c > a, b	a > b	a > b, b > a +c > a, b
	Accommodation			a > b	A > B +c > b	A > B +c > b
	Avoidance					

Figure 1.2 Learning strategies in alliances having similar cultures

Notes: Capitalization (e.g. B > A) represents strong knowledge transfer, so b > a indicates less strong transfer; +C > A, B indicates that much new knowledge is being developed, and transferred to both A and to B, and +c > a indicates a weaker transfer, and only to 'a', not 'b'; and finally ←→ maps the asymmetric learning relationships.

Source: Based on Larson *et al.* (1998).

but this is less frequent by an exchange of collaborative know-how (Simonin, 1997). We might posit that too often the firms rush into an agreement, fall into the trap of asymmetric learning and quickly become acrimonious, and so dissolve their alliance.

There is one further mode that is of considerable interest: this is when the firms are normally in competition with each other. In the past they would not have even acknowledged the existence of the other – being competitors. Now, under the new market conditions that extol the benefits of partial co-operation, we enter the mode called 'co-opetition'. By definition there can be no new knowledge development in this mode, but by the CEOs directing the players to co-operate to a limited extent – perhaps to jointly cross-market a limited product range – we will achieve some limited learning. More perhaps than when players jointly compromise, but less than when they voluntarily co-operate in an alliance crossing cultural boundaries.

Often firms create cross-border alliances with a global reach – we illustrate this in Figure 1.3 where we may posit that sometimes, too often in fact, the partners overlook the fact they will operate with 'others not like themselves' and so deny the possibility of jointly collaborating because of mutual confusion. In this case, we might find their learning strategies become much more restricted and indeed may become pathological if the firms jointly deny that any collaboration can take place between them due to lack of 'cultural literacy' (Merry, 2001).

Figure 1.3 has been developed from the concepts expressed above by Larsson *et al.* (1999). It may be seen that the option set has been shifted down and inwards because the individuals are now unwilling to collaborate. The CEOs of the firms in the alliance may have had good exploratory meetings, and the due diligence process been enacted correctly, but the realization of the value of the merger has, in this case, not filtered down to the operatives who make the goods. The option set becomes more restricted given the joint avoidance options shown in Figure 1.2 are ruled out. However, there is still the possibility of developing a co-opetition strategy although under these circumstances, with

		\multicolumn{5}{c}{Learning strategy of Firm A}
		Avoidance	Accommodation	Compromise	Competition	Collaboration
Learning strategy of Firm B	Collaboration					Shift due to cultural incompatibility
	Competition		$B > A$ $+c > a$	$b > a$	Co-opetition	
	Compromise		$b > a$	$b > a$ $a > b$ $+c > a, b$	$a > b$	
	Accommodation		Anomie	$a > b$	$A > B$ $+c > b$	
	Avoidance					

Figure 1.3 Restricted learning under conditions of cultural illiteracy

much suspicion at the level of the operatives, there will be considerable opposition to 'telling the enemy what we know' as 'they will steal it'. The target mode should be a joint compromise strategy as this is likely to yield the best results with both sides benefiting from knowledge exchange, and with new knowledge being generated for both A and B. However, the results here will be at a lower efficacy than those that may have been achieved if the firms had collaborated fully (see Figure 1.2).

Under the assumption of 'non-collaboration' due to mutual misunderstanding and the lack of cultural literacy, the strategic learning modes become quite limited (only 3 modes), when compared with the earlier assumptions of an alliance between firms from the same culture (when there are 10 modes in which some new knowledge is created).

We may posit further that when there is a lack of compatibility the two firms may behave pathologically: instead of attempting to engage in co-opetition they sink into anomie, a state in which their behavior becomes increasingly uncertain. We suggest here that anomie is totally undesirable in a joint alliance (in any situation in fact), but it is easy to slip into when there is considerable cultural illiteracy. This mode will be somewhat worse than the joint 'avoidance' modes since individuals in Firms A and B will actively be angry and upset at the other firm's members. They will be so angry that they will forget to discharge their own core activities. Under the 'avoidance' modes the operatives of both firms will at least follow their own tasks competently, though not jointly across the alliance. If the firm has been operating in an anomic state, its employees should attempt to move to the shared knowledge state. They may note that the co-opetition mode might be less fruitful than grasping for asymmetric learning (in the short term) while they learn how to fully collaborate and achieve a 'win-win' situation. Powell *et al.* (1996: 119–20) have stressed:

> The development of co-operative routines goes beyond simply learning how to maintain a large number of ties. Firms must learn how to transfer knowledge across alliances and locate themselves on those network positions that enable them to keep pace with the most promising scientific and technical developments

Learning in alliances – searching for a future

Dunning (1993) defined that Foreign Direct Investment (FDI) will proceed when three conditions are perceived to be favorable to the incoming firm – the ownership advantage, the location advantage and the international advantage. Yet, these models are viewed from the outsider's perspective (often as a western firm looking to enter Asia – but not exclusively – as they may be attributed to any cross-border venture). With respect to China, Hill (2000) has discussed the location aspect with its abundant labor force, often well skilled, and certainly willing to be employed. From a local perspective Zhao and Zhu (2000) note an accelerator effect. When there is a perception of good export performance from a city or region this knowledge attracts greater FDI to that location. However, not all the Chinese ventures are 'rosy' – there are detractions due to (a) partner-related problems, and to (b) operational-related issues (Wong *et al.*, 1999; Ye and Valentine, 2000) (as we noted above, in Figures 1.2 and 1.3).

(a) With respect to *Partner* problems it is said that the Chinese have too strong a political agenda that negatively impacts on the venture, thereby reducing reciprocity. This would tend to support our observation that anomie might be one outcome in these particular firm's relationships, especially if the Chinese work strongly within their *guanxi* networks and exclude the outsider. This has been a worrisome point in ventures developed from a base in Hong Kong. We are warned against becoming involved in any relationship predicated on Chinese cultural values, such as *guanxi*, as we, the westerners, do not understand the (mainland) Chinese indigenous networks (Child *et al.*, 2000).

(b) With respect to *Operational* problems we find that many Oriental firms appear to be overstaffed against western 'lean & mean' standards. The filial relationships in Asian cultures allow the subordinate to seem subservient to the masters, and these attitudes were rewarded by lifetime employment once widely promoted by heads of firms. There is also much in this with respect to nepotism and cronyism – both of which the western firms are said not to support. In addition, many western business practices seem to be conducted in an inverse way in China, which makes them less understandable and opaque (Martin and Larsen, 1999). Again we stumble over the problems of co-operation, co-opetition, and over mutual compromise within the alliance. The development of Larsson's model leading to anomie, which we outlined above (Figure 1.3), looks increasingly plausible.

Kautz and Vendelø (2001) explored the 'gathering together' of individuals for the purpose of knowledge sharing. They refer to the work of Hayek (1973) who described the grouping of individuals as being 'designed' or 'spontaneous'. In our context, we find that Kautz and

Vendelø echo much of what has been said above – that people lower down the organizational hierarchy are likely to strive for organizational learning which they do spontaneously unless their leader is despotic. Even in this extreme case, the cultural background of the players may modify leadership pressure by permitting the 'workers' to survive through their individuality or their inclination to (local) consensuality. However, if the leaders attempt to force through a knowledge management initiative, it is likely that the HRM function in each firm has to work hard to explain why this initiative is being promoted 'top down' before they can engage the 'workers' to jointly mesh their organizational learning. This is especially difficult if the initiative is across organizational boundaries and across cultural borders.

Kautz and Vendelø invoke the concepts of 'strong' and 'weak' ties researched by Granovetter (1973). Granovetter suggested that sometimes we learn better from our weak ties (those that extend beyond the boundary of the organization) as relative strangers introduce novelty to our stable world. In parallel, we find that 'chaos' is said to be a force 'for the good of the firm' (Pascale *et al.*, 2001): bringing in outside ways that can induce chaos. On the other hand, we may be expected to learn more deeply from our strong ties, since we best understand the models of those close to us.

There is thus a dilemma facing the managers of firms in an alliance. Consider a firm that is being offered an alliance if it is, in fact, smaller than the venturing firm which may be a multinational. The SMEs need to survive in their milieu doing what they are good at (we will presume this to be the case), but they need to keep up to date with forefront technology and ideas. However life-long learning is aspirational – it relies upon a benevolent society, more especially upon CEOs who plan for and schedule the learning and networking of their staff, since it demands time and space on the part of the learners to acquire knowledge and to disseminate it. One thematic model is suggested by Nonaka *et al.* (1994, 1995, 1998) though this model relies upon the traditions of Japan to promote its operation. That is, for staff to be willing and able to commune and network with each other for long after the 17:00 clock-off time – perhaps in a bar, perhaps in hot springs drinking sake – not just occasionally, but over many years. Such a role emphasis is further underscored by O'Reilly and Chatman (1996).

This process of differential knowledge acquisition and dissemination is suggestive of cultural processes that may be seen to be almost immutable over aeons. Indeed, Hofstede (1980, 1991) would suggest that as 'culture is the software of the mind' we could only slowly alter this genetic-like programming. We might also support this notion by reference to the basic programming of the Asiatic mind with its cultural antecedents developed from before the age of Confucius, though codified by him. Cultural role-playing, as a Confucian, has become de rigeur in Asia, and is now second nature to those raised in this region. We find this reflected in the general thesis of the 'differentiated network' wherein outposts are allowed to operate their own management models, yet at corporate level be fully integrated (Bartlett and Ghoshal, 1989; Nohria and Ghoshal, 1997).

One might suggest that this is potentially a reflection of the knowledge transfer and creation noted by Larson *et al.* (ibid) portrayed in Figure 1.2. However, it is more likely to incline to the perverse management of KM, the abreaction illustrated in our development of the Larson model posed in Figure 1.3, wherein cultural differences overwhelm the absorptive capacity of the firms involved, and individuals incline towards anomie. Once more we may suggest there is a huge difference between the operational model of the MNE that has the potential of enough organizational slack to learn how to absorb and learn about cultural differences, and the hard-pressed relatively tiny SME operation (with no organizational slack or absorptive capacity). SMEs are supposed to integrate fully with the MNEs in order to facilitate the supply chain, but the enforcing of a model of company governance more suited to a large firm, especially a multinational, will seem to be 'oppressive'.

The meta-organization

International business became an academic subject in the 1950s through the 1960s – not because such forms of organization began then, since international business has been undertaken for thousands of years. Possibly, this focus came about because of the large increase of business conglomerations noted as a new organizational form (Dunning, 1958; Vernon, 1966). Latterly, study in this area has been enabled greatly by the regular statistical data offered by the UNCTAD in Geneva: for instance, we note in Figure 1.4 the rapid global growth in both FDI and in Mergers and Acquisitions. We must heed UNCTAD who state there is no simple correlation between these two measures of economic activity as the underlying structural conditions are not constant over the years. Even so, the rapid rise in both measures leads us to believe that a study of 'governance' will yield beneficial results to the merging and merged parties.

Buckley *et al.* state that one area they find disappointing is the unsatisfactory integration between international business and business strategy

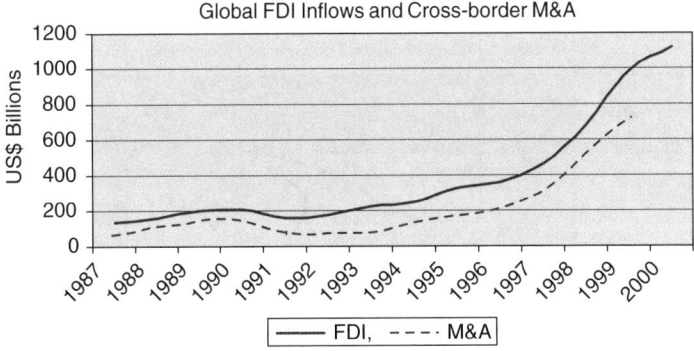

Figure 1.4 Global economic activity
Source: UNCTAD Press Releases – TDA/INF/2847@15/4/2000 and TAD/INF/2875@7/12/2000.

research (Buckley *et al.*, 1998). They go on:

> There are many bridges. And we would remember that bridges permit two-way traffic. These bridges include the analysis of culture, functional aspects of management (international marketing, international manufacturing strategy), the analysis of 'new forms' of doing international business such as alliances and organizational theory itself (ibid: 2).

We have already discussed several 'bridges' and wish to concentrate in the rest of this book upon aspects of corporate governance – not now as 'oppression' but as a means of enlightenment through better learning of its forms, aims and potentials. We might hope, as portrayed in Figure 1.5, that through a better understanding of 'governance and its purpose' an alliance will not rest in a state of anomie, and thus sooner or later be a failure. Under a generally acceptable state of 'good governance' the firms' employees should be striving to achieve a joint collaborative goal.

If the firm has operated in an anomic state its employees could move to the shared knowledge states (following the solid arrow routes). They might note however, that for them, the co-opetition mode may be less fruitful than grasping asymmetric learning (in the short term) while they learn how to fully collaborate and achieve a 'win–win' situation. But this is a risky strategy as it may result in the break up of the alliance.

Of course, we must briefly note the high profile cases of corporate misconduct that has swept though the business press in recent months.

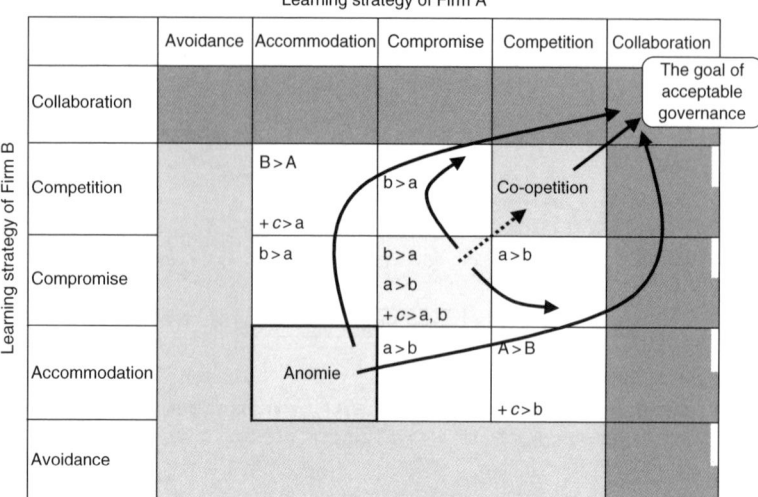

Figure 1.5 Moves towards 'better governance'

At the end of 2001 passing into 2002 was the Enron debacle which has resulted in clearer rules being made for the consulting firms who act for these major corporations – they can not be both a bean-counter 'accountants' as well as an advisor on how to make more beans. There is too much conflict especially as these consultants wish to be retained for further years of lucrative work with the MNEs. Inevitably, as this book looks to Asian matters we note that the Business Press also point at high profile misdeeds in this region also. Here software piracy is rife – for instance, even though Hong Kong spends about $8 million per annum on public awareness the piracy rate has increased by 1 per cent to 57 per cent in 2001 (Doug Nairne: Saturday 1st June, South China Morning Post). The Bank of China is looking towards a flotation in Hong Kong, but it finds an embarrassing loss of $725 million due to long-term embezzlement activity of a few former employees (David Lague: Far East Economic Review, 20 May 2002: 26). These, and other articles serve to illustrate that we have entered a time when it is almost mandatory to be clear how we account for our cash flows – even though our methods may be different, East and West. Perhaps we can close with an old quotation which illustrates that we still have to strive to educate our people to understand rights and wrongs and also to be better able to discuss with others from afar their differences in frameworks and methods – from the writings of Guanzi of 645 BC (Rickett, 1998).

48. ＜治國＞

凡治國之道，必先富民。民富則易治也，民貧則難治也。奚以知其然也？
民富則安鄉重家，安鄉重家則敬上畏罪，敬上畏罪則易治也。民貧則危鄉輕家，危鄉輕家則敢凌上犯禁，凌上犯禁則難治也。故治國常富，而亂國常貧。
是以善為國者，必先富民，然後治之。

> On Ruling over a State
>
> To govern a state it is of first importance to enrich the people. When the people are well off, they are easily governed; when they are poor, it is difficult to govern them. Why is this so? When the people are well off, they are secure in their communities and they appreciate their homes, they will refrain from crimes and respect the sovereign, and then they can be governed easily. On the other hand, when the people are poor, they are insecure in their communities and do not think highly of their homes. When they are insecure in their communities and despise their homes, they will be apt to commit criminal acts and to show no respect for the sovereign. When the people resort to criminal acts and show no respect for the sovereign, they are hard to govern...A good administrator considers it necessary to enrich people before he can properly govern his state.

That noted we might now look to our authors in the following chapters to suggest emergent models of governance that might be equally acceptable to the Asian as well as the Western manager. Hopefully this will avoid the pathologic mode of behavior achieved through poor 'understanding of the other'.

The structure of the book

Part 1: A general introduction

Chapter 1, by John Kidd and Frank Richter has illustrated the broad problems besetting many aspects of corporate governance. They looked especially at the issues, which confound alliances, when groups of individuals are brought together and who are thus supposed to learn quickly how to work in harmony together by sharing their knowledge. It is the management of the firm's intellectual capital that often causes much anxiety as the chief executive officers (CEOs) promote downwards their knowledge management initiatives, while the lower level staff engage in their own organizational learning processes. So, in a merger, joint venture, strategic alliance or other forms of 'getting together with the enemy' there is much confusion in the ranks as to how much to disclose to the 'other side'.

We have suggested that disclosure, transparency, trust and so on are the new mantra of international business linking the Oriental and the Occidental firms as the way ahead given that the WTO is now open to China. But, most importantly, we all have to learn better how to manage this new opportunity.

Part 2: Asian governance, cronyism and culture

Chapter 2 by Stephen Dearden concentrates upon the development of globalization following the cessation of the 'cold war'. He notes that the end of the cold war resulted in a far more critical attitude emerging amongst aid donors to the use of funds by recipient governments in the developing world, to issues of good governance, the rule of law and efficient public administration. Meanwhile, the globalization of production and the challenges of the regulation of the movements of capital have resulted in attempts to regulate the international financial environment.

For businesses, these demands have a profound impact upon the way that they operate in the global economy. Whilst the pressure upon developing country governments to reform is driven, in part, by a desire to improve the investment environment for the private sector, it will also place legal constraints upon the behavior of companies in these countries. Similarly, attempts at international regulation to prevent tax avoidance and evasion and to prevent money laundering, will create additional obligations upon multinational companies and international financial institutions.

Much of the discussion on corporate governance and its development is predicated upon the notions of corruption. Indeed, Dearden has noted that governments can only address a number of issues. For instance, in the UK, the House of Commons Select Committee has identified and has encouraged open tendering procedures for public contracts as one important area. They argue that audit trails are essential to the monitoring of the contracting process and that companies should be required to sign 'integrity pacts', undertaking not to engage in bribery, in order to pre-qualify for a particular contract. They have also called for the UK's Export Credit and Guarantee Department (ECGD) to more rigorously monitor companies so as to exclude those engaging in corrupt practices. Thus, he concludes, the eradication of corrupt practices will contribute greatly to creation of better mechanisms of corporate governance.

In Chapter 3, Christopher Gan illustrates that financial and corporate governance restructuring is an ongoing reform program in post Asian crisis-ridden countries. To be fully effective, corporate restructuring must be linked to bank restructuring, which, in turn, must be linked to the settlement of external debts to scale down the systemic risks. Thus, fundamental changes within the economy are necessary to create arm's-length relations between the government, corporations, and banks. Many corporations in the crisis-ridden countries are over-indebted and frequently are part of conglomerates or monopolies that are controlled by small groups: they have non-transparent accounting and close links to government and financial institutions, including commercial banks. So, here, we have a broad view of the macro effects that impinge upon firms and which demand they put in place adequate governance at their local level to absorb the broad effects.

In Chapter 4, Naresh Khatri, James Johnson and Zafar Ahmed show that cronyism is a highly prevalent phenomenon in societies and organizations holding certain cultural values such as paternalism, collectivism, and Confucianism. Despite it being cited as a major factor for Asian economic crisis and mismanagement of the Asian organizations, it is a concept that has not received due attention from management scholars. In order to better our understanding of cronyism in work organizations, they present a two-stage model, grounded in the Chinese/Asian cultural context, of the antecedents to cronyism, and present a number of propositions that follow from it. They show that Confucian values, lack of trust, collectivism, and high power distance elevate the importance of certain socially desirable behaviors – such as loyalty and close personal relationships. These behaviors, in turn, lead to three important antecedents of cronyism, which are an overemphasis on loyalty, an overemphasis on relationships, and the formation of strong ingroups. This raises the inevitable consequence following the Asian financial crisis of the late 1990s – the negative effects of cronyism on economic activity in southeast and eastern Asia have come under greater scrutiny, resulting in demands from western businesses and governments, and from supranational organizations such as the WTO and the International Monetary Fund (IMF), for greater transparency in business, economic and political affairs. In this chapter they unravel some of the cultural complexities that hinder a 'modernization' of corporate governance in China and Asia in general.

Part 3: Comparative analyses of governance processes
Reflections on China

In Chapter 5, Sui Pheng Low broadens the discussion to look at the 'mind' of the Chinese. He notes that the Orient is often viewed with a tinge of mysticism that made it almost culturally impossible for westerners to perceive. For these reasons, while there are no lack of strategic thinkers and philosophers in the East, their thoughts and philosophies are still not well disseminated, let alone popularized, throughout the world. With the economic opening up of China, an appreciation of its strategic oriental thinking and use of philosophies is of increasing importance for managerial practice. Apart from the eminent military strategist Sun Tzu, one would note the eminent philosophers, Confucius and Lao Tzu, whose teachings have had a tremendous influence on Chinese civilization and culture. Interestingly, these three great Chinese thinkers were all contemporaries in Chinese history some 2500 years ago. The tumultuous activities of this time appeared to be the main trigger for them to reflect and form their thoughts, philosophies and strategies. Perhaps in today's flux it is also opportune to reflect on their philosophy?

Matti Nojonen, in Chapter 6, continues the Chinese theme noting how, in the malfunctioning market and institutional environment of China more often than not a competitive edge is gained through extensive personal connections (*guanxi*). Gift-giving is perhaps the most consequential method used to create and to deploy *guanxi*. On many occasions gift-giving is simply associated with bribing and corruption. However, this chapter illustrates that by approaching the ethically loaded and yet theoretically and, by definition, controversial issue of corruption from a gift-giving approach, one is able to unearth the complicated logic, risks and advantages involved in Chinese business networks. He notes in detail that in expanding and utilizing *guanxi* networks in the increasingly competitive environment Chinese businessmen are actively competing with each other by differentiating their gifts in the most imaginative ways, thus forming a hidden marketplace of gifts. The emphasis is laid on illustrating the prerequisite and exacting choreography, social mechanisms and logic of action of various forms of gift-giving practices, namely 'ordinary business gift', 'hand-grenades and machine guns' and 'guided missiles' as gifts, that take place behind the cloak of visible networking (*guanxi*).

Chapter 7, by Barbara Krug and Hans Hendrischke focuses on a case in China where money, power and family relationships became entangled in a web of deceit and corruption. This led to indictments and executions – harsh perhaps, but this is one of the realities in China where (as we have said before) the State officials wish to be seen to be carrying out anti-corruption programmes. In part, this may be political – as an appeasement of the US officials who complained ahead of the

World Trade Organization accession that China should not be granted entry to this club. But harsh measures also, these same officials may explain, must be meted out as a deterrent as China is developing very fast from one in which corruption – it could be argued – was endemic from the time of Confucius, 2000 years ago.

Reflections on Japan

In Chapter 8, Teri Jane Ursacki describes the role of the *sokaiya* in Japanese business and their involvement in corporate extortion. She notes the persistence of the *sokaiya* phenomenon and considers the changes that would be necessary to eradicate it. In particular, she focuses on the impact of economic reform, and suggests that the nature of the reforms required to stamp out *sokaiya* activity would go well beyond tinkering with regulations concerning corporate governance. For instance, she notes that employing *sokaiya* is part of a wider strategy employed by poorly performing executives to keep themselves in their jobs and their companies afloat.

Economic reform must proceed far, so that uncompetitive companies have no alternative but to fall by the wayside if such dark-side strategies, of which the use of *sokaiya* are only a part, are to be made obsolete. A detailed case study of Mitsubishi Motors provides a concrete illustration of how *sokaiya* were used as part of a broader strategy to cover up underperformance. Her conclusions deal with the prognosis for current efforts to eliminate corporate extortion in Japan.

Chapter 9 by Maiko Miyake, Kathryn Gordon and Iwao Taka reviews the procedures being put in place in Japan to ensure ethical compliance based on a survey of corporate responsibility conducted by the Asahi Newspaper Foundation. Their first section discusses the conceptual definition of corruption and the legal implication of such a definition; and it also describes briefly the legal environment surrounding Japanese corporations. Their second section analyzes the voluntary initiatives on anti-corruption compliance and their third section provides findings from the survey that gives a snapshot of Japanese companies' efforts to achieve corporate conduct with higher business integrity. In conclusion, they suggest initiatives that will aid anti-corruption compliance management in Japan – in part supported further by comparative data from research in the OECD of corporate governance.

Part 4: The development of an ethical perspective

Chapter 10, by Jon Quah, is focused strongly on the strategies adopted by Singapore to clean up its own State processes and how these may be models for other nations. He notes that corruption (in Singapore) became an offence in 1871, however, nothing much was done upon this issue by the British colonial government for the next 66 years until it enacted the Prevention of Corruption Ordinance (POCO) on 10 December 1937. Since then much progress has been made, and it is widely accepted that Singapore's comprehensive anti-corruption strategy is effective as it is perceived to have been the least corrupt country in Asia during 1995–2001.

Whether Singapore's effective anti-corruption strategy can be successfully transplanted to other Asian countries depends on two important factors: the nature of their policy context, and whether they possess the political will to implement the required reforms. So far, only Hong Kong and Malaysia have adopted Singapore's anti-corruption strategy. The chapter looks carefully at the impediments to a wider acceptance across Asia of these strong governance policies.

In Chapter 11, Dennis Heaton, Thomas Carlisle and Ian Brown relate how the problem of corruption can be approached from each of three sets of factors that influence ethical behavior in organizations – individual characteristics, organizational factors, and opportunity. They emphasize individual characteristics in this chapter – in particular the development of the consciousness of the individual, including the individual's level of moral development. It is through this Vedic tradition, they suggest, that a strong moral code can be developed that will enhance corporate behavior and thus governance to meet international standards. They discuss how the Maharishi Corporate Development Program has applied this approach in numerous corporate settings in India and around the world to improve the overall effectiveness, well-being, and right action of managers and employees.

In Chapter 12, Paul Robins outlines how a Buddhist viewpoint can offer a framework upon which to base better governance and to measure its effectiveness. Buddhism is an example of an ancient and trusted tradition that places particular emphasis on the practical issues of living a moral life. It provides a source of well-founded guidance for both the individual and the organization wishing to become more moral, without being dependent on the acceptance of a particular theistic or philosophical dogma. It should therefore be possible to extract from these principles useful and practical guidelines for organizations of whatever kind.

His analysis seeks to understand the Eastern perspective although escaping from Western thought patterns is hardly complete. It is intended to offer useful guidance for those with a Western background, but it may also help to focus the minds of those with an Eastern background whose working environment has come to be influenced, if not dominated, by Western customs and practice.

Finally, in Chapter 13, Hock-Beng Cheah and Melanie Cheah discuss the dilemmas facing many governments in the region. For many, their development strategies rest on a model of corporate governance in which excessive emphasis has been placed on orthodox economic aspects. However, it is a model that is not meaningful for a large proportion of the world's population, as it has been seen to generate significant inequities. Further, it is a model that may not be sustainable in the longer term. These concerns have provoked a critical questioning of present forms and processes of development, and have led to a search for better and more viable alternatives.

The authors categorize these problems and their concerns under a rubric of issues related to an ethical imperative in the development process. In so doing, they suggest that an appropriate framework for sustainable development must focus as much attention on issues that relate to the ethical imperative, as on issues related to other kinds of governance imperatives.

Notes

Figure 1.1 was created by John Kidd and John Edwards (both at Aston Business School) who have offered it in several papers and presentations. It has been used, as here, to make clear the relationships between the CEO, the HRM function, and the management of knowledge and organizational learning within and between organizations.

Figure 1.2 is based on the fundamental work of Larsson, Bengtsson, Henriksson and Sparkes (1998) – we are grateful for their ideas and conceptualization. We have to say that the subsequent development of this model through the rest of the chapter is solely the responsibility of the authors.

Within the 'Structure of this book' sections above we have quoted proper names in the manner of the west with the family name last.

References

Bartlett, C. A. and Ghoshal, S. (1989) *Managing Across Borders*, London: Century Business.

Buckley, P. J., Burton, F. and Mirza, H. (1998) *The Strategy and Organization of International Business*, London: Macmillan Press.

Burton, J. (1995) Partnering with the Japanese: Threat of opportunity for European businesses? *European Management Journal* **13**(3): 304–16.

Chaston, I., Badger, B. and Sadler-Smith, E. (1999) Organizational Learning: research issues and application in SME sector firms. *International Journal of Entrepreneurial Behaviour and Research* **5**(4): 191–203.

Child, J., Chung, L., Davis, H. and Ng, S. H. (2000) *Managing Business in Mainland China: A Guidebook*, Hong Kong: Hong Kong Chamber of Commerce.

Cohen, W. M. and Leventhal, D. A. (1990) Absorptive capacity: a new perspective on learning and innovation. *Administrative Science Quarterly* **35**(1): 128–52.

COST 330 Action (1998) *Trends in Information Systems and Communications in European Ports*, Luxembourg: Office for Official Publications of the European Communities. ISBN 92-828-3679-7. EUR 18284.

Dunning, J. H. (1958) *American Investment in British Manufacturing Industry*, London: George Allen & Unwin.

Dunning, J. H. (1993) *The Globalization of Business*, London: Routledge.

Festinger, L. and Carlsmith, J. M. (1959) Cognitive consequences of forced compliance. *Journal of Abnormal and Social Psychology* **58**: 203–10.

Fruin, W. M. (1997) *Knowledge Works: Managing intellectual capital at Toshiba*, London: Oxford University Press.

Ghani, R. A. (2000) Few SMIs embrace ICT. *New Straits Times*, Computimes, 30/11/00: 5.

Globe Project (1999) Cultural influences on leadership and organizations. *Advances in Global Leadership* **1**: 171–233.

Granovetter, M. S. (1973) Strength through weak ties. *American Journal of Sociology* **78**(6): 1360–80.

Gray, S. J. (1996) International comparisons of business performance: measurement and disclosure issues. *International Review of Business* **1**(1): 1–15.

Hally, A. and Guilhon, A. (1997) Logistics behaviour of small enterprises: performance, strategy and definition. *International Journal of Physical Distribution and Logistics Management* **27**(8): 475–95.

Hayek, F. A. V. (1973) *Law, Legislation, and Liberty: Vol 1: Rules and Order*, Chicago: University of Chicago Press.

Hill, C. W. L. (2000) *International Business: Competing in the Global Marketplace*, New York: McGraw-Hill.

Hofstede, G. (1980) *Culture's Consequences: International Differences in Work-related Values*, London: Sage Publications.

Hofstede, G. (1991) *Cultures and Organisations: Software of the Mind*, London: McGraw-Hill.

Huber, G. P. (1991) Organizational learning: the contributing processes and the literatures. *Organizational Science* **3**(3): 383–97.

Huber, G. P. (2000) 'Transferring sticky knowledge: Suggested solutions and needed studies', in J. S. Edwards and J. B. Kidd (eds), *Knowledge Management Beyond the Hype: Looking Towards the New Millennium*. Proceedings of KMAC 2000, Aston Business School, 17–18th July: 12–22.

Inkpen, A. (1996) Creating knowledge through collaboration. *California Management Review* **39**(1): 123–41.

Kautz, K. and Vendelø, M. T. (2001) 'Knowledge sharing as spontaneous ordering: On the emergence of strong and weak ties', in C. Carter, H. Scarbourough and J. Swan (eds), *Managing Knowledge: Conversations and Critiques*. Leicester University, 10–11th April.

Kennedy, J. and Mansor, N. (2000) Malaysian culture and the leadership of organisations: A GLOBE study. *Malaysian Management Review*, December 2000.

Khanna, T., Gulati, R. and Nohria, N. (1998) The dynamics of learning alliances: Competition, co-operation and scope. *Strategic Management Journal* **19**(3): 193–204.

Kidd, J. B. and Edwards, J. S. (2000) 'Fast moving global supply chains: how organizational learning may offer bridges in crossing cultures', in the proceedings of ECKM 2000. D. Remenyi (ed.), *First European Conference on Knowledge Management*; Bled, Slovenia. October 26–7: 49–59.

Kidd, J. B. and Kanda, M. (2000) Organizational learning in practice: the behaviour of senior production managers in Britain and Japan. *Management International* **4**(2): 61–70.

Kidd, J. B. and Teramoto, Y. (1995) 'Can the Japanese localise? – A study of Japanese production subsidiaries in the UK', in S.-J. Park and M. Jovanovic (eds), *What is behind the Japanese miracle?* Megatrends I.E.C., London, pp. 136–52.

Larsson, R., Bengtsson, L., Henricksson, K. and Sparks, J. (1999) The interorganizational learning dilemma: collective knowledge development in strategic alliances. *Organizational Science* **9**(3): 285–306.

Linstone, H. and Zhu, Z. (2000) Towards synergy in multiperspective management: An American–Chinese Case. *Human Systems Management* **19**: 25–37.

Martin, B. and Larsen, G. (1999) Taming the Tiger: Key success factors for trade with China. *Journal of International Economics* **10**(May): 151–75.

Merry, P. (2001) 'Cultural literacy – its link to business success in Asia-Pacific', in J. B. Kidd, X. Li and F.-J. Richter (eds), *Maximizing Human Intelligence Deployment in Asian Business: The Sixth Generation Project*, London & New York: Palgrave.

Nohria, N. and Ghoshal, S. (1997) *The Differentiated Network*, San Francisco: Jossey-Bass.

Nonaka, I. (1994) A dynamic theory of organizational knowledge creation. *Organizational Science* **5**(1): 16–35.

Nonaka, I. and Konno, N. (1998) The concept of 'Ba': building a foundation for knowledge creation. *California Management Review* **40**(3): 40–50.

Nonaka, I. and Takeuchi, H. (1995) *The Knowledge-creating Company*, Oxford: Oxford University Press.

O'Reilly, C. and Chatman, J. A. (1996) Culture and social control: Corporations, cults and commitment. *Research in Organizational Behavior* **18**: 157–200.

OECD (2000) *No Longer Business as Usual: Fighting Bribery and Corruption*, Paris: OECD Press.

Pascale, R., Millemann, M. and Gioja, L. (2001) *Surfing the Edge of Chaos*, New York: Texere.

Powell, W. W., Koput, K. W. and Smith-Doerr, L. (1996) Interorganisational collaboration and the locus of innovation: Networks of learning in biotechnology. *Administrative Science Quarterly* **41**: 116–45.

Richter, F.-J. (2000) *Strategic Networks: The Art of Japanese Interfirm Co-operation*, New York: Haworth Press.

Rickett, W. A. (Translator) (1998) Guanzi: *Political, Economic, and Philosophical Essays from Early China*, Princeton, NJ: Princeton University Press.

Ring, P. S. and Van de Ven A. H. (1994) Developmental processes of cooperative interorganisational relationships. *Academy of Management Review* **19**(1): 90–118.

Salter, S. B. and Niswander, F. (1995) Cultural influences on the development of accounting systems internationally. *Journal of Intelligent Business Studies* **26**(2): 379–98.

Simonin, B. L. (1997) The importance of collaborative know-how: An empirical test of the learning organization. *Academy of Management Journal* **40**(5): 1150–74.

Spender, J.-C. and Grant, R. M. (1996) Knowledge and the firm: Overview. *Strategic Management Journal* **17**: 5–9.

Szulanski, G. (1996) Exploring internal stickiness: Impediments to the transfer of best practice within the firm. *Strategic Management Journal, Special Issue*, Winter, 27–44.

Vernon, R. (1966) International investment and international trade in the product cycle. *Journal of Economics* **80**: 190–207.

Wong, Y., Mather, T. E., Jenner, R., Appell, A. and Hebert, L. (1999) Are joint ventures losing their appeal in China? *S.A.M. Advanced Management Journal* **64**(1): 4–12.

Ye, A. L. and Valentine, S. (2000) More haste, less speed: the secret to investing in China. *International Financial Law Review* **19**(1): 17–19.

Zarzeski, M. T. (1996). Spontaneous harmonisation effects of culture and market forces on accounting disclosure practices. *Accounting Horizons* **10**, March: 18–37, American Accounting Association.

Zhao, H. and Zhu, G. (2000) Location factors and country-of-origin differences: an empirical analysis of FDI in China. *Multinational Business Review* **8**(1): 10–11.

2
The Challenge to Corruption and the International Business Environment
Stephen Dearden

Two factors have turned the attention of the governments of the developed world to the problems of corruption, the end of the cold war and the trends to globalisation. The end of the cold war has resulted in a far more critical attitude emerging amongst aid donors to the use of funds by recipient governments in the developing world, to issues of good governance, the rule of law and efficient public administration. Meanwhile, the globalisation of production and the challenges of the regulation of the movements of capital have resulted in attempts to regulate the international financial environment. For businesses, these demands will have a profound impact upon the way that they operate in the global economy. Whilst the pressure upon developing country governments to reform is driven, in part, by a desire to improve the investment environment for the private sector, it will also place legal constraints upon the behaviour of companies in these countries. Similarly attempts at international regulation to prevent tax avoidance and evasion and to prevent money laundering, will create additional obligations upon multinational companies and international financial institutions. This article will review the rationale for these developments and outline the various strands that are creating a new international environment for the new century.

This paper will begin by considering the nature of corruption and the attempts to evaluate its impact upon those economies in which it is endemic. It will then turn to a review of the response of the international community, especially the OECD, the World Bank and the EU. The next section examines the particular problems of money laundering and the rise of Off-Shore Financial Centres (OFC). Finally, the paper considers the likely new demands upon the private sector, and the areas of action by the UK government, the EU and other global institutions.

The nature of corruption

Corruption can take many forms. It may include payments to government officials or politicians to obtain access to a public service to which an individual or company may, or may not, be entitled, to obtain government contracts or to avoid regulatory controls and liabilities. It may involve the demand for employment of relatives or the provision of a benefit indirectly to a public official.

Corruption has usually been defined as 'the abuse of public office for private gain'. This definition has been widened recently, as attention has turned to corruption within the private sector, to cover 'giving or receiving undue advantage in the course of business activities leading to acts in breach of a person's duties' (Transparency, 1999). However, it can be argued that the role of the public sector is more significant, since it is here that the opportunities for corruption are most extensive. Also public administration creates the opportunities for corruption in the private sector by creating the necessary institutional and market conditions. In both cases, corruption can be viewed as an example of the Principal–Agent problem, where the core difficulty lies in the mechanism to monitor the actions of those to whom authority is delegated but where the information is possessed asymmetrically by the agent.

One distinction that is often made is that between petty and grand corruption. Petty corruption is often accompanied by uncertainty – who to pay, when and how much. Such payments raise costs and will inhibit the efficient functioning of the market and the delivery of public services. They are likely to have a particularly adverse impact upon the poor. They appear to be associated with low levels of public sector pay, where petty bribes become an important, and sometimes unofficially recognised, source of income.

Although petty corruption is often all pervasive in many developing and transitional economies, most attention has focused upon 'grand' corruption. Community Information Empowerment and Transparency (CIET) has observed that grand corruption '... has long been recognised as an issue in development at the macro level, with large amounts of money being stolen by corrupt senior officials and political leaders in developing countries, and large bribes being paid by international concerns in order to secure business opportunities'. It has been estimated that, worldwide, businesses pay bribes totalling $80 bn. every year. Grand corruption does not just lead to the direct diversion of funds into private hands but also distorts investment priorities. Clare Short, as UK Secretary of State for Development, believed that the debt problem could be directly related to the long run impact of persistent grand corruption.

Attempts to evaluate the economic impact of corruption are fraught with difficulties because of its multifaceted nature. Corruption can both increase or decrease the production costs faced by the firm, or the product costs faced by the individual. Bribes paid to expedite government regulatory activities, to obtain import licenses or to win government contracts, will all raise costs. By contrast, bribes paid to circumvent government regulations – for example health and safety, environmental requirements, taxation – may reduce the net cost to the company, even if it imposes social costs. In the extreme case of payments made to gain access to a valuable state resource – for example mining concessions, privatised enterprise – the existence of the enterprise itself may depend upon such payments. A government policy of protectionism, often adopted by developing and transitional economies, usually creates conditions of monopoly/oligopoly and therefore substantial economic rent for exploitation.

From the perspective of the public sector, corruption will impose both financial and economic costs. Corruption resulting in tax evasion will clearly reduce the governments' tax revenues, but corruption may also add to the governments' costs through the allocation of contracts to higher priced contractors. Such increases in prices will be essential to meet the costs of the bribes that are paid. But the economic costs may be even more substantial as projects may be undertaken merely to generate bribes rather than as a reflection of economic development priorities. Such major capital investment projects, which were never economically viable, may remain a drain on the scarce resources of developing countries for many years.

From the broadest economic welfare perspective corruption encourages inefficiency in the delivery of public services, to extract additional payments, distorts prices throughout the economy, with the cost of bribes passed onto the final consumer, and it creates delays in economic transactions and additional uncertainty, which may be a crucial element in undermining investment and encouraging capital flight. With domestic capital formation ten times the level of foreign direct investment its retention is essential for long run economic development.

Attempts to establish empirically the causes and costs of corruption have presented serious problems. Most statistical studies employ survey measures of the 'perception of corruption' in their cross-country analysis. These qualitative assessments raise questions of consistency and interpretation. Nonetheless some broad conclusions can be drawn.[1]

Johnson *et al.* (1998) confirmed the expected relationship between perceived corruption and the size of the informal sector or 'black economy', which in turn was encouraged by high levels of regulation and high perceived tax levels. Rijkeghem and Weber (1997) found a relationship between corruption and low levels of public sector pay. Although other studies have failed to confirm this relationship it has become a widely accepted view (see House of Commons, 2001). Leite and Weidemann (1999) established a clear relationship between corruption and the importance of an abundant natural resource to a country's economy; providing hard currency and opportunities for rent seeking. Finally, Ades and Di Tella (1997) employed various measures to proxy the degree of government 'interventionism' in industrial policy – for example indices for the openness of public procurement, equality of fiscal treatment, the size of public subsidies to public and private enterprises – and found a positive correlation with the extent of corruption. Other studies have focused upon the institutional causes of corruption. The 1997 World Development Report suggested that the predictability of the judiciary was an important factor, while Mauro (1995) found a high correlation with assessments of judicial integrity, bureaucratic efficiency and political stability.

Studies attempting to establish the impact of corruption have identified a clear adverse influence upon economic growth. Hall and Jones (1999) found a negative correlation between output per worker and corruption indices, while Kaufmann and Wei (1999) found an adverse impact upon GDP per capita. Keefer and Knack (1995), Poirson (1998) and Leite and Weidmann (1999) all confirmed the significance of corruption levels for growth rates. Mauro (1995) identified reduced investment as the mechanism whereby growth is diminished by the influence of corruption. However, Wheeler and Mody (1992) and Alesina and Weber (1999) were unable to establish any adverse impact upon the level of foreign direct investment, although this was contradicted by Wei's (1997) study of capital flows for 1990/91. A Worldaware survey of UK based companies found that they ranked corruption as a greater barrier to direct investment than either political stability or lack of infrastructure. Similarly, a survey of multinational companies by UNCTAD (1999) suggested that the extent of extortion and bribery were by far the most important factors in influencing investment decisions in 44 African countries. As for aid, Alesina and Weder (1999) could find no relation between OECD aid provision and the level of corruption, except for Scandinavian donors.

The international response

With the changing international political environment, the demands for more effective and poverty-focused aid programmes and the concern for the rapid integration of the transitional economies into the international economy have led various bodies to address the problems of anti-corruption measures. Here, I will be focusing principally upon the OECD, the Council of Europe and the European Union.

So far the most significant international agreement addressing the problem of corruption has been that of the OECD 'Convention on Combating Bribery of Foreign Public Officials in International Business Transactions'. This was adopted in November 1997 and came into force in February 1999. By 2000, 20 countries, including seven within the EU, had ratified the Convention, which requires the signatories to make it a criminal offence to offer bribes to public officials in order to obtain a business advantage. It also encourages States to end the ability of firms to treat bribe payments as business costs that are tax deductible. However, it does not cover payments to foreign political parties, bribery through foreign subsidiaries nor bribes offered to private individuals or firms. The success of these measures is being monitored by an OECD working group on Bribery in International Business Transactions.

The UK government ratified the Convention in 1998 on the basis of existing statutes and common law. However, in the subsequent phase 1 peer-review by the OECD, UK legislation and reliance on existing case law was found to be seriously inadequate. In the face of substantial criticism of its failure to implement the Convention with new legislation the government has now committed itself to the introduction of a Bill in the new Parliament. This legislation will include a clear definition of the concept of corruption, applicable to both the public and private sectors, and would be extraterrritorial, allowing the prosecution of British nationals even where bribes are paid abroad. It is hoped that the new law will meet all of the UK's obligations under the various Conventions, including that of the Council of Europe, and end the existing ambiguity in the treatment of the tax deductibility of the costs of bribes paid abroad.

The UK situation has been contrasted with the relative effectiveness of the US Foreign Corrupt Practices Act passed in 1997. However, even this legislation allows payment of bribes through joint ventures and for 'facilitation payments' and US companies appear to be willing to employ off-shore arrangements to circumvent these controls. Although there have been few prosecutions it has been argued that the legislation has forced US companies to adopt clear compliance procedures.

The Council of Europe has also adopted two Conventions covering Criminal and Civil Law. These cover Central and Eastern Europe as well as the EU. The Criminal Law Convention extends the definition of corruption to include the activities of the private sector, while the Civil Law Convention provides for compensation for individuals suffering a loss as a result of corrupt practices by an official. Both Conventions require legal protection for 'whistleblowers'. By 2000, twelve Member States of the EU had ratified the Criminal Law Convention, but only five the Civil Law Convention. The EC will be able to accede to the Conventions in its own right once the Conventions come into force.

Beyond the legal framework of the Conventions, international and national bodies have adopted various anti-corruption mechanisms. The World Bank, the largest international aid donor, has improved its procurement requirements and project management techniques in recent years. It also maintains a list of firms and individuals disbarred from procurement contracts on the grounds of corrupt or fraudulent practices. The Bank also has arrangements to pass evidence of criminal activity to the prosecuting authorities in which companies are registered. Further efforts are being made to facilitate information exchanges with other international financial institutions. The World Bank also maintains a successful hotline for collecting allegations of corruption and provides guarantees of protection for informants. However, the regional development banks have room for improvement in their practices. The Asian Development Bank enforces only an optional 'no bribery pledge' on large contracts and the African Development Bank has yet to seriously address the issue in its procurement procedures.

The European Union

Within the EU, two anti-corruption Conventions have been drafted. The July 1995 Convention is concerned with the protection of the EU's financial interests and the May 1997 Convention with corruption amongst EC officials or officials of the Member States. However, neither has been ratified by all of the EU's Member States. In 1997 the Commission had outlined its anti-corruption strategy in a policy paper – 'A Union Policy Against Corruption' (COM(97)192) – and in October 1998 the European Parliament accepted the Bontempi Report on combating corruption. Following this, in December, the Council committed the Member States to 'Joint Action' against corruption in the private sector through national legislation. Progress has been made on Public

Procurement Directives, the role of the Statutory Auditor and in the area of foreign aid. Public Procurement within the EU has been subject to review (COM(98)143), with the possibility of the introduction of anti-corruption pledges by all parties to contracts and the development of a coherent scheme for 'blacklisting' companies and individuals who can be identified as engaging in corrupt practices. The role of the Statutory Auditor in deterring and detecting corruption was explicitly recognised in a Green Paper (1996) and the Commission is working through the Committee on Auditing to establish the self-regulatory framework for the profession.

In terms of the EU's external relations the Common Service Relex (now Euroaid), which is responsible for executing most of the EU's development aid programme, has adopted 'ethical clauses' in its Manual of Procedural Rules for its procurement procedures. The possibility of 'blacklisting' companies or individuals who infringe these rules has, for the first time, been introduced. Unfortunately, this Manual only covers the contracting phase and the complementary rules covering the implementation phase have yet to be adopted. The Commission has however taken general powers to suspend or cancel aid if partner governments fail to take satisfactory action to combat corruption when it is discovered.

The abolition of the tax deductibility of bribes, which had been a frequent practice within EU States, will be required with the adoption of the OECD Convention. Associated with this practice has been the issue of the treatment of the costs of bribery as part of Export Credit Insurance. Bribery has been estimated to add 10 per cent to 20 per cent to the costs of any contract and these export guarantees are usually ultimately government funded. As the EU has competence in regard to external trade responsibility clearly falls upon the Commission to instigate action in this area.

The heightened priority being given by the EU to the problem of corruption in developing countries and the general approach that is being taken, is best illustrated by examining the new Partnership Agreement (Cotonou) between the EU and the ACP states that succeeded the Lomé Conventions in 2000. In this Agreement 'the respect for human rights, democratic principles and the rule of law' are regarded as 'essential elements of the partnership' while a commitment to 'good governance' is a further 'fundamental element'. In Article 8, where the process of 'political dialogue' is outlined, specific reference is made to the 'regular assessment of the developments concerning the respect for human rights, democratic principles, the rule of law and good governance.' Under Article 9 the Agreement recognises that 'democracy based upon the rule of law and transparent and accountable governance are an integral part of sustainable development'. Specifically, 'the structure of government and the prerogative of the different powers shall be founded on the rule of law, which shall entail in particular effective and accessible means of legal redress, an independent legal system guaranteeing equality before the law and an executive fully subject to the law'. Good governance is defined as 'the transparent and accountable management of human, natural, economic and financial resources for the purpose of equitable and sustainable development. It entails clear decision making procedures at the level of public authorities, transparent and accountable institutions, the primacy of law in the management and distribution of resources and capacity building for elaborating and implementing measures aiming in particular at preventing and combating corruption' (Article 9.3).

The introduction of good governance into the Agreement had faced considerable opposition from the ACP States. As Adamou Salao of Niger commented 'the main contention concerns its inclusion as an essential element in the future agreement...none of the ACP countries want to see good governance become an essential element, which, if violated, would trigger the non-execution clause and potentially lead to sanctions' (The Courier No. 177 Oct.–Nov. 1999). The ACPs were willing to strengthen the political dialogue, affirming their 'adherence to the principles of democracy, the rule of law, human rights and good governance. Nonetheless these principles should not be used by the EU to suspend development assistance unilaterally or render it conditional'. The result of the negotiations was a compromise solution distinguishing between 'essential' (i.e. human rights, democracy, rule of law) and 'fundamental' (i.e. corruption) elements of the Agreement, with two separate procedures created to address cases where there has been violation of these principles. In the case of corruption there is a consultation procedure and a strong reserve power for the EC – 'in cases of special urgency appropriate measures may be taken without prior consultation'. But the Agreement is qualified. Only 'serious cases of corruption, including acts of bribery leading to such corruption, as defined in Article 97, constitute a violation of the Agreement'. But 'if the consultations do not lead to a solution acceptable to both Parties or if consultation is refused, the Parties shall take the appropriate measures. In all cases, it is above all incumbent on the Party where the serious cases of corruption have occurred to take the measures necessary to remedy the situation immediately. The measures taken by either Party must be proportional to the seriousness of the situation. In the selection of these measures priority must be given to those which least disrupt the application of this agreement.

It is understood that suspension would be a measure of last resort' (Article 97.3).

The Agreement also qualifies the regular assessment of the ACPs progress in the 'promotion of human rights, processes of democratisation, consolidation of the rule of law and good governance' in that it is to 'take account of each country's economic, social, cultural and historical context' (Article 9.4).

Money laundering

Corruption is intimately linked with the problem of money laundering. The IMF estimated that money laundering totalled between $590 bn. and $1500 bn. in 1996, equal to between 2 per cent and 5 per cent of world GDP. The OECD, the EU and G7 are all collaborating in addressing this problem. The Inter-governmental Financial Action Task Force (FATF), created by the G7 in 1989, is composed of representatives from all of the major international financial centres and produces recommendations for anti-money laundering legislation and procedures. It encourages the harmonisation of national legislation and information exchange. In 1990 it produced 40 recommendations to counter money laundering and these were updated in 1996. FATF reviews compliance with these recommendations and maintains a 'black list' of states who fail to maintain adequate anti-money laundering controls. It also assists in the establishment of similar agreements in other regions of the world and one such has already been established in the Caribbean.

Within the EU the Money Laundering Directive (91/308/EC) provides the legislative framework. This requires all financial institutions to know their customers when opening accounts, to keep records of any transactions exceeding €15 000, and to report suspicious transfers. It requires all Member States to establish anti-money laundering programmes and to suspend bank secrecy when illegal activities are suspected. In September 2000, the EU Finance Ministers agreed to extend the monitoring requirements to cover the proceeds of all serious crime and to extend the legal obligations beyond banks to include lawyers and accountants. Further action is also to be taken to improve information exchange and cooperation between the Member States. In the UK, the EU's requirements have been embodied principally in the Criminal Justice Act 1993, the Money Laundering Regulations 1993 and the Financial Services and Markets Act 2000. The Financial Services Authority has the prime statutory responsibility to combat financial crime and has a Joint Money Laundering Steering Group addressing this particular problem.

Off-Shore Financial Centres

Closely related to the problems of money laundering has been the role of Off-Shore Financial Centres (OFC) or tax havens. There are now more than 100 such centres worldwide and it is estimated that $6 trillion to $7 trillion is now held in them, a sum equivalent to one-third of world GDP, and split roughly equally between individuals and companies. For example OFCs account for 26 per cent of US multinationals' assets and 31 per cent of their profits. Tax havens offer two advantages to international investors and international criminals alike – secrecy and low tax regimes for non-resident customers. OFCs include not only the traditional island states of the Caribbean, Pacific and Indian Oceans, but also territories such as the Channel Islands, Liechtenstein, Luxembourg and Switzerland.

As well as providing the principle avenue for money laundering OFCs have enhanced tax competition between countries, undermining the ability of states to sustain their tax base from corporate taxation. In the last ten years, OECD countries have seen the average corporate tax rate fall by ten per cent, shifting the tax burden to indirect and personal taxation. For developing countries, it has been estimated that capital flight to OFCs costs them $50 bn. per annum (Oxfam, 2000) in lost tax revenues. OFCs also contribute to the distortion of international competition, offering competitive advantages to those multinational companies (MNC) that exploit the opportunities that they offer for tax avoidance and tax evasion. Finally, OFCs are seen as contributing to the increased instability of the international financial system. The significant growth in assets and liabilities held in OFCs and the inter-bank nature of the off-shore market, all increase the risk of increasing instability in currency and capital markets. The recent crisis in East Asia demonstrated the problems that can now arise from rapid capital flows and the currency instability that accompanies it.

In 1998, the UN had published a report on 'Money Laundering', followed up in 1999 by the 'Offshore Initiative' of the UN Global Programme against money laundering. This identified a 'white list' of well regulated OFCs that were cooperating with the international organisations. Those not included were to be encouraged to adopt anti-money laundering legislation and to increase their cooperation. But the main player in international action on OFCs has again been the OECD. In 1988, it had been instrumental, together with the Council of Europe, in negotiating the Convention on Mutual Administrative Assistance in Tax Matters. This provided for the exchange of information necessary to counter tax evasion, but it was only available to members of the two organisations. In 1998, the OECD published a report on unfair tax competition (Harmful Tax Competition: an Emerging Global Issue) that identified a 'black list' of tax havens that facilitate unfair international tax competition. In the wake of the Asian financial crisis it went further and formed a Financial Stability Forum (FSF) which had examined the degree of supervision and cooperation with other jurisdictions of OFCs. In its Harmful Tax Competition Initiative it has attempted to distinguish between tax havens and 'normal' international financial centres that offer harmful preferential tax regimes to foreign deposits. For the latter, the OECD will publish a list of such practices, with an obligation upon its members to amend their tax laws by 2003. However, for those states identified as uncooperative tax havens, they will join a 'black list', with the threat of 'defensive measures' by OECD members. In June 2000, the OECD published an initial 'black list' of 35 countries which were to be required by the OECD to commit themselves to changes in the operations of their OFCs by July 2001. Opposition ensured that the deadline for compliance was delayed until March 2002.

In response, 17 OFCs, including the Cayman Islands, the Channel Islands, Malta, Mauritius, the Seychelles, St. Vincent, Antigua and Bermuda, have made serious efforts to improve their regulations and transparency. However, vociferous opposition amongst the remaining non-OECD states to this attempt to impose reform has continued and 21 have yet to indicate a willingness to cooperate. For many small island economies, their OFC represents an important contributor to their economies. The demands of the OECD for transparency, exchange of information and non-discrimination (applying the same tax regime to both domestic and foreign customer), is seen as fatally undermining any comparative advantage that these states offer for international deposits. There is also considerable criticism of what is seen as differential treatment of OECD OFCs and those of non-OECD states. The extreme example of this is the situation of Switzerland and Luxembourg, both of whom have failed to sign up to the OECD action and therefore are not liable to listing. Following a meeting of Commonwealth 'listed' countries in Barbados in January 2001[2] a joint working party of seven tax havens and six OECD states was set up to address their concerns. The non-OECD states proposed, at the first Working Group meeting, the creation of a global tax forum which was to agree to a programme of common global standards by December 2001, embodying the OECD's three principles of transparency, information exchange and non-discrimination. However, the OECD has shown little interest in this proposal nor in continuing negotiations.

But divisions within the OECD have been emerging as the US has begun to take a more hostile line in regard to the OECD's proposals. While continuing to support action to establish a global environment that allows action against money laundering and tax evasion through information exchange, the US is far more critical of any attempt to impose tax harmonisation. 'I am troubled by the underlying premise that low taxes are somehow suspect and by the notion that any country, or group of countries, should interfere in any country's decisions about how to structure its own tax system.... The work of this particular OECD initiative must be refocused on the core element that is our common goal: the need for countries to be able to obtain specific information upon request in order prevent the illegal evasion of their tax laws by the dishonest few' (US Treasury Secretary, Paul O'Neill, May 2001). By contrast the EU continues to be far more concerned about the erosion of its states' corporate tax base by the tax competition offered by the OFCs.

Even within the requirements of the OECD code, 'onshore' OFCs in OECD states, such as the City of London, continue to offer tax advantages to non-resident foreign investors. In 1984, the US had encouraged such deposits by abolishing its witholding tax on foreign investors, who are expected to meet their tax obligations in their country of residence. This has created an international environment where the imposition of witholding taxes has become increasingly problematic. Attempts by the EU to impose such a tax across the Community has been frustrated by the UK government, under pressure from the City of London which wishes to maintain its competitive position for foreign deposits. Most OECD countries attempt to counter any tax evasion and avoidance by multinational companies given their use of intra-company transactions through foreign subsidiaries by the treatment of such affiliates as Controlled Foreign Corporations. But even for OECD tax authorities this can often present serious difficulties.

The way forward

The role of the private sector

The conduct of the private sector in general, and large MNCs in particular, will be central to any attempt to tackle the pervasive problem of corruption. MNCs can influence the societies in which they operate not only through their resistance to the demands for bribes, but also through their relations with their own subcontractors and suppliers.

Some MNCs have found that a great deal can be achieved in influencing local business ethics by working with organisations such as the local chamber of commerce. But a prior requirement is that the MNCs themselves have adopted best practice.

This will require clear codes of conduct and accounting transparency, with good internal controls and external audit. In 1999, the OECD had published 'Principles on Corporate Governance' outlining the desirable improvements in the legal and institutional environment in which companies should operate. But even this does not address all of the problems. There is a need, for example, to clarify the treatment of facilitation payments. The US Foreign and Corrupt Practices Act allows such payments, where these are not locally illegal, but requires that they be explicitly recorded. This precedent has been followed in the OECD Convention, although not in that of the Council of Europe. But the House of Commons Select Committee (2001) regards the distinction between facilitation payments and bribery as entirely spurious and called for the OECD Convention to be amended to outlaw them. However, this will still leave the issue of commission payments unresolved. As part of company law reform it has also been recommended that it should be obligatory to include in annual reports any allegations of corrupt practice and assessments of the internal controls in place to prevent corruption.

But, in addition to legal sanctions, it has been argued that voluntary Codes of Conduct have an important role to play. Again, the OECD 'Guidelines for Multinational Enterprises', agreed in June 2000, provides the framework. But to be successful such codes must be supported by adequate training to ensure compliance and monitoring within the companies.

Governments

A number of issues, however, can only be addressed by governments. The House of Commons Select Committee identified the encouragement of open tendering procedures for public contracts as one important area. They argued that audit trails were essential to the monitoring of the contracting process and that companies should be required to sign 'integrity pacts', undertaking not to engage in bribery, in order to pre-qualify for a particular contract. They also called for the UK's Export Credit and Guarantee Department (ECGD) to more rigorously monitor companies so as to exclude those engaging in corrupt practices. But clearly the ECGD can only act when it has sufficient evidence of corrupt practices to defend itself against any legal challenge. Inclusion in the World Bank's list of debarred companies is regarded as just such evidence. The ECGD does require all companies to subscribe to an anti-corruption warranty and in 2000 introduced a set of Business Principles that included references to corrupt practices.

As for the EU, there have been calls for it to encourage its members to ratify and implement, in national legislation, the various Conventions to which they have subscribed. This includes not only the OECD and Council of Europe Conventions, but also the instruments already agreed by the EU itself. There are also a number of areas where the EU, in its own right, is seen as being able to make a particular contribution. In 1999, the European Council proposed that the EU should establish a justice unit to liaise between national prosecutors and the police in the fight against transnational organised crime while, more recently, the Committee of Independent Experts on Reform of the Commission suggested the creation of a European Public Prosecutor and a single European Prosecution Office. Both these proposals, if implemented, would make a major contribution to international action against corruption and money laundering.

The EC should also have a central role in the establishment of any 'black list' to sanction corrupt companies. It makes little sense for individual Member States to be maintaining their own lists given the requirements of EU wide tendering and the increasing importance of the EC's aid programme. An EU wide 'black list' would represent a far more significant sanction for any company and would result in the development of consistent and legally robust criteria. The temptation for national governments to turn a blind eye to corrupt practices by their own national companies would be severely reduced. The distortions to the single European market arising from corrupt practices are sufficient justification for EU wide action.

Similarly, the EU should be urgently addressing the tax treatment of bribe payments and the role of export credit guarantees. In both cases, the EC must insure uniform treatment across the Community. In the case of the tax deductibility of bribes, if these become illegal then tax deductibility is no longer a possibility. However, the use of ECG may prove more problematic, as governments champion their national companies in international competition for exports, especially in such sensitive areas as defence. Again, an enhancement in the role of the EC in 'black listing' could make a significant contribution to excluding companies, guilty of colluding in corrupt practices, from ECG support. Finally, the EU also has an important role in promoting best practice across the community. Short of legislation the EC will need to closely monitor the European accountancy profession as it develops common accountancy and auditing standards under self-regulation. Similarly, the

EC should encourage the development of a common approach to 'whistleblowing' across the Community under national legislation.

As for the broader global dimension three areas of development suggest themselves. First, further improvements in the international arrangements for sharing information, with a greater emphasis upon combating tax evasion as well money laundering. The OECD's Convention on Mutual Assistance in Tax Matters provides a useful model. More radically, the international community might address the issue of agreement upon a common tax base applicable to MNCs. This would not infringe the sovereignty of individual states in setting tax rates. The OECD Fiscal Committee has already introduced a loose definition of the tax base in its discussions about tax avoidance. Finally, this might be further developed into a system of global unitary taxation for MNCs, as has been mooted by the UN and the IMF. Transfer pricing within such companies offers substantial scope for tax avoidance and evasion. Global unitary taxation would require MNCs to identify the earnings of local subsidiaries as a proportion of the earnings of the company as a whole. A formula (e.g. based upon the value of national sales) would allocate the global profits to individual states, who could then apply their national tax rates.

Clearly, some of these proposals represent a considerable challenge to the national interest and national sovereignty, but it is clear that the international climate is rapidly changing. The threat of international organised crime, the scale of money laundering, with the concomitant problems of financial instability, the erosion of national tax bases and the failure of decades of international aid, compromised by endemic corruption, are all issues that are rapidly rising up the international political agenda. The environment in which multinational companies operate is inevitably going to change quite radically and they would be well advised to be 'ahead of the game'.

Notes

1 For a detailed review of the empirical evidence see Lambsdorff (1999) or Dearden (2000).
2 The non-OECD tax havens have formed themselves into the loose grouping of the International Tax and Investment Organisation.

References

ACP-EU Courier (1999) October, No. 177.
Ades, A. and Di Tella, R. (1997) Champions and corruption, some unpleasant interventionist arithmetic. *The Economic Journal* **107**: 1023–42.

Alesina, A. and Weber, B. (1999) Do corrupt governments receive less foreign aid? National Bureau of Economic Research, *Working Paper* 7108.
Commission of the European Community (1997) Policy against corruption (COM(97)192).
Commission of the European Community (1998) Public procurement in the EU (COM(98)143).
Dearden, S. J. H. (2000) Corruption and economic development. European Development Policy Study Group, Discussion Paper 18.
Hall, R. and Jones, C. (1999) Why do some countries produce so much more output per worker than others. *Quarterly Journal of Economics* **114**: 83–116.
House of Commons (2001) Select Committee on International Development: Fourth Report.
Johnson, S. *et al.* (1998) Regulatory discretion and the unofficial economy. *The American Economic Review* **88**: 387–92.
Kaufmann, D. and Wei, S.-J. (1999) Does 'Grease money' speed up the wheels of commerce? Washington, DC: World Bank Publications.
Keefer, P. and Knack, S. (1996) Institutions and economic performance, cross-section tests using alternative institutional measures. *Economics and Politics* **12**: 207–27.
Lambsdorff, J. G. (1999) Corruption in empirical research – a review: Transparency International Working Paper. See also Internet Centre for Corruption Research: Contribution 5, November.
Leite, C. and Weidmann, J. (1999) Does mother nature corrupt? Natural Resources, Corruption and Economic Growth: International Monetary Fund Working Paper 99/85.
Mauro, P. (1995) Corruption and growth. *Quarterly Journal of Economics* **110**: 681–712.
Mauro, P. (1997) 'The effects of corruption on growth, investment and government expenditure; a cross country analysis', in *Corruption and the Global Economy*. Washington: Institute for International Economics.
Oxfam (2000) Tax Havens: Oxfam Policy Papers, No. 6/00.
Poirson, H. (1998) Economic security, private investment and growth in developing countries: International Monetary Fund Working Paper 98/4.
Rijkeghem, C. and Weber, B. (1997) Corruption and the rate of temptation. Do low wages in the civil service cause corruption?: International Monetary Fund Working Paper 97/73.
Transparency International (1999) Fighting corruption: what remains to be done at EU level: Working Paper.
Transparency International (1999) The role of export credit insurance in the fight against and the prevention of corruption in international business transactions with public-sector partners. September.
United Nations Development Programme (1997) Corruption and integrity improvement initiatives in developing countries.
UNCTAD (1999) World Investment Report. Geneva, UNCTAD.
Wheeler & Mody (1992) International location decisions: the case of US firms. *Journal of International Economics* **33**: 57–76.
Wei, S. (1997) How taxing is corruption on international investors: National Bureau of Economic Research Working Paper 6030.

3
Poor Corporate Governance, Market Discipline and Cronyism in the 1997 Asian Crisis

Christopher Gan

Introduction

Corporate governance refers to the rules of the game that enables stakeholders to exercise appropriate oversight of a company to maximize its value and profits. Both financial and corporate governance restructuring is an ongoing reform program in the post Asian crisis-ridden countries. To be fully effective, corporate restructuring must be linked to bank restructuring, which, in turn, must be linked to the settlement of external debts to scale down the systemic risks. Fundamental changes within the economy are necessary to create arm's-length relations between the government, corporations, and banks. Many corporations in the crisis-ridden countries are over-indebted and frequently are part of conglomerates or monopolies that are controlled by small groups: they have non-transparent accounting and close links to government and financial institutions, including commercial banks (Iskander *et al.*, 1999).

This chapter examines the impact of corporate restructuring and governance in the aftermath of the 1997 Asian crisis in East Asia. That crisis caused an immediate clarion call to re-evaluate the issues of the market cultures and corporate governance in East Asian economies, in which the quality of governance is a key determinant to rehabilitate their financial institutions. This chapter thus addresses itself towards answering some of the questions that policy-makers themselves must answer as they strive to undertake comprehensive reforms to promote better governance. They are looking to reduce excessive risk-taking without causing distress in the financial markets; thereby they hope to minimize the chances of a second wave of crisis.

For almost a decade (1987–96), a phenomenal record of economic growth had been posted in the East Asian region. Countries such as South Korea, Hong Kong, Singapore, Malaysia, Thailand, Indonesia and the Philippines all achieved remarkable rates of growth, hosting high quality manufacturing industries in a wide range of products, from clothes to computers. The region recorded GDP growth rates ranging from 10 percent in Singapore to 4.5 percent in Philippines (von Leffern and Cheng, 1998). These economies were achieving high growth rates in what was considered a stable economic environment, with relatively low inflation and outward-oriented policy regimes. Since the 1980s, the introduction of export-oriented foreign direct investment in the region stimulated exports and import growth. The economic fundamentals were substantially strong as the region enjoyed high saving rates, relatively low inflation, and sound fiscal policy (Kawai, 1998).

However, the growth picture in East Asia has been dismally filled with corruption, cronyism and poor governance. Growth in the region was based on the "borrow and grow now, pay later" philosophy. With growth came wealth and with wealth came greed, cronyism, structural weaknesses and mismanagement. The East Asian economies mishandled the "easy money" that flowed into the region. The capital markets and financial systems did not keep pace with the extraordinarily high growth in the region: they were simply not ready for such growth.

During the region's boom, corruption and cronyism overrode laws and regulations for personal self-interest and gains giving rise to overambitious tycoons, megalomaniac dictators, and the financiers who foolishly lent them the money (Engardio and Clifford, 1999). The private sector borrowed recklessly, while financial institutions borrowed heavily offshore with exchange rate impunity. This resulted in, among other things, the construction of apartment buildings, which were subsequently left empty and unsold as the market became glutted with excessive numbers of real estate properties. In any society, we suggest, there should be a set of laws and regulations that serve productive social objectives, such as building codes, environmental controls, and prudent banking sector regulations.

The anecdotal evidence of the 1997 Asian crisis demonstrated that obscure insider lending practices diminished discipline in the financial systems, and poor corporate governance contributed to the collapse of many banks and corporate firms in Thailand, Malaysia, South Korea and Indonesia. Discipline in the financial system was being sacrificed in the place of quick wealth and prosperity. Without doubt, a financial system without discipline is a financial system without control – an invitation to financial disaster, as demonstrated in the 1997 Asian crisis. The lack of financial discipline highlighted certain institutional idiosyncrasies such as implicit government guarantees given to financial intermediaries encouraging them to engage in excessive risk-taking (Mushkat, 1998). Krugman calls this "pangloss value" which is a competition among over-guaranteed and under-regulated banks leading bankers to finance risky projects based on returns in ideal circumstances instead of a project's expected returns (The Economist, 1998: 70). International capital mobility may not always maximize economic efficiency if governments implicitly bailout banks' losses.

In trying to comprehend the magnitude and contagion effects of the 1997 Asian financial crisis, investors and policy makers from crisis-ridden countries (particularly Thailand and Malaysia) have shifted most of the blame to George Soros' speculative activities. No one can deny the fact that currency traders (such as Mr Soros) and hedge funds played a role in accelerating the financial crisis in Asia. There are many unscrupulous currency speculators and global fund managers in the financial market and likewise many "George Soros." There is no international law in the financial market to stop speculators from profiting in the market regardless of their actions. Neither is it illegal or immoral to speculate in the financial market.

Is Mr Soros solely responsible for the social ills of the 1997 Asian financial crisis? Or, is it the elite and cronies, whose substantial wealth has been eroded by the financial crisis, trying to lay the blame on an international money speculator rather than their imprudent and undisciplined fiscal behavior in the financial market? The poor weren't directly affected by the financial crisis since they do not have the wealth to be big players in the financial market. We suggest Mr Soros is simply a scapegoat of political failures. It is easier to shift the blame to others than admit one's errors and mistakes.

It became abundantly clear during the 1997 Asian crisis that the governance structure in East Asian economies needed to be improved in many aspects if good performances of corporations were to be sustained and financial distress to be avoided. As a result, the governments in the region have to be disciplined in maintaining market integrity and to restore investor's (domestic and foreign) confidence in the region. The aftermath of the 1997 Asian crisis clearly demonstrates heavy losses being sustained by many large corporations. This was heightened by revelations of dishonest or self-serving directors in the 64 failed financial institutions in Thailand who maximized their own interests at the expense of their companies. The accounting rules were lax, and the auditors entrusted with the task of checking the bankbooks and procedures were not vigorous and consistent: and that list is by no means exhaustive.

What is corporate governance?

As has been said, corporate governance refers to the rules of the game that enable shareholders to exercise appropriate oversight of a company to maximize its value and profits. It is a set of provisions that enables the shareholders through voting power to compel those in operating control of the firm to respect their interests (Scott, 1998). Corporate governance is an indirect mechanism in reducing the agency costs and transaction costs imposed by managers acting in their own interests at the expense of the companies and shareholders. However, good governance should not be judged within the shareholders–managers relationship alone. Instead, good governance should take into account actions or conduct of the company on other "parties" such as employees, suppliers, customers, auditors, regulators and the community at large (Scott, 1998; Koh, 1999). They are characterized as stakeholders, and a good governance system should be judged by how well all interests are protected by the contract.

The inescapable characteristics of good governance should include competence, integrity and empowerment.

- Corporate directors will be required to demonstrate competency in understanding of the business involved. This requires that they possess appropriate education and training to command international respect (Copp and Letza, 1998). For example, the Dresdner Bank in Britain published their directors' qualifications in their annual report as part of good governance practice.
- Integrity requires corporate directors to practice ethical values in business. This can be achieved through accountability and sanctions against fraudulent and unethical behavior.
- Empowerment should free directors from restrictive rules and regulations that could hinder their performances. Empowerment does not guarantee better governance unless the responsible public agencies are competent.

Thus, the regulatory framework must be drawn clearly to punish those who step out of bounds (Copp and Letza, 1998).

Good corporate governance integrates three coherent principles namely, process and structure, business prosperity and accountability.

This is to ensure transparency in the accounting and auditing standards and practices. Transparency, integrity and accountability in the running of a company reflect good corporate culture and governance. Good corporate governance reflects good management practices, conforming to the needs of stakeholders and the ability to challenge and absorb dynamic changes in the line of commerce such as external macro shocks (Shunglu, 1998). According to the Sir Adrian Cadbury 1992 Report:

> The country's economy depends on the drive and efficiency of its companies, (their boards) must be free to drive their companies forward, but exercise that freedom within a framework of effective accountability. This is the essence of any system of good corporate governance. (Tsang, 1999: 61)

Both financial and corporate governance restructuring is an ongoing reform program in the post Asia crisis-ridden countries. The harsh economic climate during the 1997 Asian crisis demands restructuring, and changes are needed in the economy which present a challenge to crisis-ridden countries to improve the standards of corporate governance practices so as to sustain economic growth. The quality of good governance is a key determinant to rehabilitate the financial institutions of these countries. To be fully effective, corporate restructuring must be linked to bank restructuring, which, in turn, must be linked to the settlement of external debt problems to minimize systemic risks. Fundamental changes within the economy are necessary to create arm's-length relations between the government, corporations, and banks. Many corporations in the crisis-ridden countries are over-indebted and frequently are part of conglomerates or monopolies that are controlled by small groups (like utilities, transportation and food supplies in Indonesia) and practice non-transparent accounting closely linked to government and banks. This results in cozy relationships between some politicians and their friends, which are incompatible with competitive market investment decisions.

Corporations face governance and external financing problems because different stakeholders have different preferences over how a firm should operate. For example, shareholders want their wealth to be maximized without regard to debt. Creditors want to be repaid, which implies firms taking on less risky projects than shareholders would expect. Managers, on the other hand, would like to maximize their benefits to themselves rather than outside investors (Prowse, 1999). This could sometime result in managers shirking their responsibilities, engaging in embezzlement and fraud.

In the western world, company directors' obligations go beyond maximizing the shareholders' wealth. They have a social responsibility to employees, creditors, consumers and other stakeholders (Lee, 1996). Legal actions can and have been instigated not only by shareholders but also by employees and creditors. For example, insurance claims against directors has been reported on the rise in the US, England and Australia (Lee, 1996). In Singapore and Canada, it is compulsory for public companies to have audit committees and the New York Stock Exchange requires companies listed to have audit committees too (Lee, 1996). Camdessus, the outgoing IMF chief told a summit of the 10th United Nations Conference on Trade and Development (UNCTAD) that for economic growth to be sustainable in the East Asian region it requires fundamental changes in the financial and corporate sectors and old styles of governance should be restructured or abandoned (New Straits Times, 14 February 2000: 21).

How would one undertake to measure, in a rigorous way, the effectiveness of corporate governance in the post Asian crisis region? Is there an appropriate framework to promote better corporate governance practices among companies? One response would be for the government of crisis-ridden countries to establish a prudent framework designed to encourage companies to adopt sound ethical business practices. The framework should be a set of general principles and rules supported by as small a number of detailed provisions as possible (Longstaff, 1998). This includes transparency and proper disclosure of matters such as related party transactions, and auditors having access to external and internal books. It also requires that a board of directors have effective power to oversee and monitor the management's performances on a continuous basis (Lee, 1996). It must also examine closely their incentives to act and observe their performance in actual practice.

Corporate governance problems in East Asian economies

Good governance is one of the fundamental prerequisites for sustainable economic growth in a volatile financial world. When discussing governance, most people think of prominent politicians or other leading figures in authority. The quality of political leadership does play an important role in establishing the goals and the moral tone of leadership. However, the quality of a country's civil service entrusted with the responsibility of managing the tasks of governance that directly and indirectly affect the citizen's lives, is in essence far more important for the achievement of economic growth than the leadership of a few prominent political leaders (Evans et al., 1997).

The ingredients of good governance such as transparency and accountability in the structure, which enable firms to weather through crises was missing among East Asian corporate firms during the 1997 Asian crisis. In addition, East Asian economies lack the right mechanism and regulatory agencies to handle detailed rule making and non-legal administrative enforcement such as financial disclosure and proper accounting standards and practices (Prowse, 1999). There is also a shortage of well-qualified accountants and competent auditors (e.g. Thailand and Indonesia), and the professional self-regulatory agency is inherently weak (Alba et al., 1998). Regulators lacked the expertise to monitor burgeoning markets, while loan officers relied on personal relationships to analyze credit risk, steering funds to the same over-leveraged oligarchs, which resulted in high loan defaults (Engardio and Clifford, 1999). The classification of non-performing loans was weak and inefficient allowing most banks to conceal their weaknesses. For example, the Korean banks who bought Indonesian junk bonds or lent to insolvent chaebol (conglomerates) with implicit government guarantee created a fertile ground for default loans (Delhaise, 1998).

The East Asian governments had pursued an aggressive export-oriented strategy providing incentives such as subsidized loans and tax relief to exporters (The World Bank, 1999), but the equity markets were inadequate and not well developed thereby forcing firms to borrow heavily offshore to sustain such an ambitious strategy. The lack of market discipline, plus a government safety net against systemic and external shocks, led to increased loans to firms with high leverage and low profitability. This demonstrates that corporate and financial sector governance were tolerant in allowing poor performing firms to borrow excessively given their already high degree of leverage. Foreign institutional investors were also caught in the trap of the East Asian government "too-big-too-fail" policy causing them to overlook or disregard the deficiencies in governance practices in East Asia.

Market-oriented critics also blamed the crisis on moral hazard: the inclination of creditors and borrowers to accept excessive risk because of implicit government guarantees of rescue should their businesses fail (Lachica, 1999). Many of these economies were dominated by conglomerates, non-transparent accounting practices and close relationships between the corporate and financial sectors (Iskander et al., 1999). The 1997 Asian crisis also exposed the hazards of corruption and cronyism and business conducted on the basis of "*guanxi* capitalism" (or connections) led to grotesque misallocation of funds (Engardio and Clifford, 1999). Such relations-based financial practices were cultivated over the years and have long been accepted as a business norm and culture in the

East Asian corporate world. For example, Petroliam Nasional Berhad, or Petronas (a state-owned oil and gas company) helped buy debt-burdened shipping assets controlled by the Malaysian Prime Minister's eldest son, and was also prepared to buy the cash strapped national car maker, Proton (Jayasankaran, 1999). The buy back of Malaysian Airline (MAS) at over twice the current market price of MAS's shares by the government is a violation of business ethics and good governance practices (Holland, 2001). In 1997, the top ten families in Indonesia controlled businesses worth more than half the country's market capitalization; in South Korea, the majority of the loans are made to Chaebols (well connected corporate manufacturing conglomerates) (Iskander *et al.*, 1999).

Corporate governance is not a revolutionary concept and is a well-established global issue. Good corporate governance has a multiplier effect generating benefits not only to individual companies, but also to the country as a whole. Since the 1997 Asian crisis, there has been an outburst of comprehensive corporate restructuring and improved corporate governance in the crisis-ridden countries to enhance economic performances to keep pace with globalization of corporate entrepreneurship and the regulatory regimes of other nations' corporate entities.

Importance of market discipline and good governance in the East Asian economies

Rapid economic growth in a liberalized financial world without market discipline is not sustainable. Strong regulatory and legal infrastructures are needed for the financial system to be robust and withstand macro shocks and economic distress. In designing an effective safety net for the financial system, the marketplace must be allowed to discipline financial risk-takers. It may do this by allowing insolvent and troubled financial institutions to fail and by imposing severe penalties on institutions close to failing, thus increasing overall market discipline in the financial systems (Helfer, 1999). Furthermore, shareholders should lose their equity in a failed bank. This adds to the level of market discipline by undermining the "too big too fail" philosophy. Over time, managers of financial institutions will be more cautious and pay more careful attention to risk-taking during periods of economic distress, knowing that they may lose *their* jobs and any investments *they* have in their bank if it fails (Helfer, 1999).

Restructuring and improvement of corporate governance is essential to reduce excessive debt and risk-taking. This involves a comprehensive and integrated approach linking corporate restructuring to bank restructuring in settling external debt problems (Iskander *et al.*, 1999). Fundamental changes within the relationships between the government, corporate firms and banks are required. This should diminish "relation-based" finance practices while restoring confidence in the financial system with a new and effective legal, regulatory, accounting, and institutional framework. In turn, this would lead to a competitive corporate and financial system that minimizes excessive risk-taking in a disciplined fashion. It would install equitable risk sharing and responsibility among creditors, borrowers, and the government, enhancing market discipline in the financial markets (Iskander *et al.*, 1999). There should be no artificial advantages in the financial markets in any form. Credit should be made on the principle of a borrower's ability to repay and not on some special relationship with the creditor.

Indeed, the efficiency of financial systems must be set within a disciplined legal and regulatory framework. Regional banks often lack adequate internal, market and regulatory discipline to deal with financial distress. A system of effective and reliable laws and regulations is required to stipulate the contractual rights and responsibilities of market participants so as to encourage discipline and prudent behavior. Effective bankruptcy laws must be legally enforced to ensure that unviable firms do not continue to absorb credit. The presence of an effective bankruptcy system should help create a disciplined climate for monitoring risk taking between creditors and borrowers in the financial market.

Effective and stable political institutions and bureaucrats are being recognized as prerequisites in achieving good corporate governance in an economy. This requires monitoring the performance of public agencies and authorities actively penalizing bureaucratic abuses and inefficiencies (Landell-Mills and Serageldin, 1991). Public authorities have a critical and indispensable role in establishing cost-effective policies governing economic activity. Local governments should remain the primary and core institutions in local governance and cannot delegate their responsibilities in public policy making and planning to others. According to a UN consultant at a workshop on promoting good governance, there are nine characteristics to improve governance. These include strategic vision, effectiveness and efficiency, responsiveness, participation in governance, consensus-orientation equity, and rules of law, transparency and accountability (New Straits Times, 21 February 2000: 2). Improvement in local governance will emerge if the above characteristics are adhered to and there is co-operation between private business and civil society organizations.

There is ample evidence that the long-term survival of any financial system in an economy depends on good corporate governance practices that adequately protect outside investors (Prowse, 1999). Countries that enjoy higher and sustainable economic growth are countries, which have good corporate governance and well-established capital markets. For example, the Toronto Stock Exchange Disclosure Requirements (1995) serves as a guideline and benchmark in establishing governance structure which includes giving flexibility in corporate boards, so directors have the opportunity to design the governance system that work best for their corporations. A study on the governance code by Dey (1999) reveals that the Canadian boards of directors and their shareholders have taken a more proactive role in issues pertaining to governance. The Hong Kong Stock Exchange provides board guidelines to public listed companies and they too believe that self-regulation by boards of directors is more effective and efficient than the imposition of excessive and rigid regulations in enhancing good corporate governance practices. In promoting good corporate governance, the Hong Kong Company Registry monitors closely, and enforces, the disclosure of information about directors and companies (Tsang, 1999).

Poor standards of corporate governance can be positively linked to overvalued assets, inappropriate lending, and a host of other imprudent behaviors that were said to cause the collapse of the East Asian economies (Longstaff, 1998). In a climate of harsh economic conditions how might this problem be addressed? One immediate response would be for the East Asian financial institutions as a whole to establish a prudential framework via the central bank, or monetary authorities, to encourage banks to practice good governance. The framework should make it an annual mandatory exercise for each bank to report the steps it has taken to conform to proper governance practices. The banks, in turn, should address the creditworthiness of companies to whom they lend and thereby implement a corporate governance-rating scheme. This could be the driving force in determining accessibility to financing for companies and for the monitoring of corporate behavior.

The corporate governance restructure mechanism will be a mere clanging of cymbals unless it is designed to protect outsiders (shareholders and creditors) against managerial self-denial. As stated elegantly by Milton Friedman, the social responsibility of corporate managers is wealth maximization for its shareholders while respecting the law and local customs (Cragg, 1999). Anything beyond this objective is a misuse of power that potentially could cause the firm to fail and impede its own responsibilities.

The globalization of trade and the advances in IT and telecommunications have intensified the competitive environment in the daily run of commerce (Copp and Letza, 1998). The "global village" is a reality, and this means that legislation with strong regulations and high ethical standards will promote good governance behavior among companies. Information is increasingly aggressive and pervasive in a globalized world. Computer technology can revolutionize company decision-making processes, which can lead to greater accountability and flexibility. In the developed nation, open governance within knowledge-based companies is now the norm, and they always desire more information about other companies' activities, further, they are more conscious of ethics-related issues (Copp and Letza, 1998). The timely disclosure of information is an important asset in a corporate society – shareholders need to be informed in a timely fashion on matters pertaining to their interests.

Government intervention could also act as a catalyst to promote good governance through education and training, proper disclosure, accountability and the imposition of sanctions against imprudent practices. It can promote the awareness of good corporate governance practice through exposing dishonest and self-interested directors who enrich themselves at the expense of their companies (Lee, 1996). In Malaysia, a report on corporate governance recommended that prior to a company being listed on an exchange, its directors must attend a mandatory training program pertaining to board-related issues such as the director's role in strategic planning and in implementing positive changes (Cheah, 1999). This is an efficient way to bring onboard people who are capable and competent to act as directors of listed companies, to increase investors' confidence and to contribute to the country's growth. In Thailand, the government will provide training in aspects of corporate bankruptcy and formal corporate reorganizations for judges and receivers, trustees-in-bankruptcy company managers, lawyers, accountants and others to improve corporate governance practices (Dirou, 1998).

Approaches to corporate restructuring in the East Asian economies

Promoting good governance practices in the East Asian economies is a challenging and long-term process especially as the costs to taxpayers in accomplishing this task are to be minimized. In East Asia, the immediate task is to make fundamental cultural and institutional changes to create transparent relations between the government, corporations and banks while diminishing "relation-based" financing practices

(Iskander *et al.*, 1999). The challenge for policy-makers is to fend off pressures from all parties so as to restore credibility in the financial system and to build a competitive corporate environment that will increase the investors' confidence. It requires the government to be proactive, to eliminate any obstacles to restructuring, and to establish a better and more effective legislative framework to ensure that any company in financial distress either gets reorganized as efficiently as possible, or if not, is liquidated as soon as possible. Transparency is crucial for accountability and the government has one imperative and immediate task. This is to upgrade accounting and auditing standards to be consistent with international practices, and in parallel revise relevant legislation and regulations to make it mandatory that the statements of public companies be audited in accordance to international standards (Dirou, 1998; Landell-Mills and Serageldin, 1991).

Thailand, Malaysia, Korea and Indonesia have all recognized that urgency and have committed to corporate restructuring to improve governance. The extent of their restructuring schemes and the progress differs among countries. They are influenced by the share of corporate debt held by domestic banks versus foreign banks, whether domestic banks are viably strong to engage in active restructuring, and the extent of non-performing loans in the country (Iskander *et al.*, 1999).

A different route was followed in Korea – under the International Monetary Fund (IMF) restructuring bailout program the Korean government nationalized banks to protect depositors. It also agreed to open up its financial industry to foreign investors to undertake the bank's turn-around (Lee, 2000). For example, in December 1998, the government chose Newbridge Capital of the United States to acquire 51 percent of Korean First Bank (KFB) entrusting the managerial control to Horie, an American financier of Japanese descent (Lee, 2000). One of Mr Horie's restructuring schemes was to transform KFB into an efficient and customer-oriented financial institution, instead of lending money to inefficient companies at the government's request and thus increasing market share through reckless expansion. The objective of Mr Horie's restructuring scheme was to change the KFB bureaucratic image to be business-oriented, which had been plagued by cronyism and poor governance. It is hoped that Mr Horie's restructuring scheme would send a strong signal that any attempt in the future by government to intervene in lending decisions is unacceptable.

The Korean government has demonstrated that no company is too big to fail: the family controlled and operated Hyundai has been swept away. A reformist government has helped reduce the chaebol's once limitless supply of soft bank loans. It has also sold major stakes in steel, oil-refining, aluminum, rolling stock and chemical plants (Clifford and Engardio, 1999).

The Malaysian government has taken several steps to promote and implement good corporate governance practices to protect minority interests and to ensure that there is timely disclosure of information to the market. In March 1998, the government and several key industry representatives got together to establish a framework for corporate governance and the setting of best practices for the industry at large (Yap, 1999). The framework comprises over 70 principal recommendations to raise standards in corporate governance. An Implementation Project Team was established to oversee and enforce the implementation of the recommendations. For example, to prevent abuses by controlling shareholders of publicly listed firms, the Kuala Lumpur Stock Exchange (KLSE) implemented changes to Section 176 of the Company Act requiring the consent of creditors before applications can be made to court to seek protection from creditor claims (Yap, 1999). Work has also begun in forming the Minority Shareholder Watchdog group to achieve greater transparency of ownership and disclosure in corporate transactions. The private sector has also taken an initiative to form the Malaysian Institute of Corporate Governance to promote awareness of good governance practices. In addition, the Securities Commission (SC) is committed to prosecute companies publicly where corporate activities and behaviors contravene the securities laws or exchange listing requirements. The SC is also proactive in resolving the problems of distressed brokers, and has introduced several prudent measures to strengthen the stockbroking industry as a whole.

In August 1998, the Thai government announced a comprehensive restructuring scheme on the financial sector and corporate debts. This restructuring scheme focused on a wide range of measures to resolve immediately Thailand's banking crisis, and to promote better governance practices among the industries at large. Some of the schemes include restructuring and strengthening Thailand's core financial institutions, redefining the role of financial players in a modernized Thai financial sector, strengthening market discipline to enhance transparency, developing appropriate legislative and institutional frameworks for corporate bankruptcies and reorganizations, improving the quality and reliability of key financial information provided by public corporations to regulators, shareholders and the general public, and improving accountability of boards of directors and management of public companies (Dirou, 1998).

The lack of transparency in Thai financial institutions has dramatically undermined the ability of both supervisors and investors to assess, in a timely fashion, the weaknesses and risks borne by their financial institutions, which ultimately caused distress in Thailand's financial industry. The Bank of Thailand and the Ministry of Finance are, under the restructuring scheme, committed to introducing transparency by developing accounting, external auditing and disclosure standards more in line with best international practices. This include reviewing the roles and functions of the Institute of Certified Accountants and Auditors of Thailand (ICAAT) to become an independent self-regulatory professional body consistent with international best practices. ICAAT will issue revised accounting standards for financial statement disclosures, asset classification, marketable securities, and loss recognition as well as deriving new standards for attestation, debt restructuring and impairment of assets.

Cleaning up balance sheets is just one of the many steps that the Bank of Thailand hopes will bring their banks up to global standards. But it must build a pool of professional bankers and loan officers whose lending must be based on borrowers' risk and cash flow rather than personal ties and collateral (Clifford and Corben, 1999). Thus, the role of foreign financial expertise and capital is essential. Recently, ABN Amro of the Netherlands paid approximately $185 million for a majority stake in the Bank of Asia. The Thai Danu Bank is half-owned by Singapore's DBS Bank. Standard and Charter has bought 75 percent of Nakornthon Bank, and Singapore United Overseas Bank is close to buying a 75 percent stake in Radanasin Bank, while HSBC is a front-runner to take over Bank Metropolitan Bank (Ellis, 1999).

The Stock Exchange Thailand and the Securities Commission Exchange will conduct a comprehensive review of the duties and appointment process of corporate directors, responsibilities of officers, and shareholders rights of public companies including listed companies, as well as the contingent liability. The objective is to strengthen the effectiveness and monitoring role of the boards of directors and to enhance shareholders rights (Dirou, 1998). The Thai government is also committed to reducing the debt burden of the corporate sector which has risen sharply during the crisis. Thus, the establishment of the Corporate Debt Restructuring Advisory Committee seeks to promote market-based corporate debt restructuring and enacted legal changes to its bankruptcy law to enhance economic growth and promote good governance practices (Dirou, 1998).

In Indonesia, most corporate debt is held by foreign private banks signifying the importance of foreign banks as key players in the restructuring process. Recently, the elected President Abdurraham Wahid was committed to reforms and rebuilding investors' confidence (though more recent events, in mid-2001 when he was effectively stripped of his powers might cause some alarm with respect to these matters). Even so, the Indonesian government has adopted a corporate restructuring scheme that consists of a framework to facilitate corporate restructuring, a new bankruptcy system, and a mechanism that enables debtors and creditors to hedge against exchange rate risk (Iskander *et al.*, 1999). The Jakarta Initiative Task Force was established in 1998 to provide a mechanism for out-of-court settlement between domestic and foreign creditors in a non-discriminatory manner. Necessary and relevant revision was made to the bankruptcy law, together with the Special Commercial Court to ensure that bankruptcy proceedings will be efficient and transparent. Receivers and administrators overseeing the debtors' assets against insider and fraudulent transactions will be appointed from the private sector to protect creditors from losing out (Iskander *et al.*, 1999).

Conclusions

The "global easy money" available through 1990 to 1996 has virtually fled from most of the East Asian economies, crippling their governments with huge debts and highly devalued currencies (Cheo, 1999). The message seems to be that a sound economic policy and money alone is inadequate to support high economic growth. The common symptoms among the crisis-ridden countries were long periods of growth financed with unhedged foreign borrowing and poor risk management (Delhaise, 1998). Domestic liberalization of the financial sector did not keep pace with changes in the globalized financial world. Their disclosure of financial information was below that acceptable at international level. What is needed across Asia is a clear agenda that is transparent to all, politicians who are seen to be trustworthy, and governments that have realistic and achievable goals and projects. The government should be seen as a stabilizing force, rather than a driving force in the creation of wealth, stability and harmony in the economy (Cheo, 1999).

The global financial market will continue to be volatile, risk will not be completely eliminated, and crises will continue to occur. The best each country can do is to improve its risk management practices to limit severe economic fluctuation. The challenge for East Asian policy makers is to promote good governance practices and develop effective regulatory frameworks for financial institutions with the hope of gaining credibility in the international financial markets. This includes enforcing existing laws, passing new ones on money laundering, and coming down hard on white-collar criminals perpetrating acts such as corporate fraud (Granitas, 2001). This also requires policy measures to restructure the corporate sector and untangle the solvent firms from the insolvent, and to stabilize and rehabilitate viable firms (World Bank, 1999). Banks and market participants should take a more precautionary financial leveraged approach in maximizing their wealth, given the inherent global financial risks. There are no easy solutions to the Asian financial market sector deficiencies, and rigorous restructuring and reforms must address the deficiencies adequately and quickly.

There is no single approach or golden rule to good corporate governance practices. Countries should be given the flexibility to derive their own policy options, restructuring and reform of the financial sector at a pace sustainable by their own markets. It is important for the East Asian economies to build their own surveillance system to monitor the flow of funds and be disciplined in the financial market. They should learn from the crisis mistakes that borrowing from abroad without hedging against exchange rate risk is equivalent to committing the country to suicide. There must also be greater collaboration and co-operation across agencies, sectors and borders, which positively contribute to transparency and accountability. Nothing has fundamentally changed in the global economy to prevent a second wave of the crisis from happening again. However, we suggest that a disciplined financial market will be stronger, and probably more able to react quickly and positively towards future needs.

References

Alba, P., Claessens, S. and Djankov, S. (1998) Thailand's corporate financing and governance structures: Impact on firms' competitiveness. *Mimeo*, Washington, DC: World Bank.

Cheah, F. S. (1999) Training of corporate directors. *The Star* August 24th: 9.

Cheo, R. K. S. (1999) *In Shifting Sands: Examining the Loss of Business Confidence in Asia*, Singapore: McGraw-Hill.

Clifford, M. L. and Corben, R. (1999) Putting banks on the road to recovery. *Business Week* November 29th: 76–7.

Clifford, M. L. and Engardio, P. (1999) Rebuilding Asia. *Business Week* November 29th: 68–70.

Copp, S. and Letza, S. (1998) New century, new boardroom. *Accountancy International* August: 44–5.

Cragg, W. (1999) Two models of corporate governance. *Banker's Journal Malaysia* 109: 71–6.

Delhaise, P. F. (1998) *Asia in Crisis: The Implosion of the Banking and Finance Systems*, Singapore: Wiley.

Dey, P. (1999) "Post the governance code: Positive and negative," *Corporate Governance International*, Vol. 2, pp. 104–11.

Dirou, P. (1998) *Financial Sector Reform: Policy Matrix*. Banking and Financial Sector Management Reform, Mekong Institute, Course A5, August–September: 1–62.

Ellis, E. (1999) Foreigners hired to repair Asia's banks face a tough and thankless task. *Time* November 29th: 39.

Engardio, P. and Clifford, M. L. (1999) Where Asia went wrong. *Business Week* November 29th: 82–4.

Evans, D. E. R., Angela, R. and Rigoli, R. (1997) "Governance and civil service reform: Mali," in S. C. Smith (ed.) *Case Studies in Economic Development*, 2nd edn Reading, MA: Addison Wesley, 228–33.

Granitas, A. (2001) Are your employees ripping you off? *Far Eastern Economic Review* March 8th: 42–5.

Gray, C. and Kaufmann, D. (1999) Corruption and development. *Finance and Development* March: 7–10.

Helfer, R. T. (1999) What deposit insurance can and cannot do? *Finance and Development* March: 22–35.

Holland, L. (2001) Shaking the party grip on power. *Far Eastern Economic Review* March 1st: 16–8.

Iskander, M., Meyerman, G., Gray, D. F. and Hagan, S. (1999) Corporate restructuring and governance in East Asia. *Finance and Development* March: 42–5.

Jayasankaran, S. (1999) "Saviour Complex." *Far Eastern Economic Review* August 12th: 10–13.

Kawai, M. (1998) The Asian currency crisis: Causes and lessons. *Contemporary Economic Policy* **16**: 157–72.

Koh, P. T. (1999) Responsibilities of corporate governance and control of corporate powers. *Banker's Journal Malaysia* **109**: 77–90.

Lachica, E. (1999) Asian financial crisis sparks blame game: Economists are extending finger-pointing to include markets, investors. *Asian Wall Street Journal* January.

Landell-Mills, P. and Serageldin, I. (1991) Governance and the development process. *Finance and Development* September: 14–17.

Lee, C. S. (2000) Makeover at the bank. *Far Eastern Economic Review* March 2nd: 42–3.

Lee, F. M. (1996) Towards good corporate governance practices. *Banker's Journal Malaysia* February–March: 24–6.

Longstaff, S. (1998) Moving beyond the rhetoric of corporate governance. *Banker's Journal Malaysia* **106**: 45–7.

Mushkat, M. (1998) What really caused Asia's crisis? *Times* March 9th: 21.

New Straits Times (2000) IMF Chief proposes shake-up: Move to address criticism leveled against globalisation. February 14th: 21.

New Straits Times (2000) UN consultant outlines nine characteristics of good governance. February 21st: 2.

Prowse, S. (1999) Corporate governance and corporate finance in East Asia: What can we learn from the industrialized countries? *Banker's Journal Malaysia* **109**: 3–22.

Scott, K. (1998) The role of corporate governance in South Korean economic reform. *Journal of Applied Corporate Finance* **10**(4): 8–15.

Shunglu, V. K. (1998) The role of auditor in promoting good governance. *International Journal of Government Auditing* **25**: 1–2.

The World Bank (1999) East Asia: The road to recovery. Washington, DC: The World Bank.

Tsang, D. (1999) Opening address. *Corporate Governance International* **2**: 61–3.

Von, L. E. and Cheng, K. Y. (1998) The Asian economic crisis: Causes and impact. *The Journal of Lending and Credit Risk Management* **80**(7): 50–6.

Why did Asia crash? *The Economist* January 10th: 70.

Yap, P. P. Y. (1999) Towards good corporate governance. *The Star* September 7th: 78.

4
A Two-Stage Model of Cronyism in Organizations: A Cultural View of Governance

Naresh Khatri, James P. Johnson and Zafar U. Ahmed

Introduction

The recent Asian upheaval revealed the macroeconomic risks and damages associated with political cronyism, a type of favoritism shown to associates without regard to their merit/qualifications. Cronyism is a very prevalent phenomenon in societies and organizations with certain cultural values such as paternalism, collectivism, and Confucianism. Despite it being cited as a major factor for Asian economic crisis and mismanagement of the Asian organizations, it is a concept that has not received due attention from management scholars. In order to better our understanding of cronyism in work organizations, we present a two-stage model, grounded in the Chinese/Asian cultural context, of the antecedents to cronyism, and present a number of propositions that follow from it.

First, we briefly examine the origin of the term *cronyism* and its relevance to political life and to organizations, and we provide a definition of cronyism and distinguish it from other related concepts. We argue that Confucian values, lack of trust, collectivism, and high power distance elevate the importance of certain socially desirable behaviors: loyalty and close personal relationships. These behaviors, in turn, lead to three important antecedents of cronyism: an overemphasis on loyalty and relationships, and the formation of strong ingroups.

The antecedents of cronyism in organizations: a cultural perspective

Crony capitalism, or the granting of economic favors to friends and privileged associates, is widely believed to be one of the contributory factors of the Asian financial crisis of 1997 (Dale, 1999). Although the term was coined in 1981 by a journalist at *Time* magazine (Safire, 1998), it did not become widely used until 1997. Cronyism is one of the "4 Cs" (*collusion, cronyism, corruption and complacency*) held to be responsible for undermining competition in Asia (Vogl, 1999); cronyism accounted for financial institutions extending excessive credit to those with special connections, and for governments providing financial support for failing businesses. However, this type of mentality is nothing new in business, whether in Asia or elsewhere (Asiaweek, 1999); it is the basis of the Japanese *keiretsu* and the Korean *chaebols*, which have been widely credited for producing the Asian economic miracle of the 1970s and 1980s. Societies in Asia often turned a blind eye to such behavior until the associated dangers and economic damages were brought to surface by the recent Asian upheaval.

In politics, cronyism is often used synonymously with corruption. The World Bank broadly defines corruption as "the abuse of public office for private gain" (Bottelier, 1998), which "creates favorites, loopholes, connection-based advantages, and fosters an unpredictable and opaque rule of personality" (Suite 101 Articles, 1998). Recent news articles have applied "cronyism" to political contexts as far apart as Britain, Russia, Mexico, and Indonesia. What triggered our interest in the topic is the application of cronyism, a commonly used term in politics, to the organizational context. *Cronyism* has been used to describe relationships in the upper echelons of the management of companies. For example, an AFL-CIO (American Federation of Labor-Congress of Industrial Organization) study documents how cronyism, personal friendships, and interrelationships between top executives and corporate compensation committees and boards contributed to runaway executive salaries (Washington Report, 1998). Another study has shown that individuals who are well connected have higher career attainment than those who are not (Hurley *et al.*, 1997).

In spite of these studies, and notwithstanding the presumed impact of cronyism on global business, cronyism has been a neglected topic in business literature. This conceptual study examines the phenomenon of cronyism in the context of business organizations. We start by offering a definition of *cronyism* and we distinguish *cronyism* from other related concepts. We then develop a two-stage model grounded in the Chinese/Asian cultural context, since the cultural values associated with the Chinese – especially the overseas Chinese – seem to be conducive to the emergence of cronyism: however, as we indicate later, the model might apply to other, more distant societies.

A definition of cronyism

The origin of cronyism

Cronyism is a derivative of the word *crony*, which probably originated in the seventeenth century as a slang term among undergraduates at the University of Cambridge, meaning close friend. *Crony* comes from the Greek word *khronios* meaning "long-standing" (Oxford English Reference Dictionary, 1995). The original idea was that "someone was a crony if you had been friends with them a long time, or even perhaps if you were exact contemporaries of theirs" (World Wide Words, 1998). Around 1840, the meaning of "cronyism" evolved to "the ability to make friends, or perhaps the desire to do so" (World Wide Words, 1998). It first came into use in political parlance around 1946 when a Washington columnist described as cronyism President Roosevelt's practice of appointing to public office people of doubtful competence, on the basis of personal relationships (The Oxford English Dictionary, 1989). Later, the Truman administration was similarly accused of appointing friends to government posts regardless of their qualifications. Thereafter, *crony* became a pejorative term; nowadays, it often encompasses a derogatory sense of a friendship associated with preferential advancement and/or political corruption (World Wide Words, 1998).

For the purpose of this study, we view cronyism as a form of organizational politics, a broad concept that comprises varied political behaviors. In order not to dilute the meaning of cronyism, it is important to emphasize that not all political behaviors involve cronyism. Generally, cronyism is *preferential treatment shown to select associates, without regard to their qualifications, with an expectation of reciprocity*. For example, an employee with a good performance record might not obtain a promotion or pay increase because the supervisor favored another person on the basis of a friend–friend, informal relationship. What differentiates cronyism from favoritism is that the former implies mutual dependence and reciprocity – a *quid pro quo* expectation that need not be present when favoritism occurs. This can occur even where there is a clear power difference between the two parties, because an expectation of reciprocity arises from a shared history, such as school ties, or an existing personal or family friendship.

The friend–friend and other informal relationships can override organizational charts; they involve an element of "power-seeking," where individuals exchange favors to further individual goals that cannot be met through formal channels. Such interpersonal connections often result in the formation of "cliques" (Trice and Beyer, 1993) or exclusive ingroups. We propose that cronyism is dynamic in nature since the relationships among cronies may change; for example, one may leave one crony group and join another when one sees an advantage in doing so, in particular when one's self-interests can no longer be satisfied by the existing crony group. Hence, cronyism does not necessarily reflect a long-standing relationship.

In addition, we wish to highlight the dynamic nature of cronyism from another perspective. According to Walder (1983), a particularistic reward system provides fertile ground for the growth of pervasive networks of informal ties and favoritism. Indeed, the politicization of reward systems brings about unintended consequences by creating strong material incentives for subordinates to exhibit the proper attributes in front of their superiors. Due to the ability of superiors to reward subordinates flexibly and subjectively, subordinates in turn attempt to cultivate personal ties with superiors and conform to their preferences *proactively* in order to improve or secure their positions. Often, the relationship between superiors and subordinates is one in which *active loyalty* is exchanged for reward.

Cronyism in organizations

Organizations can be seen as "complex systems of individuals and coalitions, each having its own interests, beliefs, values, preferences, perspectives and perceptions" (Ott, 1989: 165). Hence, political behavior results as they compete with each other continuously due to scarcity (i.e. limited resources, opportunities, and options in the organizations) (Pepper, 1995) and conflicting interests (Pinto, 1996; Ott, 1989). In many ways, organizational politics is highly similar to "real" politics (Warshaw, 1998); interpersonal alliances and networks are a source of power as individuals seek some form of mutually beneficial exchange organizations (Morgan, 1986). Political activity, then, is a natural part of organizational life (Graham, 1998). Thus, cronyism may be considered as a form of organizational politics in which individuals seek to enhance or protect their own or their group's interests. Beneath the cloak of formal relationships in every organization, there is a more complex system of social relationships, which emerges spontaneously as people associate with one another. Unlike the formal structure, which emphasizes official positions in terms of authority and responsibility, the informal structure emphasizes people and their unofficial relationships (Newstrom and Davis, 1993). According to Furnham (1997), the informal system evolves to fulfill needs that cannot be met by the formal system. Indeed, developing informal relationships with the right people, who may include organizational subordinates, peers, and superiors, can prove a useful means of acquiring power (Johns, 1992). Often, such informal relationships in the organization bring about more influence and power than the formal relationships (Jenks, 1990).

Distinguishing cronyism from other related constructs

Having defined cronyism, we distinguish it from related concepts in the organizational context such as *favoritism, nepotism,* and *guanxi*. *Favoritism* involves subjectivity or bias based on personal preferences (Prendergast and Topel, 1993); favoritism is broader in scope than cronyism since favoritism does not specify the connections and the reciprocal expectations that cronyism does. *Nepotism* is derived from the Latin word "nepot," meaning nephew. The negative connotation of the word dates back to the Renaissance era, when Popes used to find high-level clerical offices for their nephews without regard to their qualifications (Abdalla *et al.*, 1998). Thus, nepotism is similar to cronyism in that it involves favoritism, but it is narrower in scope as it is solely based on familial ties. *Guanxi* literally means "relationship" or "connection." It can be best translated as friendship with implications of continued exchange of favors (Pye, 1992). *Guanxi* is a long-term relationship and it, too, implies reciprocal obligations by the parties involved. A *guanxi* base must exist which comprises either a blood base or a social base, where the former includes only familial connections while the latter encompasses other social (i.e. non-familial) connections (Tsang, 1998). *Guanxi* may be seen as synonymous with cronyism in that it involves interpersonal obligations and is based on relationships rather than objectivity. However, it extends beyond our definition of cronyism, as it comprises both familial and non-familial relationships, while our definition is confined to non-familial, informal relationships in the organization. Furthermore, *guanxi* is of a long-standing nature since *guanxi* relationships can persist long after relevant social groups are dissolved (Goodwin and Tang, 1996). In contrast, cronyism is not necessarily long-standing.

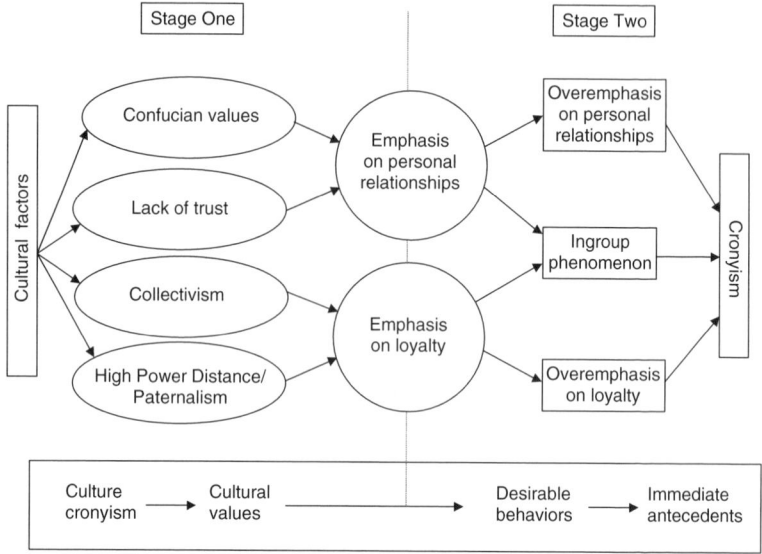

Figure 4.1 The antecedents of cronyism

In the following section, we develop a two-stage model of the antecedents of cronyism (see Figure 4.1). We argue that certain cultural values provide an environment conducive to behaviors that lead to the immediate antecedents of cronyism. Although the values that foster cronyism exist to some extent in all cultures, the Chinese/Asian culture is especially conducive for crony behavior. In the first stage, we discuss how the cultural values *Confucianism, lack of trust, collectivism*, and *high power distance/paternalism* lead to certain socially desirable behaviors. In the second stage, we discuss how these behaviors contribute to the immediate antecedents of cronyism: *ingroup phenomenon, overemphasis on relations*, and *overemphasis on loyalty*.

Stage 1: The cultural antecedents of cronyism

In the first stage of our model, we link four cultural values (Confucian values, lack of trust, collectivism, and high Power Distance/paternalism) with two highly desirable behaviors: an emphasis on loyalty and an emphasis on personal relationships.

Confucian values

Chinese culture is characterized by its stress on human interaction as the "fundamental groundwork of its philosophical systems" (Chan,

1963, 1967; Fung, 1983). The teachings of Confucius, often termed *Confucian values*, are a primary influence on Chinese culture and shape much of contemporary Chinese behavior (Ralston *et al.*, 1997). Gabrenya and Hwang (1996: 309) note that the Chinese social behavior is "a reflection of Confucian ideological beliefs." Confucianism emphasizes the importance of societal, group, and hierarchical relationships within a society (Ralston *et al.*, 1997). According to Confucius, there are five fundamental cardinal relationships, known as *wu-lun*, in which power and status differentials are prescribed: emperor–minister, father–son, husband–wife, brother–brother and friend–friend (Gabrenya and Hwang, 1996; Chen, 1995; Goodwin and Tang, 1996). Of these, voluntarily constructed friend–friend relationships are most relevant to the study of cronyism, since we have confined our scope to non-familial relations.

Confucian philosophy assumes that different relationships imply different norms of interaction; thus, social interaction is determined by the rules governing relationships. Similarly, the cultivation of external relations (beyond the family) is also governed by humanistically oriented emotions, which can be seen as the guiding spirit of Chinese cultural life. To the Chinese, being part of an integrated network of social relationships is of utmost importance (Chang and Holt, 1994). Three cultural mechanisms, *guanxi*, *renqing*, and *relational personalism*, are used to extend familial support beyond the domestic setting (Current Anthropology, 2000).

Guanxi is the key concept for understanding Chinese behavior in social, political, and organizational contexts (Bond and Hwang, 1986). According to Hwang (1987), interpersonal relationships in Chinese society can be classified into three categories: expressive ties, instrumental ties, and mixed ties. Of these, *mixed ties* are the most applicable in an organizational context since they are considered as "the *guanxi* outside an individual's immediate family" (Bond and Hwang, 1986: 224). In this kind of relationship, the affective component of the ties overshadows the instrumental part of the relationship. Due to this strong affective component, individuals seek to influence others by means of *renqing*.

Renqing indicates "the emotional responses of an individual confronting various situations of daily life" (Gabrenya and Hwang, 1996: 313). It denotes a set of social norms that one has to abide by in order to establish and maintain favorable relationships with other people. As such, resources are distributed according to the renqing rule instead of the equity rule. Special considerations apply if any of the parties involved in a social exchange is someone in power (Hwang, 1987). The manipulation of such interpersonal relationships has long been a strategy for attaining desirable resources in Chinese society (Bond and Hwang, 1986). The rule of *renqing* is a "derivative of the norm of reciprocity" (Hwang, 1987: 956). Individuals are influenced by the Confucian view that interpersonal relationships consist of an element of reciprocity (*bao*), that is, the recipient of a favor should repay it (Gabrenya and Hwang, 1996).

In an organizational context, Chinese culture places greater emphasis on seniority, relationships, and family ties (Kipling, 1996). The employment relationship is relationship-oriented rather than contract-oriented (Hampden-Turner and Trompenaars, 1997). The dyadic relationship between the superior and the subordinate is governed by their interpersonal ties rather than contractual obligations. Thus, within an organization, there is a clear demarcation between members of *ingroups* and *outgroups* (Goodwin and Tang, 1996). This phenomenon is an application of "relational personalism" in an organizational context (Gabrenya and Hwang, 1996: 311).

Personalism refers to "the mechanism used by a society to establish reliable connections for the conduct of everyday affairs" (Redding and Hsiao, 1993: 177). The exercise of personalism in interpersonal relationships allows the Chinese to overcome the problem of insecurity due to a lack of institutional systems such as laws. This traditional mechanism still persists (Redding and Hsiao, 1993).

Therefore, an emphasis on interpersonal relationships in Confucian teaching results in the development of complex networks of *guanxi* and the use of personalism in social interaction (see Figure 4.2a). This allows individuals to utilize relationships in the most beneficial way. Since cronyism is a phenomenon that involves using one's connections to obtain special privileges, its existence can be understood in culture that emphasizes the importance of personal relationships, such as a culture that is influenced by Confucian values. Hence, the following argument:

Proposition 1. The more a culture emphasizes Confucian values, the greater the importance that is placed on personal relationships.

Lack of trust

Trust is of central importance to social networks, especially in Chinese society (Redding, 1990). Trust is defined as "a willingness of a party to be vulnerable to the actions of another party based on the expectation that the other will perform a particular action important to the trustor, irrespective of the ability to monitor or control that party" (Mayer *et al.*, 1995: 712). The traditional Chinese society is structured in such a way as to negate the support of trust in institutions. Instead, trust is

A Two-Stage Model of Cronyism in Organizations   69

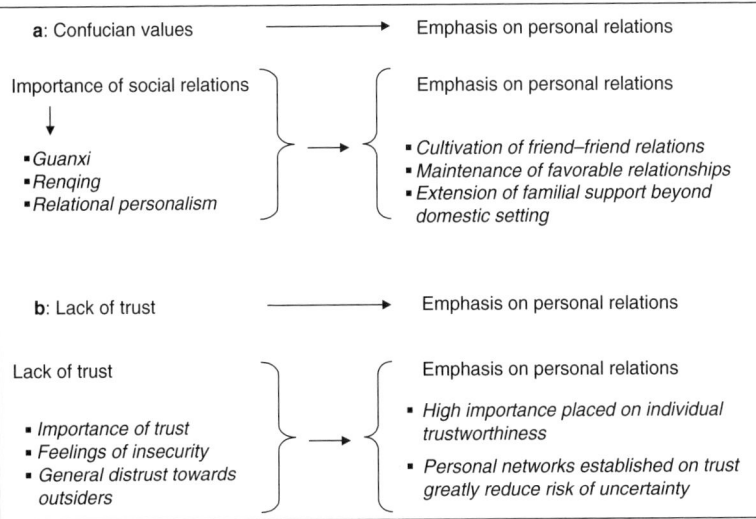

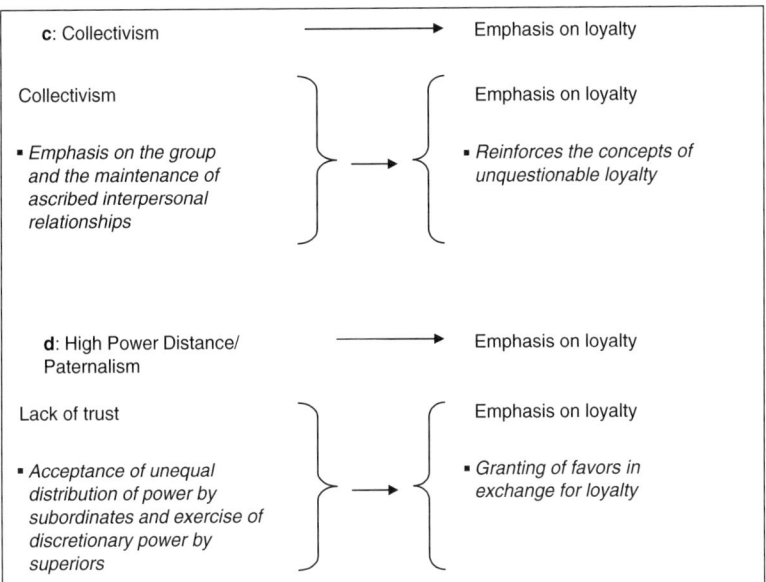

Figure 4.2 (a–d) The link between cultural values and desirable behaviors

transacted over elaborate webs of personal connections or relationships, that is, *guanxi* networks (Redding *et al.*, 1994). Trust is an essential condition for building and maintaining *guanxi* in a relationship-based society (Yeung and Tung, 1996). The Chinese have great difficulty in relationships that are of a neutral and objective nature because they cannot easily "read" trustworthiness (Redding, 1990). This implies that, for the Chinese, business relationships may evolve from their personal *guanxi* only when the counterparties are perceived as trustworthy (Tsang, 1998). In *guanxi* networks, the risks of "vulnerability" or uncertainty can be greatly reduced since opportunism is checked by trust (Bjorkman and Kock, 1995), which tends to be exclusive (Redding, 1990). Here, trust is limited to partners in the bond and it works on the basis of personal obligations, the maintenance of reputation, and "face."

Redding *et al.* (1994) identified two prominent features of societal trust processes among the Chinese: (1) the high importance placed on individual trustworthiness, and (2) the highly selective nature of the bonds in a general environment of mistrust. Therefore, to the average Chinese, the social world comprises those few whom they can trust to a very high degree, and the remainder who are not trusted at all. In general, the Chinese do not trust strangers. This characteristic of lack of trust can be attributed to the feelings of insecurity experienced by the Chinese. Hence, personal networks established based on trust become appropriate tools for the Chinese to overcome their fear of insecurity and provide comfort in the face of uncertainty (Krackhardt, 1990).

In the Chinese culture, an individual is a self-created center of an ever-expanding set of relationship "circles" (Fei, 1947). In an organizational context, interpersonal relationships can be represented by concentric circles: the central circle is the family itself and the next circle is the protofamily, whose members are treated as honorary family members, for trust bonding also extends to non-kin members (Redding *et al.*, 1994). Wong (1988) noted that bonding is "a matter of the degree of personalism in the connections" regardless of the existing family ties. The outer circle consists of the remaining employees or co-workers.

Thus, the Chinese lack of trust in others (outsiders) results in an emphasis on relationships as a mode for individuals to obtain the resources they desire (see Figure 4.2b). The development of networks based on personal relationships helps to solve the problem of insecurity in the Chinese cultural system. Hence, the following proposition:

Proposition 2. In societies where lack of trust in others is widespread, there is greater emphasis on developing and maintaining personal relationships.

Collectivism

Collectivism defines and shapes the relationships among people in a culture and the social structure they operate in (Hofstede, 1980; Earley, 1997). In this section, we discuss how an *emphasis on loyalty* can be traced to this important cultural dimension. Hofstede (1980) defined collectivist societies as those where since their birth people are integrated into strong, cohesive *ingroups* that continue to protect them throughout their lifetime in exchange for *unquestioning loyalty*. Collectivism emphasizes the group and the maintenance of ascribed and interpersonal relationships (Kim, 1994).

In a collective society, individuals are attached to a group or groups (Redding and Wong, 1986), and the sense of attachment and group identity is very strong (Triandis *et al.*, 1993). Collectivists are inclined to behave differently depending on whether or not the other party is a member of their ingroup. If the other party is an ingroup member, the behavior would be very associative (Triandis, 1994), such as providing support and assistance to that person (Triandis *et al.*, 1993). In fact, "socioemotional inputs" may be accorded a relatively stronger role than task-related inputs in the determination of payoffs and in contributing toward group maintenance (Bond *et al.*, 1982: 187). Since "loyalty to the leader is usually tied to the need of belonging and of finding group identity..." (Pye, 1985: 332), it follows that the need for attachment brings about a display of loyalty from the subordinate to the superior.

In collectivist cultures, where the emphasis is on people, ingroup relationships are intensive and interdependence is high (Triandis *et al.*, 1988). Hence, in a collectivist work unit, the employment relationship resembles a family relationship with mutual obligations of protection in exchange for loyalty (Hofstede, 1991). Therefore, there is a greater possibility that collectivists would select, evaluate, and promote individuals based on their loyalty and seniority rather than on their merit and competence (Triandis, 1995). Also, since collectivist individuals value relationships with their groups, a collectivist's sense of attachment is highly pronounced. Favoritism shown by the superior towards the subordinate and the unquestioning loyalty displayed in return characterizes the ingroup relationship found in collectivistic societies (see Figure 4.2c).

Proposition 3. In collectivist societies, individuals in organizations place great emphasis on loyalty.

High Power Distance/paternalism[1]

Power Distance is the extent to which the less powerful members of institutions and organizations within a society expect and accept that power is distributed unequally (Hofstede, 1991). Paternalism refers to a system in which superiors give favors to their subordinates in exchange for their loyalty (Husted, 1999). According to Bond (1991: 86), such "granting of 'favors' is an important component of paternalism, as it builds a network of people tied to someone in authority out of indebtedness and obligation." This distribution of resources beyond the superior's normal responsibilities is possible because paternalism is highly pronounced in high Power Distance societies (Husted, 1999).

In high Power Distance cultures, the less powerful individuals in organizations are willing to accept unquestioningly the unequal distribution of power (Blunt, 1993). The employees are at ease with the paternalistic style of management and there is no strong felt need for them to be involved in decision-making (Banks and Waisfisz, 1994). They accept the inequalities inherent in the organizational hierarchy and expect to be told what to do by their superiors. In addition, their ideal boss is a benevolent autocrat (Banks and Waisfisz, 1994; Hofstede, 1991). Hence, the superiors have considerable discretionary power as they are seldom required to justify their decisions openly. Furthermore, there is a greater possibility for mechanistic law to give way to human judgment (Bond, 1991).

One form of paternalistic behavior present in high Power Distance societies is the downward influence that can be observed in resource control, whereby individuals with control over key resources achieve the highest levels of control within an organization. Thus, "power differentials" enable the actual, unequal distribution of resources to be legitimated (Earley, 1997: 148). In such downward influencing tactics, both parties have strong obligations towards the concern and fulfillment of each other's interests (Chen *et al.*, 1998). Moreover, decisions are made based on the balance between favors and *loyalty* rather than merit (Husted, 1999). In paternalistic organizations, the preferential treatment shown by superiors to subordinates and the latter's obligation to return the favor is a characteristic of cronyism. In this process, loyalty is displayed as a valued obligation to the superiors.

In Chinese enterprises, those in positions of power and control allocate resources mostly according to their personal likes and dislikes (Cheng, 1999). In dealing with superiors, one tends to focus more on personal kinds of power tactics (Fairholm, 1993). Therefore, in order to cater to their individual agendas, subordinates may seek favors from those in key positions and, in return, provide them with personal attributes such as loyalty. In this connection, Sinha (1996) commented that power within an ingroup flows freely and that the more powerful person (the superior) shows love, affection, and care, and even takes the liberty to impose himself or herself in the interests of the favored subordinate. Further, the latter reciprocates by being personally loyal, dependent, and submissive. This reinforces the "unquestioning loyalty" that ingroup members are willing to display towards those in positions of power (see Figure 4.2d).

In light of the above arguments, we propose:

Proposition 4. In high Power Distance/paternalistic societies, there is strong emphasis on personal loyalty.

To summarize, the values of the Chinese give rise to two socially desirable behaviors: emphasis on relationships and loyalty. Confucian values and lack of trust result in an emphasis on close personal relationships, while collectivism and higher Power Distance/paternalism result in an emphasis on loyalty. In the next stage of the model, we propose that under certain conditions these socially desirable behaviors can become dysfunctional, leading to three phenomena that are immediate antecedents to cronyism: ingroup formation, overemphasis on relations, and overemphasis on loyalty.

Stage 2: Immediate antecedents of cronyism

Ingroup phenomenon

Cronyism is likely to occur whenever subjective judgment, based on personal preferences and relationships, is preferred over an objective evaluation of a person's ability. This is reflective of *personalism* or *particularism*, which is the tendency to allow personal criteria and relationships to enter into decision-making and action (Redding, 1990). Since *relational personalism* begins with a distinction between ingroup and outgroup (Goodwin and Tang, 1996), we propose that the ingroup phenomenon is inherent in cronyism and classify it as an immediate antecedent of cronyism (see Figure 4.1). In this section, we discuss two major properties of the ingroup phenomenon: *selection of ingroup members* and *ingroup bias*.

Selection of ingroup members. The concept of ingroup/outgroup has been illustrated by Graen and his associates (Dansereau *et al.*, 1975; Graen and Cashman, 1975) in the vertical dyad linkage theory of leadership, in which an individual's relationship to the workgroup is largely a function of the individual's association with an ingroup or outgroup. According to this theory, leaders develop relationships of varied degrees of closeness and distance with their subordinates. They usually establish special relationships with a small number of trusted subordinates (the ingroup), to whom they pay relatively more attention than to their remaining subordinates (the outgroup); the selection of the ingroup members is made on the basis of subordinate competence and dependability. However, this Western leadership theory is instrumental in nature and emphasizes the exchange of mutual benefits between individuals, while the formation of ingroups is based on ability and mutual trust. In contrast, the Chinese model of leadership is influenced by *bao* (reciprocity), which has a considerable degree of affective content over and above instrumental content. Thus, in Chinese societies, ingroups are determined more by hierarchical status in social relations and *bao* (Liu, 1999).

Cheng (1999) contends that Chinese CEOs categorize their employees according to three criteria:

1 relationship (*guanxi*) – whether they are ethnically related by kinship or parakinship;
2 loyalty (*zhongcheng*) – whether they possess unfailing loyalty and unreserved obedience to the CEO; and
3 competence (*chaineng*) – whether they have the ability and motivation to fulfill the goals assigned to them.

The CEO's personal values or preferences would result in differential weighing of the three aspects (i.e. relation, loyalty and competence) in employee categorization, and subsequently in dividing the employees into ingroups and outgroups.

In view of this Chinese leadership model and our earlier discussion of the cultural values underlying the importance of personal relationships and loyalty in cronyism, we propose that the selection of ingroup members is premised on *relationship* and *loyalty*. That is, given a choice between an employee who has a close relationship and high loyalty but low competence, and another employee who has high competence but a distant relationship and low loyalty, the former would be favored and recognized as an ingroup member (see Figure 4.3a).

Proposition 5. An emphasis on ingroups in Chinese culture, whereby relationships and loyalty take precedence over one's ability and competence, is a major source of crony behavior.

Ingroup bias. Studies have suggested that the mere act of categorizing people into ingroups and outgroups tends to result in favoritism toward one's ingroup (Tajfel *et al.*, 1971; Turner *et al.*, 1983). Indeed, due to this tendency to differentiate among subordinates (either knowingly or

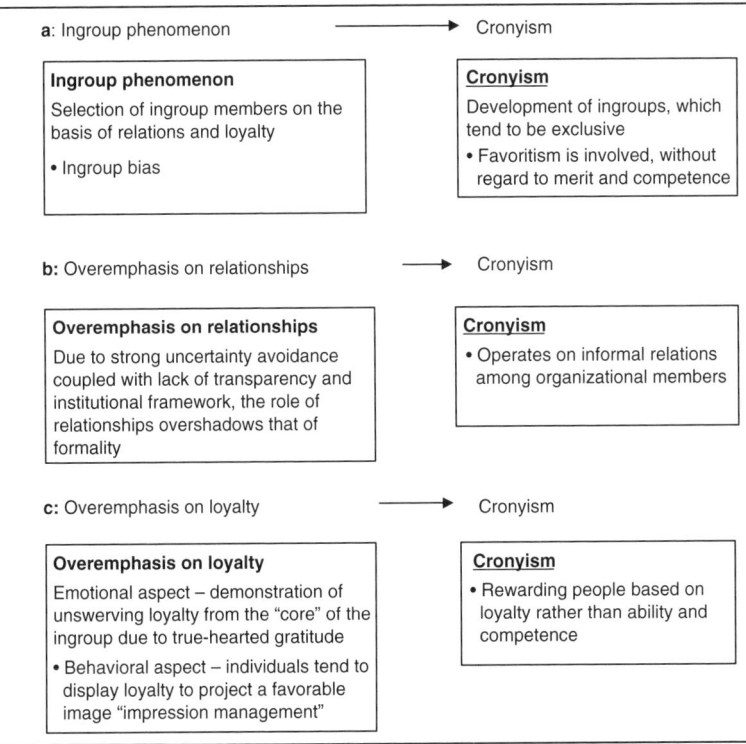

Figure 4.3(a–c) The link between immediate antecedents and cronyism

unknowingly), bias is inevitable and is reflected in various organizational behaviors. In particular, superiors tend to be more human-relation oriented towards ingroup subordinates and more task-oriented towards outgroup subordinates (Cheng, 1999). In addition, ingroup members enjoy considerable benefits, while outgroup members are denied valuable opportunities (Vecchio, 1997). Graen and Cashman (1975) have suggested that ingroup members are given high levels of trust, interaction, support and rewards, while outgroup members receive low levels of each. Since the distinction between ingroups and outgroups is at the very root of people's consciousness, such preferential treatment of one's ingroup is seen as natural and sound (Hofstede, 1991).

Proposition 6. Where the ingroup phenomenon is widespread, ingroup bias leads to crony behavior.

Overemphasis on personal relationships

As discussed earlier, both *Confucian values* and *lack of trust* give rise to an emphasis on personal relationships. This emphasis results in the formation of strong personal ties among the Chinese, and such ties constitute a basis of trust that can provide comfort in the face of uncertainty (Krackhardt, 1990). In our earlier discussion of Hofstede's Collectivism and Power Distance dimensions, we argued that the values underpinning these dimensions lead to an emphasis on loyalty; in this section, we highlight the role of uncertainty avoidance, suggesting that when an emphasis on personal relationships is combined with strong uncertainty avoidance, the result can be an *overemphasis on relationships* (see Figure 4.3b).

Uncertainty Avoidance is defined as "the extent to which members of a culture feel threatened by uncertainty or unknown situations" (Hofstede, 1991: 113). It reflects the level of tolerance for ambiguity within a given culture. Thus, individuals in societies with strong Uncertainty Avoidance feel more comfortable in a structured environment due to strong preferences for written rules and regulations (Hofstede, 1980). Hence, the emotional need for a proper institutional framework, if not satisfied, can result in the use of alternative obligation networks to fulfill that need. Chinese society, in particular, is one where the role of relationships often surpasses that of formality (Yeung and Tung, 1996).

In an organizational context, Uncertainty Avoidance relates to "formalization: the degree to which people feel the need for formal structure in the social or work environment" (Banks and Waisfisz, 1994: 81). Organizations characterized by strong Uncertainty Avoidance are more resistant to change, and there is a desire for well-established organizational structures in which clearly expressed rules and regulations are obeyed (Blunt, 1993). Thus, there is a preference for a proper institutional framework and a more transparent system in organizations. However, Chinese organizations are characterized by a lack of transparency. Management processes are neither clearly defined nor formalized. Employees' responsibilities are often left unspecified and ambiguous (Redding, 1980). Furthermore, due to a general distrust towards outsiders, disclosure is low in organizations and company policies, decisions, and plans are not openly shared and communicated to all. Hence, a lack of transparency results in the face of such ambiguity and poor disclosure.

In political contexts, the lack of transparency has been established as a major contributing factor to corruption (Suite 101 Articles, 1998). Similarly, in the organizational context, uncertainty or ambiguity has been highlighted as one of the principal conditions under which political behavior occurs (Ferris *et al.*, 1993). Since we have identified cronyism to be a form of political behavior, this phenomenon is likely to exist in organizations where there is a lack of formality. Thus, when the need for a formal structure by organizational members cannot be met, they attempt to reduce the uncertainty they face through the maintenance of close relationships with key figures in the organizations. In this way, strong Uncertainty Avoidance along with a lack of transparency and a weak institutional framework results in an overemphasis on relationships over time. Instead of relying on formal rules and procedures, organizational members often rely on the backdoor relationships they have established to achieve their goals. Hence:

Proposition 7. Strong Uncertainty Avoidance, coupled with a lack of transparency and a weak institutional framework, leads over time to an overemphasis on relationships, which in turn leads to crony behavior.

Overemphasis on loyalty

Having examined how an *overemphasis on relationships* can lead to cronyism, we explore loyalty in a similar fashion. In our view, although loyalty itself is a virtue or a desirable behavior, overemphasis on loyalty can lead to dysfunctional consequences. Pye (1985: 297) noted that "the virtue of loyalty *unquestionably* enjoys a loftier position in the Chinese political system than it does in liberal Western politics...." In a Western context, Becker *et al.* (1996) distinguished identification and internalization as the two major dimensions of loyalty. However, Chen *et al.* (1998) found that in the Chinese organizational context the dimensions of loyalty to one's supervisor include a uniquely Chinese dimension that reflects one's personal attachment to and gratitude towards the supervisor. In addition, Chinese societies are characterized by *personalism and paternalism*, suggesting that loyalty to supervisor (person) rather than loyalty to organization (system) plays a more important role in driving employee behaviors (Redding, 1990).

To explore further the concept of loyalty, we extend the discussion to Chi's (1999) study of *chin-shins* (confidantes) who hold special positions in their superiors' relational networks. *Chin-shins* are more than ingroup members; to be more exact, they are the "core" of an ingroup. The relationship between *chin-shin* and superior goes beyond instrumental social exchange. A *chin-shin* perceives the superior as someone who deserves sincere gratitude and in turn s/he demonstrates unreserved loyalty to the superior. Indeed, the unreserved devotion and unswerving loyalty that are expected of employees are based on the link between *patronage* and gratitude (Cheng, 1999), where *patronage* is the act of dispensing favors to individuals regardless of their abilities (Redding and Baldwin, 1991).

The same principle appears to be entrenched in cronyism. Cronies are tied by bonds of obligation in which *patronage downwards* and *loyalty upwards* are exchanged. This explains why traits such as loyalty and "followership" are valued more than ability and competence in cronyism. At this point, it is important to highlight that loyalty has two dimensions, that is, *the emotional aspect* and *the behavioral aspect* (Goman, 1991). Although the above literature regarding the demonstration of unswerving loyalty from the core of the ingroup due to sincere gratitude provides some support for the emotional aspect of loyalty in cronyism, we cannot overlook the role of the behavioral aspect. Since emotions are invisible, Goman (1991) suggests that one's loyalty is often evaluated through the behavioral dimension. Hence, with an overemphasis on loyalty, whereby people are rewarded based on their demonstrated loyalty rather than ability and competence, individuals are encouraged to display loyalty (McGrath *et al.*, 1995) in order to capture benefits such as favorable evaluations and more rapid promotions. Such a projection of a favorable image to orient oneself to the achievement of desirable ends may be termed broadly as *"impression management,"* which refers to the process by which individuals attempt to control the impression others have of them. Indeed, one way to gain rewards or desired ends is to appear as though one is enacting appropriate and desirable attributes and conforming to the preferences of supervisors (Turner, 1991). Thus, to elicit the desirable attribute of loyalty, individuals may adopt various impression management tactics such as ingratiation, generally defined as "an attempt by individuals to increase their attractiveness in the eyes of others" (Liden and Mitchell, 1988: 572). In view of the above discussion, we believe that the "right amount" of loyalty is laudable; however, an overemphasis on loyalty perpetuates cronyism in organizational life (see Figure 4.3c). Hence, we propose the following:

Proposition 8. In societies where demonstrated loyalty is rewarded, an overemphasis on loyalty leads to crony behavior.

Discussion and conclusions

We have defined cronyism and discussed the antecedents of cronyism in organizations. A two-stage model explained the antecedents of cronyism, using a particular cultural perspective in order to examine the interplay of various factors that give rise to cronyism. The rationale was that four cultural values present in Chinese societies – Confucianism, lack of trust, collectivism, and high Power Distance/paternalism – give rise to two socially desirable behaviors in organizations: strong loyalty to superiors and an emphasis on personal relationships. These two desirable behaviors lead, in turn, to three immediate antecedents of cronyism: formation of strong ingroups, an overemphasis on personal relationships, and an overemphasis on loyalty. Our model illustrates the effect of cultural values on cronyism in the context of societies in which the teachings of Confucius strongly influence individuals' behavior in organizations. Since the Asian financial crisis of the late 1990s, the negative effects of cronyism on economic activity in southeast and eastern Asia have come under greater scrutiny, resulting in demands from Western businesses and governments, and from supranational organizations such as the World Trade Organization and the International Monetary Fund, for greater transparency in business, economic, and political affairs. In this chapter, we have attempted to show that cronyism in Chinese societies has deep cultural roots. Although culture forms the underlying basis of the model, we are not implying that culture alone can explain cronyism, but rather we are suggesting that certain cultural values can magnify this behavior. As nations succeed in building sound political, financial and legal institutions that people can trust to be effective and impartial, individuals' dependence on ingroups and reciprocal favors is likely to diminish. However, as Hofstede (1980) has pointed out, societal values change at a very slow pace, over generations, so it is over-optimistic and simplistic to assume that cronyism is likely to disappear in a short time at the behest of outsiders.

To assess the generalizability of the model, however, we need to look at two basic elements that lead to cronyism in the model: emphasis on personal relationships and loyalty. Whenever there is overemphasis on personal relationships or on unreserved loyalty or both in an organization, cronyism is a likely outcome. The strength of cronyism will be determined by the strength of personal relationships and loyalty orientation. It is not necessary for both factors to be present to cause cronyism. The presence of one factor, if sufficiently strong, can lead to cronyism, although classic crony behaviors in organizations will be observed in organizations where both personal relationships and loyalty orientation are strong. This brings us to the notion of variants of cronyism; that is, crony behaviors observed in Asia and the West may be somewhat different. Although loyalty is a desirable attribute in all cultures, it has a much loftier position in Chinese societies (Earley, 1997). Loyalty will not be desired and rewarded in the Western context to the same degree as in the Chinese context. The other element of cronyism, personal relationships, can occur in all sorts of cultures and organizations, though the underlying dynamics is likely to be different from one culture to another. For example, in collectivist cultures, the relationship of the individual to the ingroup is stable: even when the ingroup makes harsh demands on the individual, the latter tends to stay with the group. The individualist, on the other hand, belongs to multiple ingroups and has a tendency to change group membership and status (Triandis *et al.*, 1988). The other major difference lies in the goal of personal relationships. In the West, a relationship is likely to be based more on instrumental considerations. In Chinese culture, the relationship serves many purposes, such as providing emotional support, protection, and instrumental gains.

An obvious extension of this study is to examine the model empirically and to examine the organizational consequences of crony behavior, which would be most appropriate in an Asian context. However, it should also be possible to adapt the model to other non-Confucian societies where crony behavior is common. Russia and much of Latin America are relatively collectivist societies where Power Distance is high and paternalism is evident. In Latin America, as in Chinese societies, there is a strong emphasis on personal relationships (Lenartowicz and Johnson, 1999), suggesting that the cultural roots of crony behavior would be observed in that region. By modifying the model presented here or proposing new ones, researchers will enhance our understanding of this important and prevalent phenomenon.

Note

1 We assume high Power Distance and paternalism to be concurrent phenomena and thus have used them interchangeably in this paper.

References

Abdalla, H. F., Maghrabi, A. S. and Raggad, B. G. (1998) Assessing the perceptions of human resource managers toward nepotism: A cross-cultural study. *International Journal of Manpower* 19: 554–70.

Asiaweek (1999) Editorials: Curb the cronies, 25(6): 14–16.

Banks, P. and Waisfisz, B. (1994) "Managing inter-cultural teams: A practical approach to cultural problems," in H. Shaughnessy (ed.), *Collaboration Management – Inter-Cultural Working: New Issues and Priorities*, New York: John Wiley & Sons.

Becker, T. E., Billings, D. M., Eveleth, D. M. and Gilbert, N. L. (1996) Foci and bases of employee commitment: Implications for job performance. *Academy of Management Journal* **39**: 464–82.

Bjorkman, I. and Kock, S. (1995) Social relationships and business networks: The case of Western companies in China. *International Business Review* **4**: 519–35.

Blunt, P. (1993) "Cultural consequences for organization change in a Southeast Asian state: Brunei," in P. Blunt and D. Richards (eds.), *Readings in Management, Organization and Culture in East and South East Asia*, Darwin, Australia: Northern Territory University Press.

Bond, M. H. (1991) *Beyond the Chinese Face: Insights From Psychology*. Hong Kong: Oxford University Press.

Bond, M. H. and Hwang, K. K. (1986) "The social psychology of Chinese people," in M. H. Bond (ed.), *The Psychology of the Chinese People*, Hong Kong: Oxford University Press.

Bond, M. H. Kwok, L. and Kwok, C. W. (1982) How does cultural collectivism operate? The impact of task and maintenance contributions on reward distribution. *Journal of Cross-Cultural Psychology* **13**: 186–200.

Bottelier, P. (1998) *Corruption and Development*. Remarks for International Symposium on the *Prevention and Control of Financial Fraud*, Beijing (19th October). (http://www.worldbank.org/html/extdr/offrep/eap/pbsp101998.htm)

Chan, W. T. (1963) *A Sourcebook in Chinese Psychology*. Princeton, NJ: Princeton University Press.

Chan, W. T. (1967) "Chinese theory and practice, with special reference to humanism," in C. A. Moore (ed.), *The Chinese Mind*, Honolulu, HI: University of Hawaii Press.

Chang, H. C. and Holt, G. R. (1994) "A Chinese perspective on face as inter-relational concern," in S. Ting-Toomey (ed.), *The Challenge of Facework: Cross-Culture and Interpersonal Issues*, Albany, NY: State University of New York Press.

Chen, M.-J. (1995) *Asian Management Systems: Chinese, Japanese, Korean Styles of Business*, New York: Routledge.

Chen, Z. X., Farh, J. L. and Tsui, A. S. (1998) Loyalty to supervisor, organizational commitment, and employee performance: The Chinese case. *Academy of Management Proceedings*.

Cheng, B. S. (1999) "Chinese CEOs' employee categorization and managerial behavior," in H. S. R. Kao, D. Sinha, B. Wilpert (eds.), *Management and Cultural Values: The Indigenization of Organizations in Asia*, Thousand Oaks, CA: Sage Publications.

Chi, S. C. (1999) "The role of chin-shins of top managers in Taiwanese organizations: Exploring Chinese leadership phenomena," in H. S. R. Kao, D. Sinha, B. Wilpert (eds.), *Management and Cultural Values: The Indigenization of Organizations in Asia*, Thousand Oaks, CA: Sage Publications.

Current Anthropology (2000) Guanxi: A nestings of groups. *Current Anthropology* **41**(1). (http://orion.oac.uci.edu/~dbell/html/body_guanxi.html)

Dale, R. (1999) Crisis stills apologists for corruption. *International Herald Tribune*, January 21st. (http://www.egroups.com/group/beritamalaysia/5560.html)

Dansereau, F., Graen, G. and Haga, W. J. (1975) A vertical dyad linkage approach to leadership within formal organizations: A longitudinal investigation of the role making process. *Organizational Behavior and Human Performance* **13**: 46–78.

Earley, P. C. (1997) *Face, Harmony, and Social Structure: An Analysis of Organizational Behavior Across Cultures*, New York: Oxford University Press.

Fairholm, G. W. (1993) *Organizational Power Politics: Tactics in Organizational Leadership*, Westport, CT: Praeger.

Fei, H. T. (1947) *Country China*, Shanghai, China: Observatory Publishing Co.

Ferris, G. R., Brand, J. F., Brand, S., Rowland, K. M., Gilmore, D. C., King, T. R., Kacmar, K. M. and Burton, C. A. (1993) "Politics and control in organization," in E. J. Lawler, B. Malkovsky, K. Heimer, J. O'Brien (eds.), *Advances in Group Processes*, Vol. 10. Greenwich, CT: Jai Press.

Fung, Y. I. (1983) *A History of Chinese Psychology*, Vol. 1 (D. Boddie, Trans.), Princeton, NJ: Princeton University Press.

Furnham, A. (1997) *The Psychology of Behavior at Work: The Individual in the Organization*, Hove: Psychology Press.

Gabrenya, W. K. and Hwang, K. K. (1996) "Chinese social interaction: Harmony and hierarchy on the good earth," in M. H. Bond (ed.), *The Handbook of Chinese Psychology*, New York: Oxford University Press.

Goman, C. K. (1991) *The Loyalty Factor: Building Trust in Today's Workplace*, New York: MasterMedia Ltd.

Goodwin, R. and Tang, C. S. K. (1996) "Chinese personal relationships," in M. H. Bond (ed.), *The Handbook of Chinese Psychology*, New York: Oxford University Press.

Graen, G. and Cashman, J. F. (1975) "A role making model of leadership in formal organizations: A developmental approach," in J. G. Hunt and L. L. Larson (eds.), *Leadership Frontiers*, Kent, OH: Kent State University Press.

Graham, G. (1998) Eliminate office politics and end many problems in companies. *Wichita Business Journal* (9th February). (http://www.amcity.com/wichita/stories/020998/newscolumn4.html)

Hampden-Turner, C. and Trompenaars, F. (1997) *Mastering The Infinite Game: How East Asian Values Are Transforming Business Practices*, Oxford: Capstone.

Hofstede, G. (1980) *Culture's Consequences: International Differences in Work-related Values*. Beverly Hills, CA: Sage Publications.

Hofstede, G. (1991) *Cultures and Organizations: Software of the Mind*. New York: McGraw-Hill.

Hurley, A. E., Fagenson-Eland, E. A. and Sonnenfeld, J. A. (1997) Does cream always rise to the top?: An investigation of career attainment determinants. *Organizational Dynamics* 26(2): 65–71.

Husted, B. W. (1999) Wealth, culture, and corruption. *Journal of International Business Studies* 30: 339–60.

Hwang, K. K. (1987) Face and favor: The Chinese power game. *American Journal of Sociology* 92: 944–74.

Jenks, V. O. (1990) *Human Relations in Organizations*, New York: Harper and Row.

Johns, G. (1992) *Organizational Behavior: Understanding Life At Work*. New York: Harper Collins Publishers.

Kim, U. (1994) "Individualism and collectivism: Conceptual clarification and elaboration," in U. Kim et al. (eds.), *Individualism and Collectivism in Cross-Cultural Research and Methodology Series*, **18**. Thousand Oaks, CA: Sage Publications.

Kipling, R. (1996) *East meets West: East is East and West is West and ne'er the twain shall meet*. An Arthur Anderson Business Consulting Report: *A Survey of Management Culture, Styles and Practices in Asia and the West*.

Krackhardt, D. (1990) "The strength of strong ties: The importance of philos in organizations," in V. Nohria and R. G. Eccles (eds.), *Networks and Organizations: Structure, Form and Action*, Boston, MA: Harvard Business School Press.

Lenartowicz, T. and Johnson, J. P. (1999) *Managerial values in Latin America: A twelve nation comparative study*. Presented at the *Seventh Cross Cultural Research Conference*, Cancún, Mexico.

Liden, R. C. and Mitchell, T. R. (1988) Ingratiatory behaviors in organizational settings. *Academy of Management Review* **13**: 572–87.

Liu, C. M. (1999) "The concept of 'bao' in organizational research," in H. S. R. Kao, D. Sinha and B. Wilpert (eds.), *Management and Cultural Values: The Indigenization of Organizations in Asia*, Thousand Oaks, CA: Sage Publications.

Mayer, R. C., Davis, J. H. and Schoorman, F. D. (1995) An integrative model of organizational trust. *Academy of Management Review* **20**(3): 709–34.

McGrath, N., Janssen, P. and Hulme, D. (1995) Scheming workers can ruin business. *Singapore Times* (1st September). (http://web3.asia1.com.sg/timesnet/data/ab/docs/ab0429.html)

Morgan, G. (1986) *Images of Organization*, Newbury Park, CA: Sage Publications.

Newstrom, J. W. and Davis, K. (1993) *Organizational Behavior: Human Behavior At Work*, 9th edn, New York: McGraw-Hill.

Ott, J. S. (1989) *The Organizational Culture Perspective*, Chicago, IL: Dorsey Press.

Oxford English Reference Dictionary (1995) Oxford, UK: Oxford University Press.

Pepper, G. L. (1995) *Communication in Organizations: A Cultural Approach*, New York: McGraw-Hill.

Pinto, J. K. (1996) *Power and Politics in Project Management*. Project Management Institute, Sylva, NC.

Prendergast, C. and Topel, R. H. (1993) Favoritism in Organization. *NBER Working Paper* No. 4427, National Bureau of Economic Research.

Pye, L. W. (1985) *Asian Power and Politics: The Cultural Dimensions of Authority*, Cambridge: Becknap Press.

Pye, L. W. (1992) *Chinese Commercial Negotiating Style*, New York: Quorum Books.

Ralston, D. A., Holt, D. H., Terpstra, R. H. and Yu, K. C. (1997) The impact of national culture and economic ideology on managerial work values: A study of the United States, Russia, Japan and China. *Journal of International Business Studies* **28**: 177–207.

Redding, S. G. (1980) Cognition as an aspect of culture and its relation to management processes: An exploratory view of the Chinese case. *Journal of Management Studies* **17**: 127–48.

Redding, S. G. (1990) *The Spirit of Chinese Capitalism*, Berlin, Germany: Walter de Gruyter.

Redding, S. G. and Baldwin, E. (1991) *Managers for Asia/Pacific: Recruitment and Development Strategies*, Hong Kong: Business International Asia/Pacific Ltd.

Redding, S. G. and Hsiao, M. (1993) "An empirical study of overseas Chinese managerial ideology," in P. Blunt and D. Richards (eds.), *Readings in Management and Culture in East and South East Asia*, Darwin, Australia: Northern Territory University Press.

Redding, S. G., Norman, A. and Schlander, A. (1994) "The nature of individual attachment to the organization: A review of East Asian variations," in H. C. Triandis, M. D. Dunnette and L. M. Hough (eds.), *Handbook of Industrial and Organizational Psychology*, 4, 2nd edn. Palo Alto, CA: Consulting Psychologists Press.

Redding, S. G. and Wong, G. Y. Y. (1986) "The psychology of Chinese organizational behavior," in M. H. Bond (ed.), *The Psychology of the Chinese People*, Hong Kong: Oxford University Press.

Safire, W. (1998) Crony capitalism. *New York Times Magazine*, February 1st: 16.

Sinha, J. B. P. (1996) "Indian perspectives on leadership and power in organizations," in H. S. R. Kao and D. Sinha (eds.), *Asian Perspectives in Psychology in Cross-Cultural Research and Methodology Series*, **19**. Thousand Oaks, CA: Sage Publications.

Suite 101 Articles, (1998) *Corruption and democracy*. Part Four of a five-part series on *The Clash of Capitalism and Democracy in East Asia*, Suite 101 Articles (3rd April). (http://www.duke.edu/~jason1/s980403.htm)

Tajfel, H., Flament, C., Billig, M. G. and Bundy, R. F. (1971) Social categorization and intergroup behavior. *European Journal of Social Psychology* **1**: 149–77.

The Oxford English Dictionary, 2nd edn (1989) Oxford, UK: Clarendon Press.

Triandis, H. C. (1994) *Culture and Social Behavior*, New York: McGraw-Hill.

Triandis, H. C. (1995) *Individualism and Collectivism*, Boulder, CO: Westview Press.

Triandis, H. C., Bontempo, R., Villareal, M. J., Asai, M. and Lucca, N. (1988) Individualism and collectivism: Cross-cultural perspectives on self-ingroup relationships. *Journal of Personality and Social Psychology* **54**: 323–38.

Triandis, H. C., Brislin, R. and Hui, C. H. (1993) "Cross-cultural training across the individualism-collectivism divide," in Blunt, P. and Richards, D. (eds.), *Readings in Management, Organization and Culture in East and South East Asia*, Darwin, Australia: Northern Territory University Press.

Trice, H. M. and Beyer, J. M. (1993) *The Cultures of Work Organizations*, Englewood Cliffs, NJ: Prentice-Hall.

Tsang, E. W. K. (1998) Can *guanxi* be a source of sustained competitive advantage for doing business in China? *Academy of Management Executive* **12**(2): 64–73.

Turner, J. C. (1991) *Social Influence*, Milton Keynes, UK: Open University Press.

Turner, J. C., Sachdev, I. and Hogg, M. A. (1983) Social categorization, interpersonal attraction and group formation. *British Journal of Social Psychology* **22**: 227–39.

Vecchio, R. P. (1997) "Are you in or out with your boss?" in R. P. Vecchio (ed.), *Leadership: Understanding the Dynamics of Power and Influence in Organizations*, Notre Dame, IN: University of Notre Dame Press.

Vogl, F. (1999) Business ethics: Asian crisis stimulates establishment pressures for fundamental reforms. *Earth Times* (16–28 February). (http://www.egroups.com/group/reformasitotal/6851.html)

Walder, A. G. (1983) Organized dependency and cultures of authority in Chinese industry. *Journal of Asian Studies* **43**: 51–76.

Warshaw, M. (1998) The good guy's (and gal's) guide to office politics. *Issue* **14**, (April). (http://www.fastcompany.com/online/14/politics.html)

Washington Report (1998) Cronyism bloats corporate CEO pay. *Washington Report* **38** (May 15). (http://www.uaw.org/publications/wash__report/3809/wr380902.htm)

Wong, S. L. (1988) *Emigrant Entrepreneurs: Shanghai Industrialists in Hong Kong*, Hong Kong: Oxford University Press.
World Wide Words (1998) Topical Words: *Cronyism*. (http://clever.net/quinion/words/topicalwords/tw-cro 1.htm)
Yeung, I. Y. M. and Tung, R. L. (1996) Achieving business success in Confucian societies: The importance of *guanxi* (connections). *Organizational Dynamics* Autumn: 54–65.

5
Understanding the Mind of the Chinese: A Historical Perspective
Sui Pheng Low

Introduction

In the West, the English language has popularized western management thinking, but the same cannot be said of eastern beliefs and philosophies. Apart from being constrained by the Chinese language that is neither spoken nor written in most parts of the world except Asia, the Orient is often viewed with a tinge of mysticism that made it almost culturally impossible for westerners to perceive. For these reasons, while there are no lack of strategic thinkers and philosophers in the East, their thoughts and philosophies are still not well disseminated let alone popularized throughout the world. With the economic opening of China, an appreciation of its strategic oriental thinking and use of philosophies is of increasing importance for managerial practice. With her rich wealth of history and talents, China has never been short of strategic thinkers and great philosophers. Apart from the eminent military strategist Sun Tzu, there were the eminent philosophers – Confucius (and his disciple, Mencius), and Lao Tzu (and his disciple, Chuang Tzu) – whose teachings have had a tremendous influence on Chinese civilization and culture. Interestingly, these three great Chinese thinkers – namely Sun Tzu, Confucius and Lao Tzu – were all contemporaries in Chinese history some 2500 years ago. The tumultuous activities of this period appear to have been the main trigger for them to reflect and form their thoughts, philosophies and strategies. Socrates, in Europe, was a contemporary of Confucius, though in fact he lived some 80 years later. However, European philosophy and thought developed along lines different to those emerging in the Orient.

The history of China is besieged with bitter encounters with foreigners since Marco Polo's visit to China during the Ming Dynasty

(AD 1368–1644). More recently, China was humiliated by the 1842 Nanjin Treaty, the 1858 Tienjin Treaty, the burning of the Summer Palace in 1860, as well as the invasion of China by French, British and Russian troops shortly thereafter and the so-called Rape of Nanjin by Japanese troops in 1937. Yet, from long before Marco Polo's time, China has always received foreign guests with politeness. Naturally, the events of the last century have created a deep but understandable distrust of foreigners by China. All these unfortunate events of the last century have collectively molded the Chinese to become practitioners of Lee Zhong Wu's *Thick Black Theory:* forced by their circumstances in order to thrive, win and succeed in all their dealings in their marketplace.

Having been peppered by numerous hardships throughout the history of China, the Chinese people have developed within themselves the stoicism for hard work, pain and suffering. A "typical" Chinese would therefore find within himself a conflict as he struggles to remain morally upright (Lao Tzu's teachings) and deport himself as a gentleman (Confucius' teachings) – and yet at the same time, be a person who strives to protect his self-interests both strategically (Sun Tzu's *Art of War*) and ruthlessly (*Thick Black Theory*). This natural struggle in the minds of the Chinese people must be remembered and assimilated by those who venture into China.

This chapter will examine the teachings of Confucius, Lao Tzu and Sun Tzu. It will also, in the process, extrapolate how the value systems of these sages have influenced the cultural values of the Chinese people in their day-to-day activities. The chapter will also highlight the *Thick Black Theory* to explain how the Chinese value system has evolved over time to what it is today. An appreciation of this philosophical evolution in Chinese history is essential for understanding current Chinese business practices not only in China but also in countries with sizeable overseas Chinese communities. What may initially come across as cronyism or corrupt practices from the viewpoints of western developed nations may be, in the final analysis, a phenomenon that is peculiar to the Chinese people by virtue of their historical circumstances.

The Confucian philosophy

It is not the intention of this chapter to cover the teachings of Confucius in an all-encompassing manner as different eminent scholars, both in the East and the West, have examined his writings on many occasions. Confucius was born in 551 BC in the State of Lu in modern Shantung (Dollinger, 1988). The golden rule of the Confucian tradition has been: "Do not do to others what you do not want others to do to you." Reciprocity and consideration are emphasized in all relations, and the way of loyalty and compassion is the thread that holds together all the core values in one's dealings with others. Hence, every man should always pursue self-cultivation through learning to become a responsible contributor towards the achievement of a moral society. This ethical philosophy has, over a long period of time, formed the Asian culture that regards *Jen*, based on mutual trust, as the binding force of society. Four core areas can be identified as important aspects of Confucianism:

1. Education – The Confucian philosophy views education reverently: it stresses the importance of pursuing learning, not only as an end in itself, but also as a vehicle to self-betterment. More importantly, through education, one can optimize one's contributions to society.
2. Commitment – Ethics can be taught to most people, but it will be the people that make the difference. Thus, there has to be individual commitment to adopt and use ethics in everyday business activities if ethics is to be part of an organization.
3. Collective responsibility – This stems from the tradition of distrusting formal rules and regulations, and a dislike of written contracts: both activities emphasize ethics rather than the general adoption of legal norms of conduct.
4. Mutuality and respect – The major thrust of Confucian teaching is that human society should be constructed on the basis of humanism: this attitude always emphasizes conciliatory human relations as a basis of mutual understanding.

The Confucian philosophy is often cited as the major factor determining the Chinese approach to doing business in the modern world today. Consequently, Chinese contracts are typically sketchy three- or four-page affairs, that pay more attention to trust and personal relationships than western-type contractual obligations and penalties (Knutt, 1997). While this is so, the mind of the Chinese may not be as simplistic as it seems to be. Mr Lee Kuan Yew, Singapore's Senior Minister observed that, "You have to be flexible. We are not going to change them; they are not going to change us. But if we want to do business in China, this is something we have to remember. It's different from doing business in other countries because the Chinese are clever people, in fact, too clever" (Lee, 1998). The complexity inherent in trying to understand the Asian style of management (or for that matter, the Chinese style of management) led Speece (2001) to query if there is indeed such a style and if so, what is it? The problematic issues that can arise were important enough for Kidd (2001) to observe that there is a lack of understanding of how East–West differences might collide in the daily execution of conjoint management practices. It is therefore crucial to understand aspects of inter-personal networking or *guanxi* from the Chinese viewpoint. Kidd (2001) pointed out that the Western notion of "networking" or dealing with people is far removed from the Chinese *guanxi* and that when Westerners copy *guanxi*, they do so without the finesse understood by the Chinese. This observation arose because the silent communication associated with intangible *guanxi* is somewhat unfathomable for the Westerner. It is a well-known hypothesis that the concept of *guanxi* is tacitly embedded within the Confucian philosophy and that it subtly defines the Chinese moral code. Leung and Wong (2001) posit that the Confucian social hierarchical theory concerning the five relationships of emperor–subject, father–son, husband–wife, brother–brother and friend–friend (referred to as *wu-lun* in Chinese) has been perpetuated to influence modern China. The Chinese word *lun* describes concisely the *guanxi* among these five relationships. Consequently, an individual will fall into a natural *guanxi* web in his/her socialization process after he/she is born. If every individual subsumes his/her proper position, social harmonization can be achieved in a country – even one as vast as China (Leung and Wong, 2001). It is for this reason that the Social Hierarchical Theory has prompted many Chinese rulers in the past to adopt Confucianism as a strategic tool to achieve social stability in their country (Man and Cheng, 1996). However, it should be noted that the traditional Confucian concept and modern practice of *guanxi* have significant differences. The former advocates a set of moral codes that can be manipulated by Chinese rulers and political leaders to regulate the Chinese people into achieving ideal social harmonization. The modern practice of *guanxi*, on the other hand, treats it as a strategic tool to achieve business goals: it may, in effect, be bought and sold through alliance making. Leung and Wong (2001) conclude that the modern day concept of *guanxi* could be looked at from the four dimensions of opportunism, dynamism, business interaction and protectionism.

Kidd (2001), therefore, argued rightly that when management gurus from the West "tell" Chinese managers that they should forget history and do as Americans do – that is, to venture as though there were no historical encumbrance – they overlook the innate sense of history sensed as a living force, that is totally real for most Chinese, which makes them hesitate. It is important to remember that the teachings of Confucius has suggested a way of life that has been internalized over

2000 years in China during which time there has been a continuing debate about *yi* and *li* – where *yi* is ethical value (justice) and *li* is economic value (profit) as determined within society. Thus, for the Chinese people, their ethical value structure is related to a utility informed by moral norms: *yi* may be thought of as *li* "in conformance with morality." But there is another form of *li* – Kidd (2001) explained that the Chinese people connect *yi* and *li* through a publicly declared *li* (as they obey the rule by law, accepting the declaration of a chief). Thus, the clever leader may use deep-seated Confucianism to control his subordinates. Acquiring an understanding of the *internalization* process is an important first step to penetrating the Chinese mind of rationalizing, analyzing and decision-making.

Lao Tzu's *Tao Te Ching*

While historical records about Lao Tzu have remained sketchy and are still debatable today (Chan, 1963), the *Tao Te Ching* was said to be written by a man named Lao Tzu (551–479 BC). He was a native of the Chu Jen Hamlet in the Li village of Hu Hsien in the State of Chu. Lao Tzu was a "pen name" whereas his family name was Li, his personal name was Erh and he was styled Tan. He was the Historian in charge of the archives in Chou. The records kept by the Official Historian, Ssu-ma Chien, showed that Confucius once dubbed Lao Tzu a dragon for his wisdom, insightfulness and virtue.

As the Historian in charge of the archives in Chou, Lao Tzu was able to cultivate the way (*Tao*) and virtue aimed at self-effacement. He lived in Chou for a long time but departed on seeing its decline. When he reached the Pass (or City Gate), the Keeper there was pleased and said to him, "As you are about to leave the world behind, could you write a book for my sake?" As a result, Lao Tzu wrote a tome in two books, setting out the meaning of the way and virtue in some 5000 characters, and then he departed. None knew where he went to in the end (Lau, 1963).

The text of Lao Tzu is divided into two books. There are a total of 81 chapters – 37 in Book I and 44 in Book II. Specifically, Book I was known as the *Tao Ching* and Book II the *Te Ching*. There is nothing unusual about this division except for the simple fact that the first word in Book I is *Tao* while the first word in Book II is *Te*.

As a contemporary of Confucius, Lao Tzu was the founder of Taoism, one of the most influential philosophies in Chinese civilization. Confucianism, the dominant system in Chinese history and thought, emphasizes social order and an active life. Taoism, on the other hand, concentrates on individual life and tranquility, thus suggesting that Taoism plays a secondary role to Confucianism in the Chinese society. Lao Tzu was a wise man who not only taught people to have a gentle and meek presentation, but also to be motiveless, selfless, pliant, yielding, pure-minded and natural. It is generally difficult for people to accept Lao Tzu's thoughts because most will only notice the superficial features and not their essence. Because Lao Tzu's thoughts are abstract (e.g. "The *Tao* is an empty vessel; it is used but never filled"), or illogical (e.g. "Give up learning, and put an end to your troubles"), most people would tend to dismiss his teachings as being irrelevant in their daily lives (Tsai, 1989). The emphasis on simplicity has also led people to regard the teachings of Lao Tzu as negative and defeatist. Its focus on primitivism and renunciation of civilization, taken literally, is entirely contrary to modern civilization (Chan, 1963): yet the *Tao Te Ching* teaches man how to live, embracing ethics, government and diplomacy. When *Tao Te Ching* is compared with Confucianism, it can be noted that there are more similarities than differences between Confucius' and Lao Tzu's teachings. Both are primarily interested in moral, social and political reforms; they cherish the same basic values such as humanity, righteousness, deep love and faithfulness; they oppose the use of force and punishment; and they esteem highly the integrity of the individual and social harmony even though their approaches are different. In short, both emphasize the goodness of human nature and the potentiality of everyone to become a sage. It is because of these similarities that Taoism and Confucianism exist harmoniously in parallel throughout Chinese history so that every Chinese is at once a Taoist and a Confucianist (Chan, 1963).

Tao is simply the Way of Life. It is about living naturally, effortlessly, spontaneously and correctly. *Te* can be translated to mean virtue or morality. Translated literally, *Tao Te Ching* can be taken to mean the Book (*Ching*) of how (*Tao*) things happen or work (*Te*). While it is difficult to define what *Tao* is, the Book itself has three topics:

- The natural law or how things happen.
- A way of life or how to live in conscious harmony with natural law.
- A method of leadership or how to govern or educate others in accordance with natural law (Heider, 1992).

The main focus of *Tao Te Ching* is concerned with man: 80 per cent of this Book is devoted not to the substance of *Tao* but to its function, particularly to its operation in society.

The desirable leadership style advocated by Lao Tzu is basically gracious and non-competitive. The virtues propounded in the *Tao Te Ching* include meekness, purity of heart, selflessness, righteousness, faithfulness and one's unfailing love for others. These are useful virtues and attitudes that can be valuable for leaders in managing people in general, and personal conflicts/stresses in particular.

While Lao Tzu's sayings hold a wealth of wisdom in so far as leadership qualities are concerned, it should be noted that not all his ancient sayings are relevant in the modern-day context. In effect, some of Lao Tzu's teachings may be defeatist and negative when viewed today. For example, one cannot imagine a modern-day leader who is without motive, and who will sit back and wait for events to unfold: modern-day leadership is projected as being dynamic and proactive, but the *Tao Te Ching* suggests passivity. Likewise, while modern-day leaders demand constant feedback and communication, the *Tao* emphasizes silence as a desirable virtue. Perhaps we might interpret this as a suggestion that leaders should be thoughtful?

Nevertheless, the most defeatist of Lao Tzu's teachings (e.g. to give up all of one's worldly possessions) is not meant for the modern man to attain. It is only for him to strive towards as an ideal, and to consciously keep this ideal continuously in mind if he aims to achieve fair play and inner peace. Likewise, although Lao Tzu's *Tao Te Ching* may has its origin in China, its influence on Chinese societies may not be entirely foolproof today because of the infusion of more liberal and individualistic teachings diffusing from the West into Chinese societies. While Taoism and Confucianism may still predominately form the basic social fabric of Chinese communities, exposure to and reception of western ideals have already caused some erosion to occur in Chinese societies in so far as the practice of Taoism and Confucianism is concerned.

Sun Tzu's *Art of War*

Despite the argument over its authorship, it is generally believed that the *Art of War* was written by Sun Wu (or more frequently called Sun Tzu) in the 5th Century BC which coincides with the then Period of the Warring States in China. Although Sun Tzu's strategic thoughts are of immense importance in the Chinese military arena, and the *Art of War* is reputedly the oldest and best known military treatise among the Chinese classical works, relatively little is known about Sun Tzu, or when he wrote the *Art of War*. According to the SiMa Qian's *Shi Ji* (Records of the Historian), Sun Tzu was a native of the Qi State. However, the *Art of War* was specially written for Prince He Lu of the Wu State. When Sun Tzu wrote the *Art of War* some 2500 years ago, the Prince of Wu, He Lu, was so impressed by what he read that he granted an audience to Sun Tzu. Although he was clearly impressed by what he had read Prince He Lu wanted to test Sun Tzu's ability in drilling troops to the limits – but using women. For this purpose, Prince He Lu sent for 180 ladies from his palace. Sun Tzu was, however, undaunted by this task. He divided the ladies into two companies, each headed by one of the Prince's two most favorite concubines.

Upon arming all the ladies with spears, Sun Tzu asked, "Do you know what is front and back, right and left?" When all the ladies replied in the affirmative, Sun Tzu went on to instruct them, "When I give the command 'front', you must all face directly ahead; 'turn left' and you must all face to your left; 'turn right' and you must all face to your right; 'turn back' and you must all turn around towards your back." As all the ladies replied in the affirmative, Sun Tzu laid out the executioner's sword to show his seriousness for discipline. Thereafter, the drill began as usual with the sounds of drumbeats and shouts of command. None of the ladies, however, moved. Instead, they burst into laughter.

Sun Tzu patiently told the ladies that it would be the commander's fault if the commands were vague and not thoroughly understood by the troops. He then proceeded to instruct them once more. When the drums were beaten a second time and the commands repeated, the ladies again burst into laughter. Thereupon, Sun Tzu said, "It would be the commander's fault if commands are vague and not thoroughly understood by the troops. But when the commands are clear and the soldiers nevertheless do not carry them out, then it is the fault of their officers." Having said this, Sun Tzu then ordered out both leading concubines for execution.

Prince He Lu who was observing the drill from a raised pavilion was greatly alarmed when he saw his two leading ladies were about to be executed. The Prince immediately sent an aide to Sun Tzu with the message, "I believe the general is capable of drilling troops. However, without these two concubines, my food and drink will be tasteless. It is therefore my wish that they be spared."

Sun Tzu replied that since he had received the royal commission to lead the troops in the field, he could disregard any of the ruler's commands as he saw fit. Thereafter, Sun Tzu ordered the two concubines to be beheaded as a deterrent, and accordingly appointed the two ladies next in line to replace them as company leaders. Subsequently, the drill proceeded smoothly with every women turning left, right, front or back, kneeling or rising, with perfect harmony and precision and without uttering any dissent. Sun Tzu then dispatched a messenger to Prince He Lu to inspect the troops, which he declared as having been properly drilled, disciplined and prepared to go through fire and water for the Prince. When Prince He Lu declined, Sun Tzu remarked, "The Prince is only fond of words which he cannot put into practice." Greatly ashamed by what he had heard and recognizing Sun Tzu's generalship ability, Prince He Lu promptly appointed Sun Tzu as the supreme commander of the Wu armies.

Sun Tzu proved his extraordinary ability in actual warfare after he became a general of the Wu State. From 506 BC, Sun Tzu led a total of five expeditions against the State of Chu that had regarded Wu State as a vassal. He defeated the armies of Chu and forced his way into the Chu capital, Yingdu, causing King Zhao to flee for his life. For almost 20 years thereafter, the Wu armies continued to gain victories over their neighbors, the States of Qi, Qin and Yue. After the death of Sun Tzu, his successors however did not follow his strategies as recorded in the *Art of War*. Thus, following defeat after defeat, the Kingdom of Wu was finally exterminated in 473 BC.

The thirteen chapters of Sun Tzu's *Art of War* deal with the fundamentally ideological system of strategy. A summary of these thirteen chapters is listed in Table 5.1.

Sun Tzu's *Art of War* is a very short book. It contains less than 6200 characters of classical Chinese literary writing – its longest chapter has about 1070 characters, while the shortest chapter has only about 250 characters (Low and Yeo, 1993). Sun Tzu had long recognized the

Table 5.1 Sun Tzu's *Art of War* – its chapter headings

1	Planning	Proper planning of strategy
2	Waging war	Avoidance of protracted campaign
3	Strategy	Subdue enemy without fighting
4	Depositions	Grasp enemy's vulnerability
5	Forces	Exploitation of situation
6	Opportunism	Unpredictability of strategy
7	Maneuvers	Relief of enemy's vigilance
8	Variations	Adaptability of strategy
9	Marches	Exploration of enemy's situation
10	Terrain	Diligence in command
11	Battleground	Stimulation of subordinates
12	Incendiarism	Caution in completing tasks
13	Espionage	Use of human intelligence

importance of a general's leadership qualities and classified these qualities into the six categories: wisdom, sincerity, benevolence, courage, strictness and composure (ibid). We expand on these below:

1 Wisdom

> The general who wins a battle makes many calculations in his temple before the battle is fought. The general who loses a battle makes but few calculations beforehand. Many calculations lead to victory, and few calculations to defeat; how about no calculation at all? By this measure, I can foresee victory or defeat (Planning).

A leader must therefore have the relevant knowledge and experience in the area he is leading. The ability to plan is crucial:

> The adept in warfare seeks victory from the situation, and does not rely on the efforts of individuals. Thus he is able to select suitable men to exploit the situation (Forces).

The leader must be able to select the right persons and the right methods to do the right job at the right time and right location:

> Military tactics are similar to water. As flowing water runs away from high places and speeds downwards, an army avoids strengths and strikes weaknesses. As water shapes its course according to the ground, an army works out its victory in relation to the enemy it faces. Therefore as water retains no constant shape, there are no fixed conditions in warfare. He who can modify his tactics according to the enemy's situation and thereby succeed in winning may be called a divine (Opportunities).

2 Sincerity

Sincerity means the general must have the complete trust of his ruler and of his subordinates. Likewise, the leader must have the complete trust of all the parties involved in his plans. He must maintain objectivity and impartiality in judgment.

3 Benevolence

> Regard your soldiers as your children, and they will follow you into the deepest valleys. Look at them as your own beloved sons, and they will stand by you even unto death (Terrain).

However, a general who is overly concerned with the welfare of the layman is likely to encounter difficulties:

> If over compassionate to the people, he can easily be harassed (Variations).

The leader must guard against being overly benevolent which others may interpret as a weakness.

4 Courage

> The general who advances without seeking fame and who retreats without fear of being punished, and whose main concern is for the welfare of the people and the interests of the ruler, is the jewel of the State (Terrain).
>
> He who exercises no forethought but makes light of his opponents is sure to be captured by them (Marches).

Decisions should not be made based on courage alone but on information gathered, and after due consideration of the pros and cons of each possible course of action.

5 Strictness

> If the general pampers his troops but cannot use them; if he loves them but cannot enforce his commands; if the troops are disorderly but he cannot discipline them – then they are like spoilt children and are useless (Terrain).
>
> When discipline is regularly enforced, they will be obedient. When discipline is not regularly enforced, they will not be obedient. When orders are consistently executed, it is because of the mutual trust between the commander and his men (Marches).

The leader must exercise discipline to control his resources that are required to ensure successful implementation of his plans.

6 Composure

> A ruler should not start a war out of anger. A general should not fight a battle out of resentment. Move only when it is in the interests of the State to do so. Quit when it is to its detriment. Anger can be restored to happiness, and resentment can become pleasantness.

A State once destroyed can never be restored, nor the dead be brought back to life (Incendiarism).

The leader must not be ruffled easily by any dispute. He needs to maintain his posture at all times.

Thick Face, Black Heart

Although Lee Zhong Wu's *Thick Black Theory* was first disseminated in 1911, its application to modern living in Chinese societies remains relevant today (Low, 1997). Lee Zhong Wu was a social philosopher and critic, and his purpose in developing and disseminating the *Thick Black Theory* was to describe the symptoms of an illness in the Chinese society of the time. He described in the *Thick Black Theory* the methods by which men obtain and hold on to power, and how they use their power and wealth to accumulate even more power and wealth. The methods, and the lengths to which men would go to achieve their own ends, are the major thrusts of the *Thick Black Theory*. Lee Zhong Wu had originally intended to publish the *Thick Black Theory* in a series of three articles in *The Chengdu Daily* in 1911. However, the violent reaction that erupted after the first article was published led to a cancellation of the series. Consequently, friends of Lee Zhong Wu published the series of three articles, of about 2000 words in total, in a single volume in Beijing. Eventually, it was reprinted several times between 1934 and 1936. Despite the controversy contained in the book, and the negative image it portrayed of the Chinese people, each edition sold out immediately before being banned eventually by the government.

The ban came about because many people felt uncomfortable by the true observations made by Lee Zhong Wu. Fundamentally, they were not used to seeing the ruthlessness and hypocrisy underlying many entrenched Chinese institutions laid bare. By merely mentioning these things, Lee Zhong Wu was perceived to be at best muckraking, and at worst, actually advocating the immorality he depicted. Having been banned for so long, the *Thick Black Theory* is relatively unknown to many Chinese today. In Taiwan, the book was banned during the thirty-eight years of martial law from 1949 to 1987. Even after the lifting of the ban, in the post-martial law years, the *Thick Black Theory* was not widely read. Lee Zhong Wu's work is better known in Hong Kong where copies were made available. The *Thick Black Theory* has never been translated. Even if it were to be translated faithfully, it will remain incomprehensible to most non-Chinese because of the highly context-oriented nature of the Chinese language. Lee Zhong Wu died in 1943 when the Japanese army was still in control of much of China.

Before examining the relevance of the *Thick Black Theory* for dealing with the Chinese people in business transactions, we will present the thrust of some of Lee Zhong Wu's thoughts. These deal with ways of obtaining and keeping an official position, and of taking care of business (Chu, 1988, 1992).

Six ways to obtain an official position

Historically, holding a government position is considered a prestigious occupation in Chinese societies. A high-ranking government official is thus placed at the top of the social and economic hierarchy; as a consequence, most people would constantly strive to secure an official appointment within the government bureaucracy. In the *Thick Black Theory* Lee Zhong Wu discusses the six steps involved in getting an appointment as a government bureaucrat. Although his discussion was set within the context of Imperial China, much of his observations concerning human nature remain relevant even today.

a. Emptiness
The first requirement is to empty a person's mind of everything that does not help in securing the appointment being sought. He must have no other goals and no other thoughts, and must concentrate on the appointment and meditate on it daily.

b. Boring in
A person must seize every little opportunity to advance his prospects.

c. Self-praise
A person must constantly seek to bring out his qualifications and importance to the attention of those who are in positions to help him.

d. Flattery
A person must ingratiate himself with those who can help him. He must praise them to others who will in turn carry his praises back to them.

e. Threats
A person must be very subtle with his threats because he may unknowingly threaten people who have the ability to harm him. Instead, threats should develop naturally out of his self-praise.

f. Bribery
Bribes should be given not only to the man who has the power to appoint a person, but also to his relatives and friends.

Six ways to keep an official position

The *Thick Black Theory* observes that a government official would need to be seen to act virtuously and to smear himself with a layer of false benevolence while at the same time, pretending to be a religious and morally upright man. The six ways to keep one's official position include:

a. Emptiness
A person should say and do nothing. He should instead talk about everything, but say nothing and do nothing.

b. Be obsequious
A person must bow, bend and nod before his superiors.

c. Be imperious
A person should cultivate a haughty and disdainful attitude toward his inferiors, and must be seen to be unapproachable by his subordinates.

d. Be ruthless
A person must be ruthless in pursuing his objective. However, in exploiting the vulnerability of others, one must continue to maintain a virtuous image.

e. Be deaf and blind
A person must not listen to criticism and worse still, be affected by it. One must therefore not see the reproaching looks of others. Reproaches must be allowed to pass him by without pricking his conscience.

f. Harvest
The purpose of a person getting his post in the first place was to put him in a situation where others would pay for his favors, just as he previously paid for the favors of others. One does not expend all his effort simply to acquire a job; he does it to enable himself to sell his influence.

Two methods for taking care of business

As noted above, the *Thick Black Theory* emphasizes the importance of avoiding accountability or responsibility for one's actions, and for making one's actions seem much more important or impressive than they really are. The two methods for achieving these objectives are:

1 to defer accountability by trying to do as little as possible, and always try to make someone else finish the job. Nobody cares if something goes wrong so long as the blame can be laid on whoever gave the final approval or finished the job.

2 to make a situation a little worse than it actually is in order to persuade others to appreciate your work even more (Low, 1997).

Power of endurance

The description *Thick Face, Black Heart* is used to describe the "must have" quality of Chinese political and business leaders as espoused by Lee Zhong Wu in his *Thick Black Theory*. This attitude is not a recent creation in Chinese societies but is a result of centuries of internal turmoil and disturbances caused by external forces in China. Chu (1988), in particular, points to the bitter distrust the Chinese people have towards foreigners. The relevance of the *Thick Black Theory* for daily life was subsequently expanded by Chu (1992) into the doctrine of *"Thick Face, Black Heart."* In line with other ancient Chinese strategic and philosophical treatises, Chu (1988) urged businessmen from the West to gain an understanding of this doctrine before making their forays into China.

Chu defines Thick Face as a shield to protect a person from the criticism and negative opinions of others. A thick-faced practitioner refuses to accept the limitations that others have tried to impose on him. Chu sees Black Heart as the equivalent of a spear used to do battle with others as well as oneself. While the black-hearted practitioner has the courage to fail, he also focuses his attention on his goals and ignores the cost. Together with a well-defined killer instinct, the ultimate courage of a Thick Face, Black Heart practitioner is dispassion. He has the courage to fight in spite of fear and is able to detach himself from the emotions associated with defeat so that its presence does not thwart him (Chu, 1992).

Like Lee Zhong Wu's *Thick Black Theory*, the doctrine of *"Thick Face, Black Heart"* was also examined by Chu (1992) from numerous perspectives, including the deceptive, mysterious and spiritual perspective. The lessons which one can learn from Chu's (1992) *Thick Face, Black Heart* doctrines are therefore numerous. For the purpose of using the lessons that businessmen from the West may learn from *Thick Face, Black Heart* while making their forays into China, the following will, however, only focus on "endurance" as a strategy for dealing with the Chinese.

To achieve his goals, the *Thick Face, Black Heart* practitioner develops the power of endurance even in the face of criticism and ridicule. The ultimate victory belongs to him who endures and persists to the end, particularly in the face of a crisis. The Chinese word for "crisis" combines two characters: those of danger (*wei*) and opportunity (*ji*). Hence, the wise Chinese recognizes that the true nature of a crisis is actually an opportunity in disguise. Chu (1992) argues that opportunity always exists within a crisis situation but when one loses the fighting spirit in a devastating crisis, he will be blinded by his own emotions. The nature of the thing is that when one is able to calmly endure the unendurable, the opportunity for a better alternative will eventually surface and reveal itself. While endurance is never easy, it is an essential element for overcoming crises.

Some of the enduring strategies that can be adopted for flowing along with the endurance characteristic of the Chinese were identified by Chu (1992). These are:

- Give up struggling
- Allow a solution to make itself clear
- Work through agony and grief
- Do not display your vulnerability
- Let the dark night pass
- Be inactive to conquer chaos
- Live your life as if it were someone else's.

Discussion

The background of the *Thick Black Theory* and its subsequent extension into the *Thick Face, Black Heart* doctrine espoused by Chu (1988, 1992) was described above to link them to the current business context. It is hoped that a clear explanation of how the Chinese mind functions has been made possible. Thus, we have explained the characteristics of the Chinese people from the deceptive, mysterious and spiritual perspectives, and both theory and doctrine suggest that a working knowledge of their respective principles would be beneficial for managers venturing into China.

Having been peppered with numerous hardships throughout the history of China, the Chinese people have developed within themselves the endurance for hard work, pain and suffering. This enduring characteristic of the Chinese people has, inevitably shifted into the marketplace. Therefore, in dealing with the Chinese, it is suggested that people from the West should at least pace their own level of endurance against that of the Chinese. Instead of counteracting endurance with impatience, people from the West must learn to flow along with the enduring characteristic of the Chinese people. *Thick Face, Black Heart* is, after all, about the state of the mind.

Conclusions

This study is an attempt to understand the mind of the present-day Chinese people from a historical perspective. All too often, the Chinese way of thinking has been assumed to be confined within a single paradigm – the Confucian perspective. While it may be true that the Chinese mind is influenced to a very large extent by Confucian teachings and philosophies, this is not the only conceptual paradigm within which a satisfactory understanding of the Chinese mind should be garnered. That approach is perhaps too simplistic. While Lee Zhong Wu's *Thick Black Theory* provides a better framework to understand how the Chinese mind thinks and works, it does not explain how its concepts came about – except for the fact that these evolved from the tumultuous period the author lived through during the early 1900s in China. While the difficult times could have accounted for Lee Zhong Wu's interpretations leading to the *Thick Black Theory*, it could not account for the other major events that occurred over the last 2500 years of Chinese civilization. During this time, the early major thinkers and philosophers aptly put their thoughts to paper (and bamboo strips) to be passed down from one generation to another to exert influence upon the Chinese mind – either subtly or overtly. Apart from the teachings of Confucius which have already been examined so many times before by scholars both from the East and West, this study has presented two other major works – Lao Tzu's *Tao Te Ching* and Sun Tzu's *Art of War* – to illustrate what had transpired and had been passed down from ancient China concurrently with Confucian teaching. While this chapter deals only with Lao Tzu and Sun Tzu, this is not to say that they (and Confucius) are the only significant thinkers and strategists hailing from ancient China. There are also other notable strategic thinkers such as Zhuge Liang who contributed the *Art of Management* (Low and Lee, 1997) as well as Tao Zhugong who provided the *Golden Rules For Business Management* (Low, 2000). The need to encapsulate various strands of thinking and philosophies into a single treatise was long recognized by the Chinese, for example, the *36 Chinese Classical Strategies of War* was compiled into a single volume to encompass all warfare strategies that were used in ancient China, and which are found to be still relevant today for modern day retail business (Low, 1998). This chapter therefore considers the approach to gaining an understanding of the Chinese mind from a historical perspective-suggesting it can only be seen as a multi-faceted and not a unitary approach. The thrust of this hypothesis is shown in Figure 5.1.

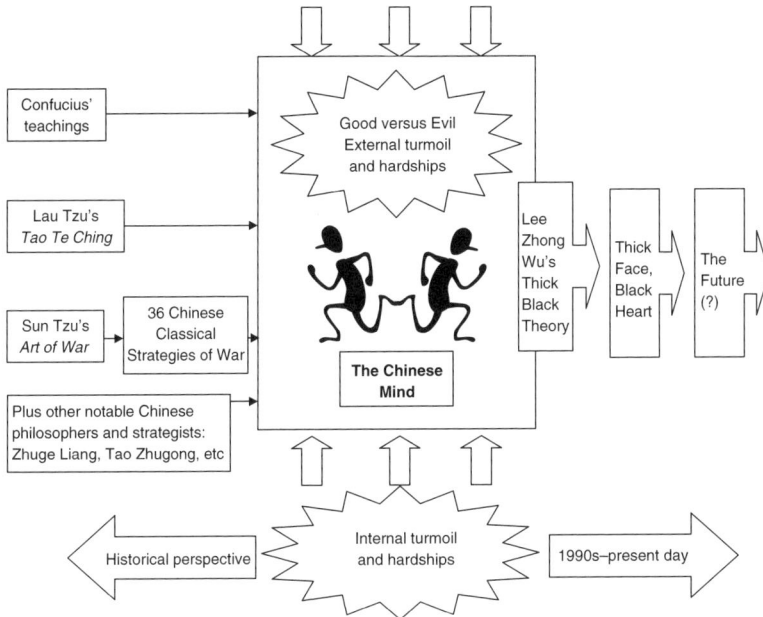

Figure 5.1 Understanding the Chinese mind from a historical perspective

The Chinese mind, as postulated in the center of Figure 5.1, is subjected to constant internal and external turmoil and hardships as recorded by history. Along the way, the Chinese mind is exposed to different strategic thinking and philosophies, which manifested themselves according to the events of the day throughout the history of China. As these thoughts and philosophies were passed down from one generation to another, either through self-learning or taught and examined in schools, they were absorbed – to be *internalized* within the Chinese mind. There is, firstly, a desire to act in a gentlemanly manner and to engross oneself with life-long learning as advocated by Confucius. There is also a concurrent desire to be in harmony with nature and to look upon emptiness as the *Tao* or way to happiness and fulfillment. In essence, the Chinese mind is taught to be compassionate and righteous. But, alas, this was not to be the case given the internal strife and civil wars between rival feudal warlords that the Chinese people have had to endure throughout history. The Chinese mind, as nurtured within the realms of Confucius and Lao Tzu, was shattered into thinking differently following the bad experience of cruelty, suffering and loss arising from internal strife and the civil wars. Wars were often fought and won by feudal warlords at all costs and without any recourse to civility and gentlemanly manners. Deception and treachery were often adopted to fight and win battles. Faced with this heart-wrenching reality, the positive aspects of the Chinese mind as nurtured in the mold of Confucius and Lao Tzu can no longer hold their ground. The mind begins to flicker, sway and strategize. As Sun Tzu so aptly put it, the hallmark of a great general is not in him winning the war. Instead, the true hallmark of a great general lies in him winning the war without going into battle. To do this, Sun Tzu advocates that it is necessary for one to know one's own strengths and weaknesses as opposed to those of the enemy's. Over time, the *36 Chinese Classical Strategies of War* recorded strategies such as "Borrowing a knife to kill someone," "Crossing the sea under camouflage," "Beauty trap," and so on (Low, 1998). The "pure" mind of the Chinese following that of Confucius and Lao Tzu, it seems, is now undermined and placed in a dilemma!

On the one hand, the Chinese mind wants to embrace fairness and equity (in today's terms). On the other hand, there is a pull towards guarding and protecting one's own self-interests through deception and ruthless strategies and tactics. Hence, Lee Zhong Wu's *Thick Black Theory* and its interpretation for the modern day *Thick Face, Black Heart* practitioner by Chu (1992) appears to be justified. There remains a conflict in the Chinese mind as to the choice between "good" (as manifested through the teachings of Confucius and Lao Tzu) and "evil" (as manifested through Sun Tzu's *Art of War* and Lee Zhong Wu's *Thick Black Theory*). Many of the thoughts associated with these teachings and philosophies are now *internalized* in the mind of the modern Chinese today, and one hears of constant references to these teachings in everyday life. Examples such as "knowing oneself and the enemy to win every battle (Sun Tzu's *Art of War*)" and "Empty city ploy (*36 Chinese Classical Strategies of War*)," as well as Taoism, continue to attract a large following from Chinese communities, including Chinese sojourners outside China.

However, this *internalization* is gradually being eroded as electronic communications and mass media technology become increasingly accessible to the Chinese – even in remote parts of mainland China. The advent of satellite television and the Internet, as the "global village," suggests that western influence will now influence the Chinese mind and its way of thinking, although the extent of this influence on the *internalization* process as described above is still relatively unknown. There are also other major events and developments in recent times that have given China an added boost to its stature on the world platform. Favorable events, such as the return of Hong Kong and Macau to China, by the United Kingdom and Portugal respectively may further reinforce the Chinese mind into thinking that its developments arising from its cultural/historical heritage are still intact, and that China is not a pushover after all. Its large population base, its growing economic prowess in the region and beyond, as well as its increasingly sophisticated military machinery may yet condition the Chinese people to reject the *internalized* mode of historical thinking described in this study. How the Chinese mind will evolve in the future, in the light of these recent phenomena, remains a question which only time can tell.

References

Chan, W. T. (1963) *The Way of Lao Tzu. Tao Te Ching*, New York: The Bobbs-Merrill Company Inc.
Chu, C. N. (1988) *The Chinese Mind Game. The Best Kept Trade Secret of the East*, Oregon: AMC Publishing.
Chu, C. N. (1992) *Thick Face, Black Heart. The Path to Thriving, Winning and Succeeding*, Oregon: AMC Publishing.
Dollinger, M. J. (1988) Confucian ethics and Japanese management practices. *Journal of Business Ethics* **7**: 575–84.
Heider, J. (1992) *The Tao of Leadership. Lao Tzu's Tao Te Ching Adapted for a New Age*, Kuala Lumpur: Eastern Dragon Book.
Kidd, J. B. (2001) Discovering inter-cultural perceptual differences in MNEs. *Journal of Managerial Psychology*, Special Issue on Asian Management Style, **16**(2): 106–26.
Knutt, E. (1997) China: building the economic miracle, *Building* **7**: 18–23.
Lau, D. C. (1963) *Lao Tzu. Tao Te Ching*, London: Penguin Books.
Lee, K. Y. (1998) When contract marks start of talk. *The Straits Times* 6 January 1998, p. 2.
Leung, T. K. P. and Wong, Y. H. (2001) The ethics and positioning of *guanxi* in China. *Marketing Intelligence and Planning* **19**(1): 55–64.
Low, S. P. (1997) *Thick Face, Black Heart* and the marketing of construction services in China. *Marketing Intelligence and Planning* **15**(5): 221–6.
Low, S. P. (1998) Applying the *36 Chinese Classical Strategies of War* for retail marketing and planning. *Marketing Intelligence and Planning* **16**(2): 124–35.
Low, S. P. (2000) An East–West business management framework for construction based on anecdotal cases from "Building" magazine. *The Malaysian Surveyor* **35**(2): 69–77.
Low, S. P. and Lee, B. (1997) Management grid and Zhuge Liang's *Art of Management*: Integration for construction project management. *Management Decision* **35**(5): 382–91.
Low, S. P. and Yeo, K. K. (1993) Sun Tzu's *Art of War* and its strategic relevance for construction project management, *RICS Research Paper Series*, Paper No. 20, London: Royal Institution of Chartered Surveyors.

Man, C. F. and Cheng, C. Y. (1996) *The Chinese Guanxiology*, Institute of Asian Pacific Studies, Chinese University of Hong Kong (in Chinese).

Speece, M. (2001) Guest Editorial, *Journal of Managerial Psychology*, Special Issue on Asian Management Style, **16**(2): 1–10.

Tsai, C. C. (1989) *The Silence of the Wise. The Sayings of Lao Zi*, Singapore: Asiapac Publication.

6
The Competitive Advantage with Chinese Characteristics – The Sophisticated Choreography of Gift-Giving
Matti Nojonen

Introduction

Every firm has a competitive strategy, whether explicit or implicit, that is employed to gain a competitive advantage over competitors. In the malfunctioning market and institutional environment of China, more often than not, the competitive edge is gained through extensive personal connections (*guanxi*). Gift-giving is perhaps the most consequential method in creating and employing *guanxi*. On many occasions gift-giving is simply associated with bribing and corruption. However, this chapter illustrates that by approaching the ethically loaded and yet theoretically and, by definition, controversial issue of corruption from a gift-giving approach one is able to unearth the complicated logic, risks and advantages involved in Chinese business networks. Based on ethnographic data, this chapter attempts to provide an insider point of view on the complex mechanisms of gift-giving in Chinese businesses. It shows that, in expanding and utilizing *guanxi* networks in the increasingly competitive environment, Chinese businessmen are actively competing with each other by differentiating their gifts in the most imaginative ways, thus forming a hidden marketplace of gifts. The emphasis is laid on illustrating the prerequisite and exacting choreography, social mechanisms and logic of action of various forms of gift-giving practices, namely 'ordinary business gift', 'hand-grenades and machine guns' and 'guided missiles' as gifts, that take place behind the cloak of visible networking (*guanxi*). This chapter attempts to avoid the definitional pitfalls of corruption by approaching the issue from a gift-giving perspective.

This enables one not only to depict how, in the marketplace of gifts, agents seek competitive advantage over each other by deploying correct social behaviour, choosing the right gift; but also in the outcome, complicate Bourdiue's notion of time in gift-giving (Bourdieu, 1990).

Why observe gift-giving and not corruption?

Contemporary research and the Press converge and point out that Chinese society operates through the realm of long-term and personal relationships, that is, *guanxi*. The reforms in China have not managed to create a reliable legal system. Thus, the officials still work in an arbitrary fashion, and so *guanxi* takes on an ever more important role as agents attempt to minimize uncertainties in society, on the one hand. Yet, on the other hand, *guanxi* is often seen as the root of corrupt practices in Chinese society. As a consequence, the Chinese themselves do not comprehend *guanxi* simply as the root of corruption, but rather refer to it in a more positivist manner as 'the science' or 'the art' of networking – *guanxixüe*. The suffix *-xüe* connotes the English suffix *-logy*, like in bio*logy*, which translates into Chinese as *shengwuxüe*.

Conducting an ethnographic fieldwork on gift-giving has certain advantages over inquiring upon corruption practices directly. The study of corruption is plagued with analytical and practical difficulties (Chabal and Daloz, 1999). First, it is virtually impossible to agree on a workable definition of corruption. Most studies on corruption analyse the issue from a normative perspective. To discuss the issue in moral terms based on our Western bureaucratic ideals, which we assume to be universal, or to observe the question in other ethical terms that are not analytically neutral: we not only risk distorting observations of the phenomena, but we are also unlikely to further our understanding of how Chinese society is actually functioning. Second, it is difficult to empirically observe deeds of corruption in a scientifically meaningful way. This is particularly so in the case of China. In China, the judicial system is mercilessly dealing with corruption, even carrying out capital punishment, so the inquiry into the actual practices of corruption becomes indubitably infeasible. As a consequence, most of the studies on corruption in China deal with the question at the macro-level, without paying attention to the actual processes of bribing or of corruption. Furthermore, there is a tendency to concentrate attention on the wrong-doings at the top, or among the princelings of the Communist leaders (Goodman and Hooper, 1994).

Hence, in order to avoid the obstacles of observing the actual practices and the definitional problems of corruption that can result in ethical, normative and judicial confusion, this study will approach the issue of corruption from the gift-giving angle and thus avoid ethical and normative judgements. Furthermore, it is notable that in collecting the data, interviewing Chinese businessmen on their personal *guanxi* experiences, the interviewees themselves did not utilize, in their narratives, words relating to bribing (*xinghui*) or corruption (*fubai*), or any other words connoting corruption. This may be due to the harsh judicial punishments on crimes of corruption. Instead, their narration captured elaborate tactics and vocabulary recapitulating the choreography of gift-giving, thus providing descriptions of the logic and practice of the commonly used categories of gifts in the Chinese business world, namely 'ordinary business-gifts', 'hand-grenades and machine guns' and 'guided missiles' as gifts.

Conceptual background

Gifts

Gifts, gift-giving, and exchange have been a frequent topic of inquiry within the field of anthropology. Recently, gifts and gift-giving have also interested other disciplines of social science and humanities (Schrift, 1997; Hendry, 1993). Marcel Mauss first addressed the problematic issue of the gift in his work *Essai sur le don* (1924) in which he theorized on the gift. According to Mauss' thesis, gifts appear free and disinterested, but in reality they are obliged and interested. Namely, gifts are parts of persons. Hence, donors do not separate themselves from their gifts completely, and recipients do not own them totally, since recipients are still bound by obligation to the donor. Levi-Strauss (1997) further explicated Mauss' thesis of the gift by presenting a three-part structural analysis of gift-giving – giving, receiving and reciprocating.

Based on the theory of practice, Bourdieu (1990, 1997) generates a thesis, on gifts, which departs from Mauss' phenomenological and Levi-Strauss' structuralist theories on gifts. In his thesis, Bourdieu focuses on the theme of time, specifically on the time lag between gift and countergift. According to Bourdieu, 'in every society it may be observed that, if it is not to constitute an insult, the countergift must be deferred and different, because the immediate return of an exactly identical object clearly amounts to a refusal' (Bourdieu, 1997: 198). Yet, the delaying or neglecting to respond can be interpreted in various ways, to be a signal of refusal, arrogance, cowardice and entailing dishonour (Bourdieu,

1997: 238). Hence, Bourdieu recognizes an important factor that agents manipulate – time.

In this chapter, the theory of gift follows the basic logic presented by Mauss, where the seemingly disinterested object of gift is never totally separate from the donor, not is it ever totally owned by the receiver. Combining this psychological insight of Mauss with the three-phase structural analysis of the gift-giving process: giving, receiving and reciprocating the gift, presented by Levi-Strauss, does not only enable us to illustrate, to bring into life the process of gift-giving in this study, but also creates an illuminating and yet simple theory of the gift-giving process. However, gift-giving is not purely a mechanistic process of giving and receiving, which then simply binds the agent to reciprocate, as is put forward by Mauss 1997. In fact, in the process of gift-giving, agents manipulate resources and circumstances, adapt personal style and charm and control time.

A gift, in this study, is understood to be a physical object which in the process of giving and receiving incorporates an additional psychological dimension that binds the receiver to reciprocate towards the donor, and in this process both the donor and the receiver bring into play the whole repertoire of collectively shared and created tacit and conversant knowledge and manipulate time in an attempt to achieve a favourable outcome. In contemporary China, an asymmetric power difference between arbitrary state officials and the subject, institutional insecurity and potential to enrich oneself, create an urge for the subject to establish a personal relationship with the official, and gift-giving is a legitimate and traditional pattern of doing it.

Guanxi and gifts

The importance of *guanxi* in Chinese society is evident. Scholars who study the business culture (Redding, 1990), business systems (Whitley, 1994) or the institutional arrangements of the Chinese economy (Nee, 1992; Boisot and Child, 1999) illustrate the relationships between firms and markets, and how the legitimacy of the institutional environment conditions agents to create and rely on *guanxi*. Moreover, the affects of *guanxi* have been vividly studied. Luo and Chen (1997) illustrate how *guanxi* affect financial outcomes, Tsang (1998) elaborates on the relationship between *guanxi* and competitive advantage, Davies *et al.* (1995) research the market benefits of *guanxi*, and recently Luo and Park (2001) have described the impact of *guanxi* on firm performance.

Scholars have unquestionably revealed the central function of *guanxi*-connections in Chinese society and market transactions. Due to the highly volatile institutional environment, agents 'share a high level of engagement in transactional networks based on relational contracting' (Boisot and Child, 1999: 622). The dynamics of this 'network capitalism' is based on the 'networked relations based on interpersonal reciprocal obligations' (ibid: 612). According to scholars, *guanxi* constitutes a key strategic factor affecting firm performance and is one of the major dynamics in Chinese society (Redding, 1990). *Guanxi* is the key determinant of business success in China: as Luo and Park (2001: 457) point out 'in China, transactions often follow successful *guanxi*, while in the West a relationship follows successful transactions'. In addition, marketing people have found the concept of *guanxi* important, especially in regard to relationship marketing (Wong and Chan, 1999).

Given the amount of research done on *guanxi*, it is striking to note that the great bulk of academic work done by management scholars on China is focused on describing the reasons causing *guanxi*, or the possible effects of *guanxi* on businesses. This must be contrasted against how little scholarly attention has been paid to divulge the actual complexities and social manoeuvres, whether it be gift-giving or bribing. This study attempts to illustrate that establishing and cultivating a successful *guanxi*-connection is not a straightforward and simple act, but a complex and resource-consuming process, more often than not involving the complexities of gift-giving.

The Chinese society is a network/relationship-based society (*guanxi benwei shehui*). Fei Xiaotong (1991), the pioneer of Chinese sociology, depicted the Chinese society by the analogy of concentric circles, like ripples of waves inside each other. The individual and his/her family form the core of the rings. The ripples around the core form a structure of various relationships. The relationships that exist at the distant ripples are plagued by low trust and instrumentality. Conversely, relationships at the ripple boundaries close to the core are more trusted and emotionally laden. When a situation arises that is beyond one's own capacity, *guanxi* strings are pulled to accomplish the desired results (Fei, 1991; Liang, 1999).

Guanxi is tightly bound together with the concept of face (*mianzi*), best understood as social capital, which can be lost, protected and enlarged in *guanxi* interaction. Interacting within the *guanxi* network, agents pay attention to giving face to others, and paradoxically, by giving face to the other people one gains face oneself. Hence, the key rule of dynamics and smoothness of *guanxi* interaction is the importance of sustaining one's own face by giving face to the other party (Huang, 1988).

Agents carry out the pulling of strings, creating or cultivating *guanxi*, through providing a *renqing*. The word *renqing* has three meanings – 'gift', 'human feelings' and 'favour'. When Chinese people establish or cultivate *guanxi* they literally mobilize renqing (*zuo yige renqing*), which can be translated either as 'to give a gift', or as 'to do a favour'. Furthermore, the expression of 'owing a *renqing*' (*qian yige renqing*) is frequently used in the Chinese language. The Chinese art of gift-giving or providing a favour embodies a strong indigenous idea of reciprocity (*bao*) and striving to maintain balance in the interpersonal flow of gifts and reciprocal favours. 'Face' is the guarantor in the process of ensuring eventual reciprocation of the *renqing*. In failing to reciprocate properly, one might endanger one's own face, and on the other hand, reciprocating gives face to the actor (Huang, 1988).

In addition, the expression of 'not understanding *renqing*' (*ta bu dong renqing*) refers to a person who is poor in managing interpersonal relationships, thus being socially handicapped. This kind of person lacks the necessary social skills of expanding and cultivating *guanxi*; being uncultivated to provide favours and gifts and thus being unable to weave people into a durable web of dependence. At worst, this kind of person can be accused of 'not having any *renqingweir*', literally the 'flavour of human feelings'. In that case he/she is lacking a sense of humanity and basic human feelings – being a non-human. In other words, in interpersonal relationships, one needs not only to have *renqingweir*, but more importantly one needs to exchange *renqing* – gifts and/or favours (Huang, 1988).

According to Lovett *et al.* (1999) '…*guanxi* is a relationship in which the participants quickly begin to cement their ties through exchange of respect and affection, as well as material objects or specific favours'. Hence, gift-giving as a part of networking practices possesses strategic importance in the increasingly competitive environment of the Chinese market; therefore it is worth the attention that ought to be given to it. However, due to linguistic differences, the separation of gifts from favours is not that straightforward in China. It is intriguing to note that while in the Germanic languages the contemporary words 'present' and 'poison' derive from a common etymological word – 'the gift' – the Chinese words for gift all share positive connotations. The word *renqing* constitutes two characters; *ren* a man, human being; and *qing* feeling, sentiment, affection and favour. Tentatively reasoning, due to the ambiguous meaning of *renqing*, human feeling, favour and gift, the Chinese are not drawing and creating a strong polarisation between gifts and favours, which is in contrast to the Occidental notion of reciprocating a gift with another gift.

Chinese people are more flexible in reciprocating gifts and favours. In social interaction, one can often hear the Chinese say *'song ge renqing'*, which can be understood as 'to give a gift', 'to give a favour' or 'give a piece of human feeling'.

However, there are two other words for gift in the Chinese language; *lipin* and *liwu*, both sharing positive connotations. Namely, the character *li* in both words has the meaning of 'a ceremony, ritual', 'etiquette', 'gift', while *pin* and *wu* stand for 'an article, a product' and 'a thing, matter' respectively. Hence, *li* shares the meanings of showing the correct etiquette, ceremonial ritual in offering the gift. Even more importantly, *li* is one of the central Confucian concepts, through which one can become a superior man and control the society. The Chinese society was kept in order through institutional forms of rituals, ceremonies and offerings (*li*), which were carried out in families, religious rites and social and political life. The most powerful ministry in Imperial China was the Ministry of Rites (Moore, 1967).

Even today, Chinese people show great aptitude in providing 'traditional' ritual gifts. When Chinese people provide ritual gifts it is possible to observe how agents reproduce the models and perceptions of proper social conduct. They carry out, in what seems to a foreigner, a well-orchestrated social play involving offering the gift by two hands, in some cases raising the present above one's own head, whilst if standing bowing (*jugong*), or if sitting kowtowing (*ketou*), a bow of the head or deeper bow by the upper part of the body. This performance is not meant to show subordination, but rather it is a means of expressing respect (*jingyi*) in a traditional form (Kipnis, 1997).

Gifts are provided as a ritual on the occasions of birthdays, funerals, national festivals, on a child's 100-day birthday, and for graduations and so on. The ritualized gift exchange provides a practical means not only to map one's *guanxi* network, but also to scan the motives of donors. 'Mapping' is the common phenomenon by which the Chinese people measure their own and other's social fame by the number and kind of gifts received. 'Scanning' refers to the practice whereby, in providing a ritualized gift, it is common that the donor writes his/her own name on the gift, thus making it clear who bought the gift. Thus, when the receiver receives an exceptionally valuable or desired gift he/she knows to whom he/she should direct gratitude and counter-favours (Yan, 1996; Kipnis, 1997).

In summary, one can state that the economic and social reforms in China (re)generate not only the institutional conditioning conditions, perceptions and practices of *guanxi* activities (Nee, 1992; Boisot and

Child, 1999), but also produce and reproduce the blossoming of gift-giving (Kipnis, 1997; Wank, 1999). In other words, the contemporary political, social and institutional environment of China conditions agents to rely on and create circumstances that allows them to expand their *guanxi* networks. In this process, gift-giving has proved to be the most common and effective method. As gifts are never separated from the donor, gift-giving connects two agents together with a sentiment, which the Chinese refer to as *renqing*, and as/when gifts are reciprocated. Thus, the whole process of gift-giving weaves neatly together past, present and future, forming a dyadic *guanxi* tie. In a similar fashion, the *li* (gift, ritual, etiquette) in Confucian China was the actual manifestation of the most important social contract that secured social stability, provided continuity of the past, content to the present, and predictability to the future for individuals and society, that is, the whole process of being a human and more precisely, a Chinese.

As the reforms have gathered pace without notably changing the arbitrariness of the state officials, agents have developed their gift-giving practices and expanded their gift-giving networks in the most imaginative manners. In the following analysis, indigenous categories of gifts are introduced; and it is illustrated how these gifts are given, received, reciprocated and what role time plays in the process. The data will show that, in addition to the importance of the time lapse between gift and countergift (Bourdieu, 1977, 1990), the mastering of the timing of gift-giving also plays a crucial role in a successful gift-giving process.

Gifts in the contemporary Chinese business world

The competitive advantage of the Chinese market is achieved through efficient management of *guanxi*, and gifts possess an essential function in establishing and utilising *guanxi* networks. In expanding *guanxi* networks in an increasingly competitive environment that is plagued by institutional insecurity, the Chinese have developed elaborate tactics and vocabulary describing the choreography of gift-giving. In this chapter, the descriptions of the logic and practice of the commonly used categories of gifts in the Chinese business world are provided, namely 'ordinary business gifts', 'hand-grenades and machine guns' and 'guided missiles'.

Ordinary business gifts

Ordinary business gifts refer to the small presents that are exchanged during the first encounter with a potential client or business partner.

These gifts are most commonly non-expensive 'small things' (*xiao dongxi*) such as pens, calendars, watches, or some other decorative small items that have been labeled with the company name. These gifts are provided as signals of goodwill and to promote the image of the company.

There seems to exist a commonly shared understanding of when one should be prepared to provide the ordinary business gift. However, it is common that agents depart from these rules of the thumb. As was stated by a salesman working in Shanghai, 'I have always with me some gifts in case someone gives me a small gift (*xiao lipin*). It is not comfortable to receive a gift without being able to return a gift. However, in these days it is not common that businessmen give gifts to each other when they meet for the first time'. However, after the interviewee continued to elaborate on the nature of gift-giving, he stated that if you have invited a person to visit your own company it is 'civilized to provide a gift for him visiting our company'. This statement confirms my personal experience of the practice of receiving and exchanging gifts when visiting Chinese companies for the first time.

If the companies are located far away from each other, like in different cities, there seems to be an unwritten rule that both parties are prepared to provide gifts during their first encounter. Usually, in this case, parties have been negotiating with each other through phone and fax and thus have formed a basis of familiarity with each other prior to the first meeting. As one interviewee noted, 'It is a question of hospitality and respect. It is important to express *renqing*. I take them out to eat local food and give them small gifts to make them feel at ease'.

Furthermore, it is necessary to be prepared to give a gift when management-level personnel meet for the first time, either to negotiate or to conclude a deal. Especially, if people meet to sign a contract, the gift-giving is a highly ritualized action that is carefully carried out in a transparent manner. Rituals regulate the gift-giving process, courtesy, speeches and toasting followed by counter-speeches, gifts and toasting, making the eulogies appear to continue without an end. For these kinds of occasions, an ordinary business gift is carefully chosen. It should be valuable, but not too valuable, so that it is clearly distinguished from a bribe.

In Western business guides on China a lot of attention has been given to the etiquette of gift-giving and wrapping of the gifts. According to the business guides, the gift should be beautifully wrapped in red paper. Furthermore, opening the gift in front of the donor should be avoided as the act signals greed and material lust, rather than showing interest in the person who gave the gift. However, based on my data and observations, the ordinary business gifts are not wrapped anymore, but are offered in red-cloth decorated storage-boxes, and the boxes are opened in front of the donor and other people. In inquiring further into this habit, business people explained that they, as well as the state officials, were careful not to accept anything too valuable in front of other people. Receiving an expensive gift in public was hazardous, and it was avoided. State officials and representatives of state-owned companies (SOE), on the one hand, did not like to end up in a judicially risky situation, while on the other hand, they avoided the entrapment of falling into a reciprocal debt to the donor.

The social practice of exchanging ordinary business gifts has been subject to change. Not only is the role and function of providing gifts evolving, but also the etiquette of gift-giving, wrapping and opening the gifts is changing. The development of domestic production of consumption products, eventual explosion of cheap mammon coinciding with the rising incomes combined with the institutional practice of gift-giving have inevitably undermined the possibility of generating true *renqing* – the feeling of indebtedness and gratitude – with the ordinary business gift. And yet, even as the local businessmen all share a collective understanding of the deflated nature of the ordinary business gift, one should still be ready to reciprocate 'ordinary gifts' at any moment.

Under these circumstances, in minimising the time-gap between receiving and reciprocating the ordinary business gift one cannot expect to receive a 'deferred or different' counter-gift. The immediate return of an identical small item (*xiao dongxi*) is an important signal of courtesy, respect expressed in the process of maintaining one's own face and to avoid causing the loss of the other party's face. Contrasting Bourdieu's (1997) thinking of 'swapping' of identical gifts 'amounts to a refusal' or 'insult', the exchange of identical gifts in China is a highly ritualized social action which generates collectively shared meaning and creates a string of commonality between two agents. More importantly, the exchange of small business gifts does not only lay the first cornerstone of the successful business, but eventually is the first stepping stone in the escalating competitive exchange of *renqing* in Chinese business.

'Hand-grenades' and 'machine-guns'

As the reforms and economic development have deflated the potential of 'ordinary business gifts' to generate true feelings of gratitude, and thus have changed the basic logic of gift-giving into a ritual of courtesy, agents have invented new categories of gifts. These new categories of gifts are colloquially called 'grenades' (*shouliudan*) and 'machine-guns' (*jiguangqiang*), commonly referring to the brand-name of liqueur and ten-packs of cigarettes, respectively.

The logic of these 'armament' gifts – the establishment of familiarity with the other party, correct timing of giving, receiving, and reciprocating the gift, departs from the function and logic of the ordinary business gift. In contrast to ordinary business gifts, 'armature' gifts are not provided as an act of courtesy, but are already calculated, carefully manipulated social and economic actions aimed at gaining competitive advantage over competitors by successfully generating a strong feeling of *renqing* debt and eventually, of receiving a favourable countergift or service.

The peculiar militarist names for these gifts derive from the actual function of the gifts. These gifts are used to dig foxholes or to win over an insider (*neiburen*) in the other party's organisation. With the help of these foxholes or insiders, companies gain information, licenses or make important shortcuts in the red-tape processes. They eventually establish long-term strategic friendship relationships, thus gaining competitive advantages over their competitors in the malfunctioning Chinese market. It is not surprising then that companies exert much effort in developing this kind of relationships.

However, as the names of the armament gifts indicate, charging trenches is always risky, takes time, consumes resources, and creates a demand for certain skills. As one interviewee, a man in his late 40s, stated about the competitive forces of the 'armament gift', 'What can you do? Our competitors do it – we have to do it. It takes a lot of time and gives a lot of headache. You see, people are different, companies are different. What is working in one company, does not work in another company. There is no pattern in this'. The interviewees shared a collective understanding on the necessity of competing in the marketplace of armament gifts. Furthermore, there seems to be a clear difference between people working in SOEs and other sectors of the economy. Interviewees stated in a convergent fashion, that individuals working for government organizations took advantage of their position, and were reluctant to co-operate without receiving face, attention and *renqing*.

Despite the difference between different sectors of the economy, the crucial question is how to know to *whom* to give this kind of gift. Interviewees informed that some of the potential receivers themselves indicate their needs by demanding certain presents for counter-favours; so saying they referred to officials or clerks working in the state sector. Most of the businessmen disdained themselves and did not trust this kind of person. Some indicated their interest in more indirect ways by hiding their appeal in other forms of signals. The most commonly used signal is to tell that 'we need to do some research (*yanjiu yanjiu*) before any action is carried out'. However, *yanjiu yanjiu* has a homonym, in cigarettes (*yan*) and alcohol (*jiu*), hence agents indicate in an indirect direct way the need to provide tobacco, liqueur and entertainment.

The actual competitive challenge and risk in offering the 'armament gift' arises from identifying the right person and creating ideal circumstances where the gift receiver has difficulties in refusing to accept the gift. The circumstances have changed and become more complicated from the late 1980s and early 1990s when it was rather common to establish an 'insider' relationship with the car drivers (company chauffeurs). As the economic reforms began in the early 1980s, government departments and SOEs rushed to purchase imported Japanese and Western cars. However, there was still a shortage of good drivers. Consequently, drivers were treated with special care and they even participated in banquets and dinners together with the people they were transporting. Hence, drivers were strategically situated in the organization. Furthermore, as was stated by an interviewee, 'When have you ever seen a driver who does not smoke? All you need to do is to ask someone from your company, like your own driver or someone else, first to talk, chit-chat (*liaotiaor*), to give face and express *renqing*. Only after this can one give the cigarettes'. However, since that epoch, the social status of drivers has decreased and they are not invited to dinners or banquets anymore, but rather wait in the vicinity of their cars. According to the interviewees the importance of drivers as insiders has decreased in recent years. Even so, drivers are still often invited to dine with little demarcation between a social or business meal: yet, conversely are often excluded from participating in a meal and thus be deprived of insider information. What determines this decision – to include or exclude – seems to depend on the political (one's rank) as well as the social levels (the driver may be assigned as a bodyguard, for example).

Gender also plays an important role in establishing foxholes in the other party's organization. If the *guanxi* target is a man, it is advisable to send a woman to deal with him. This is done in accordance with a traditional Chinese expression 'even the hero has difficulties in dealing with a beauty' (*yingxiong nanguo meiren guan*). On the contrary, if the *guanxi* target is an older woman it is advisable to send a younger man to deal with her. In addition, young women feel less constrained talking to other young women, but it is not smart to send a young woman to soften up an older woman (Yang, 1994: 83). As was stated by an interviewee, 'We knew that the secretary of the official was a young woman so we asked one young woman from our department to go over to handle the affair'. However, providing a bottle of brandy or ten-pack of cigarettes for a woman would overstep the bounds of decency in contemporary China, therefore women are instead given DVD movies and free-of-charge beauty parlour sessions, among other things.

In addition to age and gender, individual character also plays an important role in establishing a successful preliminary contact and thereafter being able to advance with the gift, if necessary. Some individuals have an eye for reading people and circumstances better than others, as was illustrated in a group interview with two Chinese businessmen, Mr Yü and Mr Ma, working for the same company. Mr Yü, working in the finance department, in referring to his friend Mr Ma, mentioned that he was extremely good at establishing *guanxi* with people. He characterized Mr Ma as 'very experienced in generating *renqing*' (*renqing lianda*). Mr Ma was working in the public relations (PR) department, where his responsibility was to cultivate good relationships with government and municipal agencies, mainly with the harbour authorities and customs officials.

According to Mr Ma, it is extremely difficult to know to whom or how to provide the 'armament gift'. The only rule of the thumb is to spend time together, to 'shoot the breeze' (*liaotiao*), generate and express *renqing* by talking about things the other party likes, to take the other party out to eat his/her favourite dishes and so on, while simultaneously observing the other party's reactions and signals. However, Mr Ma said that he 'could only feel, and not express himself in words' (*zhi ke yihui, bu ke yanchuan*) about how to identify the right signals, how to know the right string to pull in various situations, and how to be successful in charging the trenches. Even so, Mr Ma said that there were two other things that were important for succeeding – 'the more you have *guanxi* the easier it is, and finally it is always a question of luck'. In contrast to the ordinary business gift, the 'armament gifts' are not usually given in front of other people.

It is important to generate circumstances where rejecting the offered gift is difficult. One effective way is to intentionally create from the first instance a relaxed atmosphere, spend time together, chat, and gradually establish a 'friendship' relationship. As stated by Mr Ma 'after one has "shared the joys and sorrows" (*tonggan gongku*) it is difficult to refuse to receive a gift'. In practice, this means that just before departing from the joys of a long and 'wet' restaurant evening, one deliberately purchases a bottle of nice liqueur or brandy and then while leaving the restaurant gives it to the other party. In providing the bottle of liqueur the skilled gift-giver offers the gift to the other party in a contemplatively disinterested and undeliberate manner playing down the importance of the gift by bringing into play conventional cultural dispositions and models stating that 'this is just a small expression of *renqing*, please take it', while simultaneously, appealing to feelings, referring to friendship, to the joyful time shared together and to future similar evenings that they will spend together strengthening their friendship. Hence, the careful choice and construction of the occasion together with seemingly unintended and disinterested acts of gift-giving binds together the past and the mutually shared joyful evening of the present. The emotional construction of the social arena, and the future expectations, make it harder for the receiver to turn down the gift.

The commonly used Chinese expression 'eating from others makes your mouth softer, taking from others makes your hand shorter' (*chi renjia zui ruan, na renjia shou duan*) illustrates the acme of timing and tactic involved in the case described above. The first part of the expression describes a situation where after a nice banquet one has difficulty refusing the request expressed by the other side. Hence, how much more difficult it is for the guest who has been treated well to refuse the request of the host when the host appeals the guest to receive the bottle, not as a gift but as a signal of friendship, gratitude and time he had spent with the host?

In an attempt to simplify the logic of this process, let us imagine two individuals, A the host, and B the donor – the guest and the receiver. First, A entertains B, in other words gives *renqing* to B. Consequently, B, after being the guest of honour, owes a *renqing to* A. Thus, B is psychologically bound to reciprocate to A. However, when A appeals for the reciprocal favour, A in effect asks B to accept his small gift, not as a gift, but as a signal of gratitude, almost as a reciprocal favour for the time and friendship A has shared with B. As A treated B in the restaurant, B owes A a *renqing* favour. Therefore, B faces difficulties in rejecting the appeal of A, subtly coated in expressions of gratitude. Nevertheless, by accepting the gift, B does not balance his/her *renqing* debt to A because B has now received a gift. Hence, A binds B even stronger into feelings of indebtedness. In other words, B has entered the reality described in the second part of the expression 'taking from others makes your hand shorter'. Hence, after receiving the gift B faces even more difficulties in refusing to help A.

The need to rely on and expand *guanxi* networks, as in establishing insider relations, creates a need for people who possess the qualifications needed for 'working on *guanxi*' (*gao guanxi*). Several interviewees stated that people who were good in 'working on *guanxi*' usually worked in the PR departments. In fact, business organizations in China are hit by the fashion of establishing PR departments, or as the Chinese say, there is a 'fever of public relations' (*gongguan re*) in China (Pan, 1995: 197). However, the conventional notion of PR in China is purely related to the notion of 'working on *guanxi*' with government departments. Several interviewees stated that people who worked for PR departments usually were male workers in their late 20s and early 30s, and that these people were particularly skilled in 'working on *guanxi*'. As a matter of fact, these people had received their own nickname – 'an artful slippery fellow' (*huatou*, or *huatou huanao*). Several interviewees referred in a less respectful manner to PR people as 'slick and sly' (*yuanhua*).

Last but not the least important is the organization that one is dealing with. According to the interviewees, there is a great difference between bureaucrats and representatives of SOEs and the other sectors of the economy. Generally, the businessmen whom I interviewed explained that the people working in the state-sector were 'greedy and always hungry'. Especially officials who were working in certain crucial 'spots' (*quan dian*) of control: for instance, controlling the licensing, or people with special authority of supervision. Hence, in meeting with government authorities agents were more prone to pick up the concealed messages. Agents understand that these kinds of activities were determined by the asymmetrical power relationship, which Walder (1986) has discussed under the 'patron–client relationship' framework.

On the one hand, interviewees referred to this as 'the power-economy' (*quanli jingji*), which can create a lot of risks. Namely, there was a risk that the representatives of SOEs or other government bureaucrats became concierges blocking the way to information or to other important people, while they expected to be treated favourably. As was stated by an interviewee, 'You have to please them, but you never know whether it will get you anywhere'. This is reminiscent of the Qing-dynasty (1644–1911) practice where business people had to pay off at each stage of the bureaucracy before being able to establish a relationship with people who possessed the real power (He, 1998: 127).

This practice is also known as 'the exchanging power to money' (*quan qian jiaoyi*). On the other hand, interviewees stated that providing this kind of 'rather inexpensive gifts' was an effective way of expressing *renqing*. Furthermore, it is in line with the historical legacy of how merchants worked with officials. As one interviewee stated, 'it is the special character of China that "officials thousand miles away are seeking wealth" (*qian li zuoguan wei qiu cai*). You help them and they help you. Of course it is wrong, but "the legal apparatus cannot punish the masses" (*fa bu ze zhong*)'.

In addition, offering an armament gift is an effective means of generating the feeling of a *renqing* debt and is not directly considered a bribe. As was stated by an interviewee, 'paying back a debt of *renqing* is much more difficult than paying back a debt of money, because you never know how to count the monetary value of a *renqing* debt'. His statement was in accordance with the commonly used expression 'it is easy to pay off the monetary debt, but difficult to pay off debt of *renqing*' (*qianzhai hao huan, renqing zhai nan huan*).

The development of competitive advantages is always a challenging task. The enlargement of a *guanxi* network does not make an exception in this regard. Contrary to the conventional perception (Tung and Yeung, 1996; Li, 1998; Luo and Chen, 1997) of the smooth expansion of *guanxi* networks, the actual enlarging of one's *guanxi* base is a challenging task usually involving the complicated ritual of gift-giving. In providing the gift, several things need to be taken into consideration; choosing the right person, gender, age, personal and professional qualifications. Furthermore, the person has to bind his/her resources into establishing, maintaining and cultivating the relationship, and has to be capable of not only creating appropriate circumstances but also be able to decide the timing of the gift-giving in such a manner that rejecting the gift is difficult. It is also increasingly important to differentiate the gift from competitors' gifts. Hence, the competitive factor has forced the participants to develop even more delicate techniques in choosing the gift object and timing the gift-giving. The 'guided missiles' as gifts are an outcome of this competition.

'Guided missiles'

The 'guided missile' (*daodan*) gift is the most complex and resource-consuming pattern of gift-giving in the Chinese market. The actual name 'guided missile' is not, at least to my knowledge, widely used. As a matter of fact it was Mr Ma who used the category of 'guided missile' when he illustrated the fascinating complexities involved in the whole process of choosing the target of the 'missile', deciding the gift object, and deciding on the time and pattern of gift-giving.

A 'guided missile' should be of special importance and value for the receiver, who has been identified in advance. The gift item can be anything that people collect and subjectively appreciate; traditional decorative stones, stamps, minority people shoes, an art book, a traditional painting and so on. It can also be a personal favour – basically anything that is believed to generate a strong feeling of *renqing*. However, it is not a prerequisite to know the person in advance. Nevertheless, it is important to find out his/her desires and hobbies, which are then made use of in the gift-giving process. Hence, before one is able to provide the gift, it is necessary to carry out 'pre-networking', identifying the right person and finding the correct gift for him or her. As a matter of fact, gathering information begins from the first encounter with the other party. In this process, it is important to find an insider who can reveal the information on the key personnel of the company, then identify the real decision-maker in the organization.

Information is gathered not only from the 'insider'. One important stage in receiving information is through banquets. Banquets are the most common and natural platform where this kind of information is gathered and exchanged. Banqueting is one mechanism to establish *guanxi*; it is also an important stage where social exchange takes place (Yang, 1994). During banquets people socialize freely and business talk is traditionally tuned down. As one interviewee stated, 'one should try to remember everything that was said by the opposite side. Sometimes I go to the toilet to make notes on what they said'. Several interviewees believed that the more you knew of the other party, even personal matters, like hobbies, birthdays, marital status, names and birthdays of children, close friends and so on, the better off you are. As a matter of fact, this was usually stated by quoting Sun Tzu 'know your enemy and know yourself and your victory won't be threatened' (*zhi bi zhi ji zhe, bai zhan bu dai*).

An interviewee, Mr Pan, a businessman from Fujian province, illustrated the challenges involved in giving the 'guided missile' gift. Mr Pan had established a company in Beijing, attempting to lease office equipment in the capital. According to him, the competition in the market was fierce. Through his local associate he had managed to establish an insider relationship with one company, which could become his first big client in the business. During the first few weeks Mr Pan negotiated with various people in the organization, but without much progress. Mr Pan came to the conclusion, that 'his insider' did not have enough power within the organization. Finally, Mr Pan got the chance to meet with the person, Mr Zhou, who was in charge of the possible purchase. Eventually, Mr Pan found out that Mr Zhou was fond of minority people shoes. During the Cultural Revolution, Mr Zhou had been sent down to the remote countryside and during his stay in the south-western parts of China he had been in frequent contact with the local minority people. Since his return to the capital he had gradually begun to collect, as a hobby, minority people art, dresses and shoes. Mr Pan, desperate in reaching the deal, activated his network of friends to find certain minority people shoes for Mr Zhou, who was very pleased to receive the gift. However, at the time of the interview they were still negotiating the deal so the outcome of this gift-giving is not yet known.

I also encountered other similar stories illustrating the complexities involved in the 'guided missile' gift-giving. Another interviewee, Mr Wei, stated that he had found out that his 'target' was collecting stamps. Hence, Mr Wei 'activated' his own network and eventually found a friend who was also a philatelist. On the recommendation of this friend, Mr Wei not only purchased stamps to be given as the gift, but also learned some basic things about stamp collecting. In the words of Mr Wei, this was 'to catch two flies with one stroke – you do not only give the gift (*songli*), but you also give a feeling (*ganqing*)'. When the gift was received, Mr Wei continued, 'he immediately appreciated the effort that I had taken for him'.

Even though the 'guided missile' is understood to be an effective means of generating a strong sense of *renqing* debt, agents have invented, an additional, even more effective path of providing the 'guided missile'. As was stated by an interviewee, 'people are careful not to accept gifts. But if you give the gift to their children, they have more difficulties in saying no. This is what I call "different means," but equally satisfactory outcome (*yiqu tonggong*)'. The preliminary work is similar, only that this time it is necessary to inquire into the family-life of the potential decision-makers. In order to gain this kind of information, one should have an insider who is well connected and knows or can find out the necessary information on hobbies, birthdays of family members or other family anniversaries.

Usually, in generating the feeling of *renqing* debt by giving the gift to a child, one should invent an occasion for the gift-giving. As pointed out by Yan (1996), agents are inventing new opportunities for gift-giving. An interviewee in Shanghai, who in addition to commonly used gift-giving occasions, like birthdays and graduations, created a new opportunity for legitimate gift-giving. Ms Feng found out that the son of the person in charge was going to participate in the national university entrance exam. For this occasion, she ordered a special cake, bought a painting and fresh flowers, and took these gifts to the official the night before the exam and wished good luck to the whole family. This was, what Ms Feng called 'to use feeling to substitute the gift-object' (*yi ganqing daiti liwu*). She actually provided three objects, but she considered that the expression of feeling in her conduct was the decisive factor, not the gift items. This expression of feeling helped Ms Feng to get the approvals she was applying for.

Thus, the logic of providing the 'guided missile' complicates Bourdieu's notion of time – the important time lag between receiving and reciprocating the gift (ibid, 1997: 198). In many cases, especially for those people who lack the organizational backing or the leveraging power of their own personal network of people, the donor makes the decision on the time lag or interval and not the receiver, as is described by Bourdieu. For instance, Ms Feng first provided the gifts and then retreated and waited for almost two weeks before she went back to see the official at his bureau. Ms Feng considered this to be appropriate and wise, since otherwise, directly waiting for or asking for immediate reciprocation would have ruined her apparently disinterested act of gift-giving, her symbolic and ritualized expression of attachment and concern in the way that she performed the gift-giving. Hence, in the Chinese context, time is not only the resource of the receiver. On the contrary, time is a crucial resource that is carefully used by the donors in deciding on the timing of gift-giving and on deciding the length of the interval between giving and asking for the reciprocal favour.

In addition, the traditional festivals, especially the Spring Festival and Mid-Autumn Festival, are used as excuses in launching expensive 'guided missile' gifts. These expensive gifts, in contrast to the rather inexpensive, but still subjectively valuable 'guided missiles' described above, are clearly regarded as bribes. Due to the intense anti-corruption campaign the donors have recognized that the 'guided missile' pattern of providing the bribe is very efficient and safe, and thus have intensified the usage of 'guided missiles'. Furthermore, interviewees shared a collective belief that the police and prosecutors would not interfere in gift-giving during national holidays and festivals, or if they did, they would be more lenient than usual.

The 'guided missile' as a gift is the most complex and resource-consuming pattern of gift-giving in China. It usually demands extensive pre-networking aimed to gather together puzzles of information about the potential target and his/her preferences. Receiving the decisive information can take place through exchanging information during banquets or is provided by the 'insider', or sometimes it is entirely a matter of chance. When the other party feels that it is necessary to influence a decision-maker, they can utilize the information about the opposite party to provide him with a 'guided missile' that is valuable to the receiver. Depending on the nature of the gift it can be given in front of other people, but usually, at least according to the data available for this research, it is provided behind the stage of the visible networking. Due to the subjective value of the gift and due to the relatively low judicial risks of receiving the 'guided missile', it is an effective way of generating a feeling of *renqing* indebtedness and thus binds the receiver into a dyadic relationship with the donor.

Conclusion

This chapter illustrated the complicated and sophisticated art of gift-giving that forms an additional marketplace where Chinese companies compete with each other. Contrary to the conventional perception of unconstrained utilization and smooth expansion of *guanxi*, the enlarging of the *guanxi* base is a challenging task involving more often than not the complicated practice of gift-giving.

Furthermore, gift-giving can also be seen to follow an escalating pattern of competition. The first step is to give the 'ordinary business gift' in establishing the necessary basis of familiarity. As one establishes familiarity and recognizes the potential for business, one might attempt to establish 'an insider' relationship by advancing with the 'armament gift'. Often one has 'planted an insider' in the organization, so, if necessary one can launch 'the guided missile' to gain the favour of the decision-maker. Each process has its own logic of giving, receiving and reciprocating. Likewise, the role and function of time also differs at each stage. It is obvious that the mere complexities of gift-giving in Chinese networking question the conventional perception of smooth *guanxi* practice.

In addition, the empirical findings of gift-giving in a Chinese context makes more problematical the conventional Western notions of exchanging gift-object with another gift-object, and complicates the notion of time in the gift-giving process. The Chinese notion of gift-giving, exchanging *renqing*, does not mean that the transaction necessarily occurs in the conventional Western pattern, that is, the given and reciprocated gift as an object. In the Chinese context, it can be the exchange of a favour with another favour; a gift-object can be reciprocated with a favour. A favour can be reciprocated with a gift-object, and a gift-object reciprocated with a gift-object. The ambiguous word *renqing*, connoting to gift-object and favour, is frequently used in the process of providing and reciprocating favours/gifts, thus urging us to expand our conventional theory on gift-objects to include favours as well, the non-physical products.

Bourdieu (1997: 198) states that gift-giving follows a certain universal pattern where in every society it may be observed that, the counter-gift must be deferred and different, because the immediate return of an exactly identical object clearly amounts to a refusal or to an insult. Hence, according to this theory the *'swapping of identical gifts'* harms or even destroys the relationship between the agents. However, exchange of 'the ordinary business gifts' in China questions this notion of Bourdieu. In fact, 'ordinary business gifts' are small items, pens, calendars and so on, labeled with the company name and logo, which by their nature and actual monetary value are more or less identical. In the Chinese context, the exchange of 'identical' ordinary business gifts follows a different logic. The importance of exchanging identical 'ordinary business gifts' lies in the fact that it tends to *project the relationship* into a more advanced level, facilitating feelings of commonality among agents, which is a basic requirement of co-operation and even future gift-giving. The exchange of ordinary business gifts divulges that both parties have and can give *renqing* – human feelings and/or favours, which is the essence of Chineseness.

Time has a central role in gift-giving. According to Bourdieu (ibid, 1997: 198–9), time lags between giving and reciprocating are essential in gift-giving. 'The relationship between gift and counter-gift is what allows a relation of exchange to appear as irreversible, yet is both forced and self-interested, so be seen as reversible'. To abolish this interval is also to abolish the strategy of gift-giving. However, as was discovered in this study, gift-giving has several dimensions that need to be taken into consideration, and time is only one of them.

Hence, in providing the 'armament' and 'guided missile' gifts, time has additional functions that complicate Bourdieu's notion of time in gift-giving – the time lag between giving and counter-gift. Correct timing in gift-giving is an effective way of not only generating a stronger feeling of indebtedness and gratitude, but can also make it harder for the receiver to deny the gift. It is common to time gift-giving to coincide with personal anniversaries, thus making the gift appear to be more personal and disinterested. An additional ploy is to provide gifts for family members as an act of genuine care and attention, attempting to drive the receiver into a corner, where he has fewer opportunities to reject the gift. Furthermore, the time-lag between the giving and the reciprocating of the gift is in certain circumstances the reverse in China. If the agent does not have a strong organizational backing or extensive personal *guanxi* base he/she needs to apply a different strategy, namely, after one has provided the gift of 'guided missile', one should retreat and wait for an appropriate time before advancing and asking for a reciprocal favour.

In summary, in gift-giving, time has at least three different roles. First, the *time interval between giving and reciprocating*. Here, the *receiver controls time*. Second, *choosing* and *mastering the timing* of gift-giving, which is naturally *done by the donor*. Third, *controlling* the appropriate *time difference between gift-giving and asking for the reciprocal favour*. The *donor*, who does not enjoy organizational backing in facing the bureaucracy, *does this*. In fact, most of the Chinese do not have the access to organizational support that could equal the monumental state apparatus and Communist Party of China. Probably, the total time spent on the gift-giving process could also be taken as the 'fourth' aspect of time in gift-giving, as it can restrict the deployment of resources.

This then is the context within which Chinese business people have to manage. This study is an attempt to provide an insight, to see the process from the various perspectives, of the importance and logic of gift-giving in Chinese business. As a result of the institutional setting and dependency on *guanxi*, a completely different mindset and range of competences is being demanded of Chinese businessmen. The competitive advantage of Chinese businesses constitute successful management and deployment of gifts in *guanxi* networks. In addition to the delicate sensitivity of controlling time, crucial for the successful gift-giving are the manipulation of circumstances and 'style'. In providing the 'armament' or 'guided missile' gifts, gender, individual skills and choice of style are decisive factors. Due to the countless possible variables involved, displayed, conditioned and yet spontaneously created at the stage of gift-giving, it is hard to draw an abstract theory on gift-giving acts. Some individuals are more skilled than others at networking and gift-giving. They are more ingenious in reading the postures, gestures of the body and picking up linguistic nuances. They are more nimble in their reactions, guided by intuition and observation. They are able to choose the right words, adapt their style and eventually create ideal circumstances and favourable timing for gift-giving. It is a matter of timing, creation and manipulation of style and circumstances conducive to successful gift-giving. The same act of giving the gift can have completely different meanings at different times and even giving the right gift at the right moment, but with a wrong style can be disastrous.

References

Boisot, M. and Child, J. (1996) From fiefs to clans and network capitalism: Explaining China's emerging economic order. *Administrative Science Quarterly* 41: 600–28.

Boisot, M. and Child, J. (1999) Organizations in adaptive systems in complex environments: The case of China. *Organization Science* **10**: 237–52.

Bourdieu, P. (1997) *Selections from the Logic of Practice*. Quoted in Schrift, A. 'Introduction: Why Gift?' in Schrift, A. (ed.), *The Logic of the Gift*, London: Routledge, 190–230.

Bourdieu, P. (1997) *Marginalia – some additional notes on the Gift*. Quoted in Schrift, A. 'Introduction: Why Gift?' in Schrift, A. (ed.), *The Logic of the Gift*, London: Routledge, 231–44.

Bourdieu, P. (1990) *The Logic of Practice*, Cambridge: Polity Press.

Chabal, P. and Daloz, J.-P. (1999) *Africa Works: Disorder as Political Instrument*, The International Africa Institute, Indiana: University Press.

Chen, M. (1995) *Asian Management Systems; Chinese, Japanese and Korean Styles of Business*, London: Routledge.

Cheung, P. (1996) 'The Political Context of Shanghai's Economic Development', in Y. Yeung and Y. Sung (eds), *Shanghai, Transformation and Modernisation under China's Open Policy*, Hong Kong: The Chinese University Press.

Child, J. (1996) *Management in China during the age of reform*, Cambridge University Press.

Davies, H., Leung, T. K., Luk, S. and Wong, Y. (1995) The benefits of *guanxi*: The value of relationships in developing the Hciese market. *Industrial Marketing Management* **24**: 207–14.

Fei Xiaotong (1991) *Xiangtu Zhongguo*, Xianggang: Sanlian shudian.

Goodman, D. and Hooper, B. (1994) *China's Quiet Revolution: New Interactions between State and Society*, Cheshire: Longman.

He, Qinglian (1998) *Xiandaihua de xianjin – dangdai Zhongguo de jingji shehui wenti* (The Pitfall of the Modernisation – economic and social problems of contemporary China) Jinri Zhongguo chubanshe.

Hendry, J. (1993) *Wrapping Culture: Politeness, Presentation and Power in Japan and Other Societies*, Oxford: Clarendon Press.

Huang, G. (1988) *Renqing yü mianzi: Zhongguoren de quanli youxi* (Renqing and Face: The Chinese Power Game), in G. Yang (ed.), *Zhongguoren de xinli*, (The Psychology of the Chinese People), Taibei.

Kipnis, A. B. (1997) *Producing Guanxi*, Durham, NC: Duke University Press.

Levi-Strauss, C. (1997) 'Selections from Introduction to the Work of Marcel Mauss', in Schrift, A. (ed.), *The Logic of the Gift*, London: Routledge.

Li, P. P. (1998) Toward a geocentric framework of organizational form: A holistic, dynamic and paradoxical approach. *Organizational Studies* **19**(5): 829–61.

Liang, S. M. (1999) *Zhongguoren: shehui yu renshen*. Zhongguo wenlian chubanshe.

Lovett, S., Simmons, L. C. and Kali, R. (1999) *Guanxi* versus the market: Ethics and efficiency. *Journal of International Business Studies* Summer, **30**(2): 1–11.

Luo, Y. (1997) *Guanxi*: Principles, philosophies and implications. *Human Systems Management* **16**(1): 43–51.

Luo, Y. and Chen, M. (1997) Does *guanxi* influence firm performance? *Asia Pacific Journal of Management* **14**: 1–16.

Luo, Y. and Park, S. (2001) *Guanxi* and organizational dynamics: Organizational networking in Chinese firms. *Strategic Management Journal* **22**: 445–7.

Mauss, M. (1924) Essai sur le don. Forme et raison de l'échange dans les sociétés archaïques. Paris, *l'Année Sociologique, seconde série*, 1923–4.

Mauss, M. (1997) '*Gift, Gift*', in Schrift, A. (ed.), *The Logic of the Gift*, London: Routledge.
Moore, C. A. (1967) *The Chinese Mind – Essentials of Chinese Philosophy and Culture*. University of Hawaii Press: Hawaii.
Nee, V. (1992) Organizational dynamics of market transaction: Hybrid forms, property rights, and mixed economy in China. *Adminstrative Science Quarterly* 37: 1–27.
Pan, G. (1995) *Hewei 'fuwu'* (what is the meaning of 'service'), in *Gongzhong guanxixüe* (The Art of Public Relationship). Beijing: Beijingdaxüe Chubanshe. 170–202.
Redding, G. (1990) *The Spirit of Chinese Capitalism*, Berlin: De Gruyter.
Schrift, A. (1997) 'Introduction: Why Gift?', in Schrift, A. (ed.), *The Logic of the Gift*, London: Routledge.
Tsang, E. (1998) Can *guanxi* be a source of sustained competitive advantage for doing business in China? *The Academy of Management Executive* 12(2): 64–73.
Tung, R. L. and Yueng, I. Y. (1996) Achieving business success in Confucian societies: The importance of *Guanxi*. *Organizational Dynamics* 25: 54–65.
Walder, A. (1986) *Communist Neo-traditionalism*, Berkeley, CA: University of California Press.
Wank, D. (1999) *Commodifying Communism, business, trust and politics in a Chinese city*, Cambridge: Cambridge University Press.
White, L. and Li, C. (1993) 'China Coast Identities: Regional, National and Global', in L. Dittmer and S. Kim (eds), *China's Quest for National Identity*, Ithica, Io: Cornell University Press.
Whitley, R. (1994) *Business Systems in East Asia; Firms, Markets and Societies*, London: Sage Publications.
Wong, Y. H. and Chan, R. Y-K. (1999) Relationship marketing in China: *Guanxi*, favouritism, and adaptation. *Journal of Business Ethics* 22(2): 107–18.
Yan, Y. (1996) The culture of *guanxi* in a North China village. *The China Journal* 35: 5–16.
Yang, M. (1989) The gift economy and state power in China. *Society for Comparative Study of Society and History* 31(1): 25–54.
Yang, M. (1994) *Gifts, Favours, And Banquets; The Art of Social Relationships in China*, Ithica, Io: Cornell University Press.

7
The Economics of Corruption and Cronyism – An Institutional Approach to the Reform of Governance

Barbara Krug and Hans Hendrischke

Introduction

Moral outrage was the response of the Chinese press, when Cheng Kejie, one of the country's highest officials, Vice-Chairman of the Standing Committee of the National People's Congress and former Governor of the *Guangxi* Zhuang Autonomous Region, was arrested on grounds of corruption on 25 April 2000. Cheng's arrest came amidst a spate of serious corruption cases that reached into the top echelons of China's state leadership (China Aktuell, 2000). His case attracted wide public attention in national and international Chinese media because of his high office, the number of officials implicated, and the involvement of his lover Li Ping (dubbed the *"Jiang Qing of Guangxi"* by the Hong Kong and overseas Chinese press) (Ming Pao, 2000), daughter-in-law of his predecessor in the position of Governor of *Guangxi*, and for years the most influential woman in *Guangxi*. This was not just a case of a local official embezzling public funds, but a story of love and greed of a popular political leader, who had achieved much for his province. This was also not the story of an anonymous mistress, but of an ambitious, intelligent and attractive woman using the position of, first, her father-in-law, then her lover, to systematically, and on a long-term basis, exploit the powers vested in the office of provincial governor. The accusation against them focused on three crimes: appropriation and sale of real estate development and construction rights, sale of publicly subsidized goods at market prices and promotion of trusted allies into official positions of power. While the personal details of Cheng's deeds and his final execution in September 2000 fascinated the Chinese and Hong Kong press, his case also demonstrates how corruption works in China today (Hendrischke, 2001).

Research on China's major corruption cases, such as the one involving a Beijing mayor Chen Xitong, and the still unsolved case in the city of Xiamen, has often linked them to power struggles and factional alliances within the top leadership (Wedeman, 1996). More general analysis points to the Leninist state-party system that is not bound by its own rules as the deeper cause of continuing corruption (Manion, 1997). The reasons for corruption are particularly vexing issues in all societies, open to cultural, psychological and political analysis (Holmes, 1993, chap. 5) as well as anthropological (Rocca, 1992), or more focused economic explanation (Rose-Ackermann, 1999, chap. 3). On the other hand, Chinese researchers tend to emphasize the moral dimension (Yang Xiliang, 1997).

This study presents an economic analysis of corruption, with particular focus on cronyism and nepotism as a network-based form of corruption open to institutional analysis, as one group of actors positively discriminate against "outsiders" in favor of members of their own group. In effect it will take the form of an extended "case study."

Talking about cronyism

Forms of corruption and cronyism have been observed in most societies; however, their importance differs between countries and periods. Some economies seem to be almost completely run by cronyism, like Marcos' Philippines, while in others, like Switzerland, cronyism seems to be "unknown" – although one must be careful about definitions as there are always exceptions – note the secrecy of Swiss banks, and also the large differences between their cantons on many matters, not least women's liberal rights. In general, the people most concerned about corruption and cronyism seem to be politicians and journalists: they treat them as either legal issues or as moral scandals. From the perspective of political science corruption and cronyism are considered to be institutional issues, mainly occurring in transforming or weak political systems as they are often to be found in developing countries. Institutional analysis usually relates them to clienteles or patronage and focuses on the given dependency of those involved in, for example, clan systems. Consequently, corruption and cronyism in these institutional environments are not looked at in terms of voluntary exchange (Eisenstadt and Lemarchand, 1981).

Surprisingly, corruption and more specifically cronyism are rarely dealt with in economics (Boycko *et al.*, 1995). They occasionally appear in economic history concerned with changes in property rights or specific allocation systems that preceded the emergence of market economies (North, 1981). On the other hand, the literature on the shadow economy and related corrupt activities rather concentrates on the question why people find it profitable to leave the official sector, but stops short of investigating the individual calculus for engaging in corruption and cronyism (Cassel, 1986; Rose-Ackerman, 1978; Weck *et al.*, 1984; Haslinger, 1986).

These explanations look at corruption and cronyism from a macro(-economic) point of view. Yet, since both arise from the decision of individual actors, it might be useful to turn to the microeconomic perspective as first developed by Becker (Becker, 1971 and 1982; Shleifer and Vishny, 1993; Krug, 1988; Fan and Grossman, 2001). We start by contesting that preference for relatives; people from the same origin or comrades are the only determinants for cronyism. Instead, by arguing that institutions matter, we can revisit questions such as, what are corruption and cronyism and what are their causes. Do different institutional settings constrain cronyism, either by reducing incentives or by exercising more efficient control? Can the prevalence of corruption and cronyism observed in a country such as China be linked to the co-existence of a socialist and a market sector? Can it be concluded from this analysis that cronyism is the result of a weak institutional context rather than the newly emerging market sector?

This chapter is organized as follows: First, the question of honesty is addressed in order to clarify the relation between corruption and cronyism. Next, corruption and cronyism as problems in the public sector labor market will be dealt with followed by an analysis of corruption and cronyism as economic or rent-seeking problems. The final section shows that the need to "network" turns corruption and cronyism into a problem that is shaped by the interdependency of the political market and the economic sector.

Corruption and cronyism as a problem of morality

Usually, corruption refers to the sale of state provided goods by a government official in return for private gains. An individual will engage in such a scheme, if by doing so s/he can expect a higher income than by acknowledging procedural rules and working for promotion.

In moral terms, what makes a politician or bureaucrat honest is their resistance to the temptation of increased income by working in the "public interest" only. Yet, from an economic point of view, a bureaucrat does not need to be intrinsically honest; it would suffice to be indifferent to the distributional consequences of state-organized allocation of goods. For example, as long as s/he follows the usual bureaucratic practice of "first-come-first-served," her/his personal morality is not an issue. The problem starts the moment the bureaucrat "cares" who gets what. Cheng Katie's commitment to Li Ping was based on personal affection and infatuation with her refinement and cosmopolitan flair that transcended his provincial horizon. His hope was to marry her eventually, to which she agreed, provided that they would together be able to earn enough money to lead an independent life. As part of their arrangement, Li Ping took care of their finances and transferred her illegal gains to Hong Kong under her name. In Cheng's view, this was meant to provide for their later life after his retirement. This commitment by Cheng Kejie makes the corruption case special, because money gained with his support flowed primarily to his lover, to some of his family members, but hardly to himself, who was still on a nominal monthly salary of 900 yuan.

Thus, love or caring is the defining element of cronyism and nepotism as a special form of corruption. For the purpose of the following analysis the two terms will be defined as follows: Cronyism describes the willingness to break procedural rules and to forego revenues/income appropriable in a system of corruptive practices in order to provide better income earning opportunities to people for whom one cares. If those cared for people belong to one family, then we talk about nepotism.

This caring leading to positive discrimination can be based on emotions for certain people, can be subject to pressure of interest groups on whose support a bureaucrat's political or professional survival depends, or can be based on the expectation that the beneficiaries will "pay back" the favor in kind or money. In other words, cronyism and nepotism caused by affections is based on intrinsic motivation while the two latter cases point to extrinsic (monetary) incentives at the base of corrupt behavior. Unfortunately, from an analytical point of view, both can also be a mixture of all three elements as the following analysis and the story of Cheng shows.

One way to model cronyism is to conceive of it as a gift (Neilson, 1999; Yang, 1994). If most members of the society were honest, that is, immune against the monetary incentives corrupt practices promise, cronyism and nepotism would be limited to *gifts* between relatives, friends, or, indeed, lovers. In the Cheng case, at least two groups of people who might fit this description can be singled out. First, his lover Li Ping and the Hong Kong business man Zhang Jinghai, who as her

Hong Kong lover received large sums of money from her, which he converted into Hong Kong investment. Another, very broad group is the Zhuang population in *Guangxi*'s border regions to Vietnam, a national minority population to which Cheng Kejie belonged. By successfully lobbying the central leadership in Beijing, Cheng Kejie succeeded to get a six-lane motorway financed, which connects the minority counties, but could hardly be justified on technical or economic grounds. By supporting border trade as a provincial policy and turning a blind eye to large-scale smuggling along the Sino-Vietnamese border, he created major economic benefits for the minorities in these areas, which had been long neglected (Hendrischke, 1997). From a personal, moral perspective one could argue that had Cheng been indifferent to Li Ping's charm and to the needs of the minorities, he probably would not have become engaged in corruption.

The problem with that kind of argument is that it is hard to judge from the outside what the real motives were that prompted Cheng's behavior. One might be prepared to believe that he was "truly" in love with Li Ping and wanted to see her well off. His caring for the minorities is harder to judge. Turning a blind eye on smuggling could have been prompted by a wish to help the border minorities, by enforcing a development policy that made the development of the poorer regions at the border to Vietnam part of his programme (Hendrischke, 2000), or his ability to create a new revenue source from which he personally profited.

In any case, the comment in the Chinese press, that he was somebody, who had "developed an ideological style of money worship, hedonism, and extreme individualism" (FBIS-CHI-2000-0420) is premature, to say the least. Moreover, such moral judgement cannot explain how Cheng could go on with his acts of corruption for such a long time; neither can it explain how he became Vice-president of the NPC.

For this Institutional Economics suggests another way of modelling. Instead of concentrating on the motives of individual actors, that is, why they embark on corruptive practices, such an analysis concentrates on the ability to do so, and on the institutional setting that allows individuals to hand out gifts, or take bribes. The following two sections will therefore analyse the conditions that allow corruption and cronyism to emerge.

Cronyism as a labour market problem in the public sector

Not all employees working in the public sector can hand out state provided goods in return for bribes or change the allocation rules. The ability to do so requires a certain amount of power as described below.

The government official needs to hold *effective property rights*,[1] in the sense that he can first exclude anybody from using (or transferring) the assets under his control. Second, he must be able to make the use of an asset dependent on his approval. Basically, s/he controls and allocates the right to use a resource. It is the trade in permits and approvals, which in most cases dominates corruption. As officially all goods provided by the public sector are in state ownership in China, effective property rights executed by officials indicate weak institutions. Consider the following example from the Cheng/Li file which relates to a piece of land that was originally assigned to the provincial-level Nationalities Affairs Commission for development. Cheng, as the local Governor, was able to reverse this allocation and transfer the development rights for the site to his lover who sold them for a huge sum to an associate of the Governor. This is one side of weak institutions; in a setting with strong legal institutions, the Commission could have filed a case against the Governor for interference in administrative procedures. Another side is that the beneficiary of the land deal can also not be sure if his payment for the development rights secures the necessary property rights, which will still rest with the bureaucracy. Contracts between the bribe taker, that is, the person in control of state provided goods, and bribe payer, the individual who complies with the payment, are unenforceable in any political system, resulting in a (high) risk premium. In our case, enforceability was secured through the promotion of personal allies of the governor into bureaucratic positions in charge of development approvals and allocation of goods.

The official also enjoys managerial *discretion*[2] – which quantity (or quality) to sell to whom, or which permit/approval to give to whom. In the Cheng/Li case goods and permits were first offered to his lover as a middle person and to associates. In this case, cronyism refers to weak government rather than weak institutions. It is a problem of *principal–agent relations* in which the principal, that is, the central government, cannot monitor the provincial agents closely enough to enforce behavior. The most striking feature of the Cheng/Li case is certainly that Cheng as the provincial Governor was entitled to monitor the behavior of the provincial state administration, in other words he would have been entitled to monitor and punish himself, or to make sure that appropriate legislation would limit the managerial discretion of people like himself. It is this blurred distinction between the principal, that is, legislation, and the executive side of the government as the agent, which offers the chance to embark on corruption to beneficiary groups. These groups then ensure through networks of cronyism that their members occupy positions, which allow them to engage in corrupt practices at low costs.

As the revenue from corruption also depends on the *monopolistic position*, the ability to limit the number of competing suppliers of the same good is crucial (Olson, 1965: chaps 1–2). Otherwise s/he has to share the monopolistic rent, with the threat that competition will drive the bribe-price down. An easy way to do so is to control production of the good in question. As long as a few large state firms are the only suppliers of certain goods, control of these firms allows appropriation of the monopolistic rent. Another way is to design regulation for local jurisdiction, or control export/import licences. In all cases, the strength of the monopoly depends not only on the ability to block "market entry" of other suppliers but also on the mobility of resources that are subject to regulation.

Cheng was able to exclude lower level bureaucrats from the process of issuing land development rights and from the distributive mechanism for centrally subsidized scarce goods, such as edible oil and white sugar.

As will be shown presently, the effectiveness of such a corruptive network will ultimately depend on a proper job placement policy. Personal sympathy might play a role as, for example, when Cheng made Li head of the *Guangxi* trade representation in Hong Kong. Another condition is that the person will collaborate with the corruption practices established so far. Otherwise, the fine-tuned system of bribes might collapse or at least become harder to enforce. It might be fatal to place a kinsman who is honest into a position where he is expected to collaborate.

This is basically the reason why it is so hard to judge from outside to which extent single acts of cronyism indicate "caring" or self-interest. Simple microeconomics can show how corruptive practices work.

Corruption and cronyism as a problem of (mis-)appropriating rents

In the Cheng case, the press summarized the costs of his behavior as shown in Table 7.1. These sums represent the costs from a legal point of view, namely the income earned by illegal behavior. An economic analysis does not limit itself to the actual money transfers but includes the distributional effects as well as the indirect costs that accrue out of the misallocation of resources. In order to understand corruption in China it is essential to distinguish between "rights," first the control right over the operational side of a business or bureaucratic procedures and the "property" right over net return or cash flow.

Table 7.1 An indication of corruption flows

Years	Item	Foreign currency amounts	RMB Yuan
1994–97	Real estate development and contract construction	HK$8 040 000	17 300 000 8 603 000 2 200 000
1994–98	Promotions of officials	US$35 000 HK$20 000	595 000 290 000 21 400
1992–97	Quotas and allocations		9 030 000
Total		US$4 583 000	38 040 200

Source: Central News Briefing on the "Cheng Kejie Corruption Case", Beijing Xinhua Hong Kong Service in Chinese, 20/4/2000, FBIS-CHI-2000-0420. Xinhua Hong Kong service the Chinese press agency in Hong Kong.

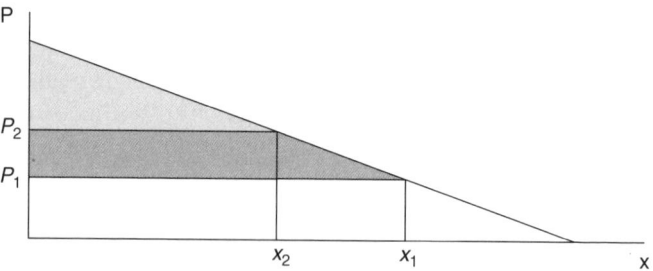

Figure 7.1 Price vs. consumers

Take the following example from the Cheng/Li file, where corruption occurred in the distribution of sugar and oil. In general the following practices can be distinguished.

Assume that sugar is controlled by a state agency and distributed at a fixed price (P_1) so that x_1 consumers can be served (Figure 7.1). The light shaded area is the consumer rent that all buyers enjoy who would have been willing to pay a higher price. By asking for a bribe, which raises the total price for sugar to P_2, the bribe taker can appropriate part of the consumer rent, the dark shaded area. The higher total price works like a tax and will lead to a decline in total demand depending on price/income elasticities. Thus, if white sugar is regarded as essential for cooking then the drop in demand will be low. This explains why corruption concentrates on goods whose demand is relatively inelastic, such as energy, water, food, housing and so on. In this case the bribe taker (Cheng) would have acknowledged the property right of the national treasury which would see the revenues generated by the sale of sugar at the state fixed price transferred. The loss for the treasury would be the difference between the lower demand (x_2-x_1) multiplied by the state price. At a general level, the consumer would not be hurt as long as the number of people who had been willing to offer a higher price does exceed the number of consumers no longer able (or willing) to pay the higher price. The bribe taker gains from the appropriation of the consumer rent.

In the Cheng/Li case rent seeking involved the conversion of government allocations of subsidized goods and import quotas into options that could be sold on the market. Such allocations to the provincial government are routinely channelled from the central State Planning Commission to the provincial Planning Commission, which is in charge of distributing them to local import/export firms, which in turn have to provide the goods to provincial users. This process normally takes place in March/April every year. Items for which such import quota are allocated are essential goods in short supply on the domestic market, such as fertilizer, edible oil, and indeed, refined sugar. Local sources state that Li Ping became involved in this type of business activity in 1993 by trading allocations of low-priced refined sugar when there was a shortage of sugar in the market leading to high market prices.

Another situation occurs when the state agency in control of the sales of sugar acts as a monopolist. Then we have a case of corruption plus embezzlement of funds. In this case, the state agency would ask for a monopolistic price, and appropriate the whole monopolistic rent. In other words, the bribe taker will not respect the property rights of the national treasury over the revenues generated by the sales of sugar. He will not transfer revenues from the sale of sugar at the state fixed price but instead keep everything himself. Subsequently, both the consumers and the national treasury are hurt. The bribe taker needs to pay attention to two constraints. In order to keep his (local) monopoly he must be able to limit competition from other state agencies (or private firms) offering the same product or a close substitute. As his profit depends on (marginal) costs for the input, that is, white sugar "bought" within the state controlled bureaucracy, he has to make sure to know people willing to sell him the sugar even if they know his business practices. One way to ensure a steady supply of low priced sugar is to agree to share the monopolistic rent with the supplier agency. Another way is to make sure that like-minded people are appointed to those agencies that allocate sugar within the bureaucratic system. The same means need to be employed to keep out competitors. Provincial legislation/regulation offers powerful tools to limit entry to local markets by means of taxation, regulation, or registration. Offers to share the monopolistic rent here, too, is an attractive means to "buy votes," that is support, in the provincial, or county, administration. In the latter case, the regulation can be advertized as a policy to protect local farmers, local (infant) industry, or certain groups such as minorities. As in all cases of protectionism the distributional effects are such that the producers benefit to the detriment of the consumers (plus the national treasury).

In both cases, corruption with or without embezzlement, the ability to appropriate part of the consumer or the monopolistic rent, depends on the ability to coerce others into collaboration or to "buy" their support. The minimum requirement is that the state controlled price agreed upon in the political arena is lower than the market price. Otherwise there would be no rent to appropriate (Cheung, 1996). Coercion turns corruption into a political problem, buying support turns corruption into a problem of a malfunctioning bureaucracy, that is, a principal–agent relation problem in economic parlance. The analysis shows that corruption, in order to survive, needs to expand and include more and more people in positions that are able to limit free trade.

For this reason, in the long run, the social costs of corruption and cronyism need to include the re-allocation of resources to those opportunities that offer high gains. Thus, for example, it can be expected that goods and regulation which private economic agents cannot avoid, that is, low price and income elasticities, will be favored. This might explain better the focus by Cheng/Li on sugar and oil deals, as they are two ingredients in Chinese cooking for which substitutes are hard to find. Other examples are prestigious large-scale infrastructural investment projects to which the national budget has itself committed. The large sunk costs that would have to be accepted if the investment should fail allows participating (construction) firms to heavily overcharge the government as customer. Part of the gain from overcharging can be used for bribing those who decide which company will be involved. At the same time construction firms are also willing to offer bribes for getting contracts, knowing that they can retrieve these costs by later overcharging the government as a customer. Knowing this, one no longer wonders how the six-lane motorway in the province fits into this picture.

Another example, and the one that led to the demise of Cheng Kejie, was Li Ping's involvement in the construction of the Nationalities Palace. This brought her into conflict with the provincial Party School. The Nationalities Palace was one of the government projects for the

50th anniversary of the People's Republic of China in 1999. It was built in the center of Nanning on land that was partially owned by the Party School. Because it was a government project, the Party School could not raise any objections against losing its apartment buildings on the site. However, when it turned out that Li Ping, with the consent of Cheng Kejie, had become involved and had transferred the construction contract from the Nationalities Affairs Commission to her ally Zhou Kun, who in turn included members of Cheng's family in the project, the Party School started to pressure the Central Discipline Inspection Commission in Beijing to get involved in the case. Reportedly, this case was also initially referred back to *Guangxi* and suppressed by Cheng Kejie. The Party School finally approached the Head of the Central Party School and required his personal intervention. As a result, in May 1999, one of the Deputy Secretaries of the Commission was sent to *Guangxi* to personally head the investigation. After the conclusion of her investigations, Cheng Kejie was put under a specific form of house arrest (*lianggui* or *shuanggui*), which restricted his movements and contacts.

The other long-term effect is that private investment will be crowded out by corruption. The difference between control rights over the operational side of a business and the property rights over net return or cash flow are crucial in this case, too (Shleifer and Vishny, 1993). Assume a company where the management has complete rights with respect to production, investment, price, and output. It has to pay taxes on profit, but is free to allocate net returns according to its own policy, for example, using part of its profits for paying dividends, part for re-investment, part for upgrading technology or research, and part for intra-firm consumption. In short, after tax, the company enjoys full property rights over its revenues. These property rights are respected by state agencies at all levels. Even if one state agency, say a city government, were to ask for an additional tax or fee, companies could cope with this as long as the additional fee is low enough to allow the company to stay in business and as long as the fee can be anticipated and remains stable. Corruption again would take the form of a local tax, affecting total production costs which, depending on price and income elasticities, can be transferred to consumers and clients of the company. The negative effect would be shared between consumers and producers, the bribe takers could appropriate part of the producers' rent. Corruption becomes destructive when part of the net profit is confiscated by local authorities asking for part of the cash once they become aware of the profit situation of the company. That can take the form of "voluntary contributions" to the building of local roads or a new football stadium, cash hand outs to state officials, or participation in intra-firm consumption budgets by obtaining invitations to banquets, access to the firm's car park, free airplane tickets, or seeing relatives of officials employed by the firm. Empirical surveys have shown that the more corrupt a country, the lower the level of private investment.

Another form is regulation concerning the use of cash flow. When, for example, state agencies force companies to re-invest in infrastructure, such as housing, or research, the state agency might not directly profit (in monetary terms) from the regulations. Yet, the property rights of the company over net profit are affected nevertheless.

So far, the analysis suggests that with increasing liberalization and deregulation, corruption would disappear. That is, indeed, how many Western economists argue (Stigler, 1988: chaps 6–8). Yet, this kind of an analysis overlooks the interdependency between the economic sector and politics. It is within the political "market" that monopolies are created or broken up. As long as bureaucrats are not controlled by a government – the executive or parliament – or a strong constitution the principal–agent problem will not disappear. The effectiveness of corruption and cronyism under such a condition will then depend on running an effective network of co-ordinated price policy.

Cronyism as a network for discrimination

So far, the analysis offered a static view of corruption and cronyism. In order to understand the dynamics of corruption, the supply side in the market of corruption needs to be analysed further. As was said before, to the extent that a bureaucrat cannot control a monopoly over goods and/or over lucrative positions within the bureaucracy (is not an independent "price setter"), s/he needs to rely on collaborators. Thus, Li Ping entered this business by establishing a network of local officials who had the power over land allocations and building approvals. The core members of this network were arrested at the same time as Cheng Kejie. Their ranks were at the provincial departmental level – corresponding to state-level ministers. As will be seen presently the kind of relationships between collaborators (or competitors) strongly influences the level and content of corruption.

It was argued before that contracts between bribe takers, that is, bureaucrats in control over state provided goods and their customers are not legally binding or otherwise (socially) enforceable. The same is the case when two or more bribe takers on the supply side need to co-ordinate their action. In this case too, all partners in the network of corruption cannot rely on binding contracts. This "institutional weakness" is an inherent feature of corruption and cronyism, which leaves the system of bribes and cronyism a fragile construction. In order to understand this, consider the following cases:

In order to avoid competition, (bribe) price setters must carve out local monopolies whose heads pledge to stay within the territory assigned to them at the beginning. Different cost structures or demand might then lead to different monopolistic prices. There is, therefore, an incentive to shirk the original agreement and move the "business" to the territory that offers the highest rent. As in all cartels, compliance with the original agreement is hard to enforce.

Officials are able to "create" complementary state provided input on whose use the total value of assets depends. One example would be the acquisition of land for the purpose of building a factory. The land remains "useless" if in order to do so permission needs to be "bought" from other state agencies. One state agency might ask for a bribe for the permission to build the factory, another for firm registration, a third for access to water and electric power, each of which knows that without this permission the whole venture might collapse. The chain reaction that can be observed starts when the bribe revenues appropriated by one agency will attract the attention of another branch of the bureaucracy, which will invent another monopoly in the form of licenses and permissions. This chain reaction finds its end only if the total sum of bribes to which the customers are (over-)charged will lead to a drop in total demand. Then, by ignoring cross-elasticity in demand, the result will be that all interdependent bribe takers are worse off. In order to avoid this, a strategy of joint profit maximization is needed. Once more, the problem of co-coordinating the action of different bribe takers shows up as the crucial one, if unilateral increases in bribes are to be avoided. It is worth emphasizing that the final breakthrough for an enquiry against Cheng and Li by the Central Discipline Inspection Commission did not come as the result of State and Party watchdog institutions pursuing their duties, but when economic interests of powerful institutions were negatively affected.

As Institutional Economics has shown, the co-ordination problem knows a monitoring and an enforcement aspect. The fact that corruption and cronyism are illegal makes secrecy an essential pre-condition for their functioning (Posner, 1980: 1–53). One effect is that not only law-enforcing agencies, but also all collaborating members face high costs for detecting a violation of rules. In the first case, the violation of rules refers to the illegality of corruptive practices, in the latter the violation of rules refers to the original agreement between all partners in the network of bribes and cronyism. As such networks cannot rely on the "official" law enforcement agencies, they need to "police" themselves with the effect that the costs for running a system of corruption increase progressively over time and with increasing number of members at the supply side.[3] One way to keep the monitoring costs down is to employ only people on whose trustworthiness one can rely as a "police force." These people might be relatives, members of the same ethnic groups, or those bound together by special pledges of allegiance. The "mafia" still serves as the proto-type of such an organization (Gambetta, 1993). In the case of Cheng, it is known that he used the powers of his office to appoint a network of officials to those positions where their trustworthiness was crucial for his corrupt dealings. It is no wonder that the official report on corruption would later claim that "All major policy decisions, the appointment or dismissal of leading cadres (...) must be fully discussed by the collective, and no individual or small group is allowed to take arbitrary decisions" (FBIS-CHI-2000-0420).

Yet, even if the individual behavior of network members can be effectively monitored at low costs, there is still the enforcement problem. Here again, the Mafia-organizational structure and policy can serve as a model (Posner, 1981, chaps 5 and 8). When no recourse to the law is possible, then three other institutional devices are available: first, revenge with or without violent means that works as a deterrent; second, hierarchy within the network of corruption and cronyism, to the effect that one person controls the network while other members comply to his/her commands; third, an alliance with politicians that allows to prosecute rule-violators with the help of the official law enforcement agencies. Thus, Cheng during his time as provincial governor acted as a "Godfather" for the network of corruption and cronyism. In this case, he did not need to seek an alliance with politicians since he himself held the top political position in the province. Therefore, he could use or threaten to use official law enforcement agencies for controlling the network. In the Cheng/Li case, there were reportedly large numbers of letters of complaints to the Central Discipline Inspection Commission from county level officials concerning the sale of quota. While Cheng was the Governor, these letters were sent back and suppressed at the provincial level, where institutions could not act against the Governor. Other examples of institutional complaints from the provincial level that were not followed through are reports by the Head of the Guangxi Customs Office to his headquarters in Beijing on Li Ping being caught on many occasions taking cash and gold to Hong Kong. In such cases, the Governor's personal secretary had to interfere on her behalf to secure her release and prevent further prosecution.

It is noteworthy, that Cheng became vulnerable only when he left the province in order to become the Vice-chairman of the Standing Committee of the National People's Congress in Beijing, a move for which he had to give up his position as provincial Governor, and subsequently his "godfather" position. Hierarchy as a way to co-ordinate the network failed once he got promotion, as did his ability to buy support for covering up schemes.

Conclusions

An economic analysis shows what the real life case so vividly illustrates: Institutions matter. Regardless of what the motives are, love, greed, passion or caring, corruption and cronyism depend on institutions that create the opportunity. Clearly defined property rights are essential as are state regulated prices and state controlled "monopolies" over licences, permissions, and approvals. Consequently, market liberalization via the introduction of private property rights and free prices plus deregulation would destroy the rents that can be appropriated by corruptive practices. The total profit from corruptive practices would decline, so would the number of people who might find it profitable to embark into such activities.

As the analysis further shows, however, two other institutions need to be taken into account for explaining corruption and cronyism. There is first the bureaucracy, more precisely the principle–agent relation problem that characterizes bureaucratic discretion at all levels of state administration. There is second, the political sector, which can be modelled as the political market where the supply of and demand for regulation, state monopolies, and national price policy is co-ordinated.

Through its dynamics corruption creates a costly economic system. It drives resources to such investment opportunities, and into sectors that promise the highest net gain from corruptive practices, instead of directing the resources to their "best use" as allocative efficiency would expect. Second, networks for corruption are costly co-ordination devices. In order to protect the networks' rent-seeking powers, more and more people need to be taken in, which in turn leads to actively searching for more and different opportunities. Moreover, the co-ordination of activities of individual network members also asks for an institutional solution. As Cheng was to learn, the moment he lost his position as provincial

Governor of *Guanxi*, he became vulnerable. He, but not all of his former cronies, came under investigation and was prosecuted.

The ultimate loss might be seen in the fact that Li Ping could have contributed to the development of China's emerging private sector in terms of cleverness and innovativeness. She undoubtedly had entrepreneurial talent, and demonstrated this over ten–fifteen years as she superbly and systematically exploited the institutional weaknesses of China's economic and political system.

Notes

1 The following is based on the conceptual frame as developed first by Demsetz, 1967; Fama and Jensen, 1983; and the contributions in: Furubotn and Pejovich, 1974.
2 The seminal papers are Arrow, 1985; Niskanen, 1974; Pratt and Zeckhauser, 1984.
3 It is worth mentioning that this mechanism can help to explain why economies relying on cronyism and/or nepotism, such as Indonesia or the Philippines can survive for some time, but at one point implode. The "implosion occurs when the costs for maintaining the corruption system exceeds the gains in the official sector." For other cases see Sanchez and Waters, 1974.

References

Arrow, K. J. (1985) "The economics of agency," in J. W. Pratt and R. J. Zeckhauser (eds), *Principals and Agents: The Structure of Business*, Boston, MA: Harvard Business School Press, 37–54.

Becker, G. S. (1971) *The Theory of Discrimination*, 2nd Pd., Chicago: University of Chicago Press.

Becker, G. S. (1982) *Der ökonomische Ansatz zur Erklärung menschlichen Verhaltens*. Tübingen: Siebeck/Mohr.

Boycko, M., Shleifer, A. and Vishny, R. (1995) *Privatizing Russia*, Cambridge, MA: MIT Press.

Cassel, D. (1986) Funktionen der Schattenwirtschaft, im Koordinations – mechanismus von Markt – und Planwirtschaften. *ORDO* 37: 73–104.

Cheung, S. N. S. (1996) A simplistic general equilibrium theory of corruption. *Contemporary Economic Policy* 14(3).

China aktuell (2000) Kampagne zur Korruptionsbekaempfung in *Guangxi*: harte Massnahmen gegen Cheng Kejie und andere hochrangige Partei- und Regierungsmitglieder. April: 367–8.

Demsetz, H. (1967) Toward a theory of property rights. *American Economic Review* 57: 347–58.

Eisenstadt, S. N. and Lemarchand, R. (eds) (1981) *Political Clientelism, Patronage and Development*, Beverley Hills/London: Sage.

Fama, E. and Jensen, M. C. (1983) Separation of ownership and control. *Journal of Law and Economics* 26: 301–25.

Fan, S. and Grossman, H. I. (2001) *Zhongguo jingji tizhi gaige zhong de jili yu fubai (incentives and corruption in the reform of China's economic system)*, in Hu Angang (ed.). *Zhongguo: Tiaozhan fubai (China: Fighting against Corruption)*. Hangzhou, Zhejiang Remnin Chubanshe: 149–63.

FBIS-CHI-2000-0420. RMRB commentator slams Party Corruption. *Beijing Xinhua Domestic Service*, 20/04/2000.

Furubotn, E. G. and Pejovich, S. (eds) (1974) *The Economics of Property Rights*, Cambridge, MA: Ballinger.

Gambetta, D. (1993) *The Sicilian Mafia: The Business of Protection*, Cambridge, MA: Harvard University Press.

Haslinger, F. (1986) Reciprocity, loyalty, and the growth of the underground economy. *European Journal of Political Economy* **1**(3): 309–23.

Hendrischke, H. (1997) "*Guangxi*: towards Southwest China and Southeast Asia," in D. S. G. Goodman (ed.), *China's provinces in reform – Class, community and political culture*, London and New York: Routledge, 21–47.

Hendrischke, H. (2000) Smuggling and bordertrade on the South China Coast. *China Perspectives*. November–December: 22–35.

Hendrischke, H. (2001) *Corruption, networks and property rights; the demise of a local leader through love and greed*. Bochum, Festschrift Helmut Martin (forthcoming).

Holmes, L. (1993) *The End of Communist Power – Anti-Corruption Campaigns and Legitimation Crisis*, Carlton: Melbourne University Press.

Krug, B. (1988) "The Economics of Nepotism," in K. Alewell and A. Bohnet (eds), *Leistungswille und Leistungsanreize im Systemvergleich*. Giessen: Justus Liebig University.

Manion, M. (1997) Corruption and Corruption Control: More of the Same in 1996. *China Review* 33–56.

Ming Pao, Hong Kong, 1/6/2000. "*Ren cheng Guangxi Jiangqing*," *qingfu gangdao yong haozhai* (the mistress, who people call the *Jiang Qing* of *Guangxi*, owns a luxury apartment on Hong Kong Island).

Neilson, W. S. (1999) The economics of favours. *Journal of Economic Behaviour & Organization* **39**: 387–97.

Niskanen, W. A. (1974) "The peculiar economics of bureaucracy," in E. G. Furubotn and S. Pejovich (eds), *The Economics of Property Rights*, Cambridge, MA: Ballinger, 187–99.

North, D. (1981) *Structure and Change In Economic History*, London/New York: Norton.

Olson, M. (1965) *The Logic of Collective Action*, Cambridge, MA: Harvard University Press.

Posner, R. A. (1980) A theory of primitive society, with special reference to law. *Journal of Law and Economics* **1**: 1–53.

Posner, R. A. (1981) *The Economics of Justice*, Cambridge, MA: Harvard University Press.

Pratt, J. W. and Zeckhauser, R. J. (1984) "Principals and agents: An overview," in W. Pratt and R. J. Zeckhauser (eds), *Principals and Agents: The Structure of Business*, Boston, MA: Harvard Business School, 1–36.

Rocca, J.-L. (1992) Corruption and its shadow: An anthropological view of corruption in China. *The China Quarterly* **130**(2): 402–16.

Rose-Ackerman, S. (1978) *Corruption: A Study In Political Economy*, New York: Academic Press.

Rose-Ackerman, S. (1999) *Corruption and Government – Causes, Consequences, and Reform*, Cambridge: Cambridge University Press.

Sanchez, N. and Waters, A. R. (1974) "Controlling Corruption in Africa and Latin America," in E. G. Furubotn and S. Pejovich (eds), *The Economics of Property Rights*, Cambridge, MA: Ballinger, 279–95.

Shleifer, A. and Vishny R. W. (1993) Corruption. *NBER Working Paper 4372*, Cambridge, MA: National Bureau of Economic Research.

Smart, A. (1998) Gifts, bribes, and *guanxi*: A reconsideration of Bourdieau's social capital. *Cultural Anthropology* **8**: 388–408.

Stigler, G. J. (1988) *Chicago Studies in Political Economy*, Chicago/London: University of Chicago Press, chapters: 6–8.

Weck, H., Pommerehne, W. W. and Frey, B. S. (1984) *Schattenwirtschaft*. München, WISO-Studien.

Wedeman, A. (1996) Corruption and politics, *China Review* 61–94.

Yang, M. (1994) *Gifts, Favors, and Banquets: The Art of Social Relationships in China*, Ithaca, NY: Cornell University Press.

Yang, X. (1997) *Fubai lun* (a theory of corruption), Beijing: Zhongguo shehui kexue chubanshe.

8
Taming the *Sokaiya*: Can Economic and Corporate Reform Eliminate Extortion in Japan?

Teri Jane Ursacki

Introduction

Sokaiya literally means "general meeting handlers." More specifically, they are corporate extortionists with (typically small) holdings of shares in targeted companies who extract payments from them in exchange for ensuring their annual shareholders' meetings proceed quickly and smoothly. If not paid off, they may harass company executives at the meeting for hours with embarrassing questions about real or imagined corporate or personal shortcomings or wrongdoings. If paid off, they will not only refrain from causing trouble at the meeting themselves, but may also use verbal or physical intimidation to ensure no one else, including ordinary shareholders with grievances, is able to raise a question. It is illegal for the *sokaiya* to request such payments and for companies to provide them, yet many companies have been caught doing so in recent years, and some *sokaiya* groups still operate quite openly.

Sokaiya activity has been a well-known part of the seamier side of the Japanese business world for decades, but attempts to control them have been sporadic, with relatively few arrests and seemingly rather lenient punishments both for corporate executives and the *sokaiya* themselves. In 1997–98 there was a major crackdown that revealed a large number of scandals involving many of Japan's top companies. Over 100 executives and many *sokaiya* were arrested, and most have subsequently been convicted. The companies involved included the Dai-Ichi Kangyo Bank, one of the nation's largest, all four (now three) big securities companies, and a wide cross-section of other firms from retailer Matsuzakaya and food processor Ajinomoto to electronics giants Toshiba and Hitachi, and automaker Mitsubishi Motors.

There was a high profile for this crackdown, which was front-page news for months, and there were widely publicized campaigns by the National Police Agency and business organizations such as Keidanren. Despite this, and despite a stiffening of the penalties for *sokaiya*-related infractions, surveys continue to show that a large (though declining) number of firms employ the services of the *sokaiya*. Moreover, several more firms have since been embroiled in *sokaiya* scandals, including Japan Airlines, Kobe Steel and heavy equipment manufacturer Kubota. Known *sokaiya* continue to show up at many shareholders' meetings; and there is at least one major *sokaiya* group that maintains a clearly marked headquarters and a web site.

This study considers the persistence of the *sokaiya* phenomenon and the nature of the changes that would be necessary to eradicate it. In particular, it focuses on the impact of economic reform, and suggests that the nature of the reforms required to stamp out *sokaiya* activity would go well beyond tinkering with regulations concerning corporate governance. Employing *sokaiya* is part of a wider strategy employed by poorly performing executives to keep themselves in their jobs and their companies afloat. Economic reform must proceed far enough so that uncompetitive companies have no alternative but to fall by the wayside if such dark-side strategies, of which the use of *sokaiya* are only a part, are to be made obsolete.

We begin by clarifying the origins and nature of *sokaiya* operations. A brief history of attempts to control this form of criminality and an overview follows a variety of alternative explanations for the existence of the *sokaiya* in Japan. A detailed case study of Mitsubishi Motors provides a concrete illustration of how the *sokaiya* were used as part of a broader strategy to cover up under performance. We conclude with the prognosis for current efforts to eliminate corporate extortion in Japan.

Origins

Szymkowiak (1994) traces the origins of *sokaiya* activity to the Meiji era and the pre-modern take-off of Japanese industrialization in the late nineteenth century. The notion that in the new, joint-stock companies shareholders were anything more than passive sources of funds were slow to take root. Companies were quick to turn to those with connections who could prevent "interference" with managerial prerogatives.

Although *sokaiya* influence was deeply ingrained even before World War II, it was only in the 1960s and 1970s that their numbers took off with the influx of large numbers of thugs who had learned an important lesson from social activists. Protestors at that time were opposed to the pollution emitted by companies such as Chisso Corp. (the source of mercury-induced Minamata disease). Others were against the involvement of major Japanese corporations, such as the Mitsubishi Heavy Industries in supplying the US military in Vietnam. These protestors had successfully used the strategy of buying one share each in order to be able to attend the companies' meetings. They then turned these meetings into a forum for the airing of their grievances. Targeted companies turned to established *sokaiya* for protection from these "invasions" and low-class thugs quickly realized that threatening to disrupt the shareholders' meeting was an easy way to extort cash payments from major companies with little risk. As a result, the number of active *sokaiya* swelled from a few hundred to 6783 by 1982 (*Sokaiya no Shinso*, 1997). Subsequent countermeasures have returned the number of active *sokaiya* to a few hundred. But those holding out have deep roots in the businesses – they are not the mere "hangers-on" who crowded in during the brief heydays when the *sokaiya* could be seen in major business districts lining up around the block to receive their annual envelopes of cash. Thus, the decline in reported numbers considerably overestimates the actual impact countermeasures have had to date.

Modus operandi

By definition, a *sokaiya* must own, or have the wherewithal to credibly threaten to buy, at least enough shares in a company to gain access to the company's shareholders' meeting. At one time, this might have been as little as one share, but today this generally means 1000 shares, the minimum specified by the Commercial Code of Japan. In some cases, the *sokaiya* have purchased large shareholdings in targeted companies in order to obtain access to privileges such as speaking rights and insider information. Firms sometimes use the euphemism *"tokushu kabunushi"* (special shareholders) to refer to the *sokaiya*.

Typical *sokaiya* operations would include some combination of the following functions:

(a) gathering information about poor corporate performance;
(b) gathering information about misconduct by firm managers such as embezzlement;

(c) gathering information about the private actions of managers or their families (a manager's extra-marital affair, a son's drug addiction, a daughter's unplanned pregnancy, etc.);
(d) suppressing the results of their own research into corporate or personal wrongdoing;
(e) preventing the release of any of these kinds of information by other *sokaiya* by buying them off or intimidating them;
(f) preventing ordinary shareholders from asking awkward questions through verbal or physical intimidation, or simply by filibustering; and
(g) providing support to cooperative managers in internal power struggles.

At least some of these functions may at times have the potential to be of positive value to society. For example, as West (1999) points out, Japanese financial statements are typically very opaque and provide much less disclosure than those of comparable US companies. The upper echelons of *sokaiya* use their skills in financial analysis to distill information about the true performance of the company, including where investments may be under performing or be complete failures. In principle, the revelation of such information could be a useful public service as the resulting changes in stock prices and corporate management could result in a superior allocation of capital. However, since the *sokaiya* only generate such information in order to extract a payment for not revealing it, this potential benefit remains largely unrealized. In other cases, the information is obtained by more surreptitious means, such as by eavesdropping on inebriated or disgruntled company employees in bars, or by the use of private detectives. And of course, where the information concerns private personal matters that are not criminal, but merely embarrassing, the public interest is in no way served.

The *sokaiya* who threaten disruption themselves are referred to as "*yato sokaiya*" ("opposition party *sokaiya*"), while those who offer to ensure the silence of other *sokaiya* and/or legitimate shareholders through payoffs or verbal or physical intimidation are referred to as "*yoto sokaiya*" ("incumbent party *sokaiya*"). Many firms have long histories of using *yoto sokaiya*, and in some cases a firm has been "passed down" from a *sokaiya* nearing death to one of his proteges.

The use of *sokaiya* is one of several tactics that ensure most shareholders' meetings in Japan are of extremely short duration – by North American standards. Other methods include the use of phalanxes of uniformed security officers and company personnel with security armbands to dissuade potential disrupters from entering, and packing meetings with "reliable" company employee shareholders who swiftly, positively and loudly respond to any suggestions by the management. Most companies also hold their meetings on the same day in late June to ensure *sokaiya* and other potentially troublesome shareholders are unable to attend more than one meeting even if they own shares in several companies (this phenomenon will be discussed in greater detail later). A total duration of 30 minutes for the annual general meeting of a major corporation is typical, and meetings of 15 minutes or less are quite common. The main exceptions are a few companies such as electric utilities that are continually harangued by environmentalists, and some that have adopted Western-style, free-wheeling meetings as part of a more investor-friendly style. Apart from these rarities, companies with meetings of over an hour in duration are usually reported prominently on the front pages of Japanese daily newspapers. West (1999) used an event-study methodology to find that firms that typically have short meetings, but suddenly have long ones, suffered small but significant drops in their stock prices. Thus, there may be reasons beyond avoiding embarrassment for Japanese executives to want short meetings.

Although easily confused with *yakuza* (Japanese "mafia," i.e. organized crime groups) in the popular mind, in fact NPA (National Police Agency) documents suggest only about 10 percent of *sokaiya* are actually members of *yakuza* groups (more officially known as *boryokudan*, or "violent groups"). Many do, however, maintain links with figures from the underworld. Such connections can give added poignancy to *sokaiya* threats, as numerous cases of violence directed at executives, including shots fired at homes, fire-bombings, slashing of family members and occasionally murders, have been linked to firms' attempts to cut *sokaiya* ties. *Yakuza*-affiliated entertainment establishments may also be good listening posts for the latest rumors on the less savory aspects of corporate activities.

The part of the company that is generally used to deal with *sokaiya* is the "general affairs" department. As mentioned earlier, at one time it was common to see the *sokaiya* lined up at companies' headquarters to receive their annual "retainers" in cash. These sums varied from a few hundred to many thousands of dollars, depending on the individual's reputation and history with the firm. However, since it was formally made illegal to pay off the *sokaiya* in 1982, more cunning ways have been devised to reward them. Payments are often disguised as inflated payments for goods or services, for instance, the rental of potted plants, advertising in *sokaiya*-controlled publications or billboards, the use of a beach house or a training center for company employees or, most commonly, subscriptions to newsletters and magazines. During the 1997–98 series of scandals, it was revealed that some firms were paying for subscriptions to hundreds of *sokaiya*-run "newsletters," many of which existed for no reason other than to serve as a cover for illicit payments. Retailers have often given gift certificates, while in the case of financial firms rewards have included preferential access to "loans," which were never repaid, or compensation for losses on stock portfolios. The latter, which is illegal in Japan, is an example of the peripheral crimes which managers are often drawn into when they try to hide payments to the *sokaiya*. Other common examples of such crimes are falsification of accounting records and tax evasion by misreporting payoffs as legitimate expenses.

The *sokaiya* often attempt to paint themselves as shareholder activists. One major organization which has had associates linked to numerous scandals is Rondan Doyukai. In 1999, their headquarters indicated that they were the headquarters of a "shareholder rights" group, and their web page included links to legitimate shareholder rights groups around the world (photo and web page printout are on file with author).

Why do the *Sokaiya* exist in Japan?

Explanations for why the *sokaiya* exist in Japan can be categorized as cultural, economic or universalist.

Cultural factors

A cultural explanation points to traditions and customs in Japan with deep historical roots. It does not suggest that the traits of a given culture result in more or less crime than any other, but rather that these traits may shape the nature of the crimes committed. Ursacki (2000) has summarized several aspects of the cultural explanation for the *sokaiya* phenomenon as follows:

- The importance of saving face and preserving harmony in Japanese culture makes individuals there vulnerable to blackmail.
- *Sempai–kohai* (senior–junior) relationships make it difficult to resist organizational pressures for conformity to norms of illicit behavior (Chikudate, 2000).
- Customs such as gift-giving and extravagant entertaining provide a convenient cover for illicit payments.
- Relativistic ethical reasoning allows managers to justify to themselves the breaking of rules and laws if there is a higher good at stake. Thus,

steeped as they are in a group-oriented culture, the perceived need to protect the group (their company) where they have spent all of their working lives is held to be such a higher good.

Economic factors

West (1999: 781–96) provides a detailed exposition of the reasons for the existence of the *sokaiya* based on the economics of information as commonly used in the economic and financial literature on corporate governance. West argues that institutions in Japan such as extensive cross-shareholding between group firms (in the *keiretsu*) and the main bank system mean that important stakeholders can be informed of important developments without the necessity for market-wide release of the news. Because such "stable" shareholders hold around 70 percent of the shares in many companies, the float of shares that actually trade is small, and stock prices can be highly volatile in the face of unexpected news. The fact that most Japanese boards of directors are comprised exclusively of insiders (company executives) also ensures companies are better able to prevent leaks of negative information than their Western counterparts. Japanese disclosure law is not only weak, but also little enforced, so managers have little to fear when they keep secrets. Indeed, West argues that the regulatory bureaucracy is often so concerned with industry stability that it facilitates an implicit agreement among firms not to disclose certain negative information.

Through ties to the *yakuza*, the *sokaiya* are able to obtain such negative information. Due to legal and institutional barriers they are largely unable to profit from it by the means typically used in other countries, such as lawsuits, greenmail, or short-selling. This combination of structural conditions in Japan leads them to engage in extortion.

Universalist argument

A third explanation emphasizes that *sokaiya* payoffs are simply a uniquely Japanese manifestation of the worldwide phenomenon of poor managers misusing company resources to try to keep their jobs. In South Korea and Italy, there are somewhat similar actors known as *chongheoggun* and *disturbatori*, due to similarities in their national institutions. In other countries a variety of actors try to derive profits from information they have in ways that reflect the specific circumstances of their operating environments. More familiar mechanisms to North American observers would be greenmail, options trading and lawsuits. In some cases (e.g. options trading, short-selling), the individual with the negative information does not have to deal with the target firm's managers directly, while in other cases (greenmail, lawsuits), there may be direct contact which makes the parallel to the *sokaiya* phenomenon more striking. However, in each case, the essence of the situation is the same: the firm's managers have negative information about the firm that they do not want to reveal while someone outside the firm finds out about it, and tries to profit from it; thus shareholder wealth is transferred to the discoverer.

Attempts to control *Sokaiya* activities

Under 1982 revisions to the Commercial Code of Japan, it became illegal for companies to convey benefits to shareholders in connection with the exercise of their rights as shareholders. *Rieki kyoyo*, the legal name for this practice, was forbidden under Article 294-2. Directors could be sued for the amount of such illegally conveyed benefits under Article 266-2. Conviction for violations carried a maximum sentence of six months imprisonment or a fine of up to 300 000 yen. In a series of *sokaiya* scandals in 1997–98, over a hundred executives from the nation's largest companies in the banking, securities, retailing, automobile, electronics and food processing sectors were arrested. Almost all were subsequently convicted, however, the executives concerned invariably had their sentences suspended, as did the vast majority of convicted *sokaiya*. While this may appear lenient, as Haley (1991) has noted, Japan sends very few of its convicts to prison, and few of those that do go spend much time there. The arrests were followed by a major campaign to shame companies into publicly committing to abandoning ties with the *sokaiya*. Major business organizations encouraged members to make such declarations and prominent signs on entrance doors announcing that the *sokaiya* were not welcome rapidly appeared throughout Kabuto-cho, home to the Tokyo Stock Exchange and to most of Japan's leading securities companies. The penalties for requesting or making *sokaiya* payments were also stiffened, becoming effective by 23 December 1997. Demanding or making such payments now carries a maximum penalty of three years or a fine of three million yen.

A uniquely Japanese response has been a tendency for companies to hold their shareholders' meetings on the same day so that *sokaiya* resources are spread too thin to affect many companies. With encouragement from the authorities, the number of companies holding their meetings on the same day in late June rose sharply starting in the 1980s. By 1998, over 2000 listed companies met at 10 AM on the same day, including 95 percent of those listed on the First Section of the Tokyo

Stock Exchange: this is an elite group which includes almost all the nation's leading corporations. The meetings proceeded under the protection of more than 10 000 police officers as well as countless private security personnel and corporate "volunteers."

The scandals of 1997-98 led many major corporations to adopt policies intended to increase the transparency of their shareholders' meetings. Some were even broadcast on the Internet. Criticism of the "meeting day" phenomenon also led to a decline in the number of simultaneous meetings: by June 2001 the number had declined for four consecutive years, with a drop of 56 in 2001 over 2000. Even so, there were still over 2000 companies holding their meetings in this "traditional" way – including 1345 First Section TSE firms.

The impact of these countermeasures is difficult to assess. The number of *sokaiya* officially recorded in NPA statistics dropped from 6783 in 1982 to 1682 in 1983 following the introduction of the Commercial Code reforms. This appears to have reflected primarily a re-classification of extortionists from the *sokaiya* to other categories as some failed to meet the new, higher minimum number of shares required to attend meetings (Szymkowiak, 1994). Moreover, in most cases, securities firms had begun restricting odd-lot sales and selling only in units of 1000 shares even before the reforms. Thus, what may have led many peripheral *sokaiya* to withdraw was the signal that greater attention to *sokaiya* activities on the part of authorities had increased the likelihood of arrest. A similar drop from around 1100 or 1200 down to 600 was noted following the 1997-98 crackdown, which signaled that the authorities were once again focusing on this issue after many years of neglect.

It is difficult to ignore the fact that for many years the *sokaiya* had operated with relative impunity as the authorities turned a blind eye to their activities. When major companies were able to go for years at a stretch without a single shareholder question, when many were able to wrap up their annual meetings in 15 minutes or less, when companies were attacked for hours at one year's meeting only to have the next meeting last less than 30 minutes, and when surveys published in major newspapers reported large percentages of public companies admitting to dealing with the *sokaiya*, it is simply not credible to believe that the authorities were unaware of the scale of the problem, or that the roughly two dozen cases prosecuted between 1982 and 1997 were anything but the tip of the iceberg.

Indeed, with the heat of the 1997-98 scandals dying down and a spate of recent corporate scandals providing ample fodder for criticism, *sokaiya* activities appeared to rebound. NPA statistics showed that the number of *sokaiya* attending meetings dropped from 202 individuals at 139 meetings in 1999 to 113 persons at 58 meetings in 2000. However, early figures for 2001 show a reversal of this trend. After declining from 86 *sokaiya* at 46 companies on the "meeting day" in June 1999 to a low of 43 at 31 companies in 2000, the number rose to 64 individuals at 44 companies on the "meeting day" in June 2001. At 13 of these 44 meetings, a total of 20 *sokaiya* spoke, double the number in 2000. This confirmed a trend noted earlier in the year when 46 *sokaiya* attended 30 meetings between January and April 2001, up from 11 meetings attended the previous year.

The persistence of the *sokaiya* in the face of efforts to control them is also evidenced by the results of polls conducted by the National Center for the Elimination of *Boryokudan* (violent groups), an affiliate of the NPA. In the 2001 survey of listed firms 1977 (about two-thirds) responded, and 513 (26.9 percent) of those were the recipients of demands by *sokaiya*. Almost half of the demands were for less than 100 000 yen, but 28 were for over 10 million yen, including eight that exceeded 100 million yen. These figures showed little change over surveys conducted by the same organization in 1995 and 1999 (*The Japan Times Online*, 16 March 2001).

A closer look: Mitsubishi Motors Corporation and the *sokaiya*

Understanding the operations of the *sokaiya* may be facilitated by a detailed look at one specific case. A string of incidents involving Mitsubishi Motors Corporation between 1997 and 2001 were chosen for this purpose. This selection is not intended to imply that this particular case was any more egregious than others that came to light around the same time. Rather, the case has enough richness to illustrate some basic aspects of *sokaiya* operations while still being simple enough to summarize in a case study of reasonable length. (Unless otherwise indicated, the facts of these incidents have been summarized from press reports in English and Japanese from the newspapers listed in the references. All Japanese personal names are reported in Western style, i.e. with the family name last.)

By late 1997, the Japanese media were full of reports of several major *sokaiya* scandals. A well-known *yoto sokaiya* named Ryuichi Koike had borrowed a massive sum from the Dai-Ichi Kangyo Bank and had used the money to buy 300 000 shares in each of Japan's top four securities companies, Nomura, Nikko, Daiwa and Yamaichi: he then used these shareholdings to extort a variety of benefits from these companies. After all five companies had been raided by the police, numerous executives were arrested for paying off Koike. Yamaichi would later fail as it was revealed that it had hidden over US$2 billion in losses through a practice known as *tobashi* (shifting worthless assets from one affiliate to another so no one ever held them at year end and hence no one was required to declare the losses). Earlier in the year, top food processor Ajinomoto had been caught making payoffs, and the courts were still dealing with the fate of those arrested in a 1996 incident involving Takashimaya, a leading department store.

Against this background of an apparent crackdown, on 22 October 1997 the police raided Mitsubishi Motors Corporation's (MMC) headquarters and ten private residences in a search for evidence of *sokaiya* payoffs. Yuichi Ueki, 43, the head of the general affairs department, Atsushi Ueba, 56, his predecessor, and Yoichi Shima, 38, a senior member of the general affairs department, were all arrested under suspicion of violation of the Commercial Code. They were followed the next day by Yasuo Shimizu, 59, a managing director of the firm and president of the Urawa Red Devils, a J-League professional soccer team owned by MMC. Also arrested were Terubo Tei (a.k.a. Teiji Nakamoto or Jo Mo Chung), 53, and his assistant Kaoru Hamada, 40. Tei was the head of Nakamoto Sogo Kikaku ("Nakamoto General Planning"), a long-established *sokaiya* group. The timing of the news was particularly unfortunate for MMC, as its President was forced to hold two news conferences on 22 October to deal with the two waves of arrests – this on the very day that the Tokyo Auto Show was to open. News of the arrests forced the company to scale back its presentation at the show, and cancel most of the advertising for a month at this key point in the sales season.

These arrests soon led to others, once it became known that around thirty companies had been paying off Tei, including Mitsubishi Electric, Mitsubishi Estate and several other members of the Mitsubishi *keiretsu* (industrial group), as well as electronics manufacturers Hitachi and Toshiba. Tei's wife owned Honma International, an auto repair and sales company that ran a beach house (*umi-no-ie*) in Fujisawa, a resort town southwest of Tokyo. The companies involved had been paying substantial sums to Honma for the use of this beach house, though in most cases few if any employees used the facilities. Tei had reportedly received between 200 and 300 million yen from these companies in the years after the beach house was opened in July 1986. Hitachi and Toshiba had been paying Tei since before the beach house was opened, and it (the beach house) simply became the vehicle through which their payments were channeled.

MMC had been spun off from its parent, Mitsubishi Heavy Industries, in December 1988, at which time Tei purchased 3000 shares. Although he never attended the company's annual meetings, he began to receive payoffs from the company in 1989 after submitting a list of questions to the management and requesting three million yen. Shimizu, the then head of general affairs, began by paying him two million yen in 1989. This was subsequently raised to 2.5 million yen in 1991 and three million yen in 1994. His successors in the "general affairs" office – Ueba and Ueki – continued the payments and reported them to Shimizu, by then their superior. The payments were reported as "special entertainment expenses" to the tax authorities, as this category requires no receipts. Tei appears to have delivered the peaceful meetings that the management was seeking. From the initial shareholders' meeting in 1989 to the breaking of the scandal in 1997, not one meeting lasted over 30 minutes, and after 1994 not a single question was asked from the floor.

The *Umi-no-Ie* case, as it came to be known, came to light as a result of a 1993 *sokaiya* incident involving Kirin Beer, then Japan's largest brewer and a fellow member of the Mitsubishi *keiretsu*. In the process of investigating the various *sokaiya* Kirin had been paying off, police found that the company had been delivering beer to the beach house owned by Honma International, which was known to be owned by the wife of a *sokaiya*. Further research showed that many other companies had been making payments to Honma International, supposedly for the use of the beach house. These payments were suspicious because it became apparent that most of the companies were not using the facilities, and the payments were concentrated around the date in June when most listed companies hold their annual shareholders' meetings. Most such beach houses receive their corporate payments in September, when figures on actual usage by the firms' employees have been established. Moreover, unlike most others in the area the beach house in question did not put up a list of companies with whom it had contracts for the benefit of visiting employees. Finally, Tei was found to own shares in a dozen Mitsubishi group companies, most of whom were transferring funds to the beach house.

In 1996, the Metropolitan Police Agency advised companies that had been paying off *sokaiya* that they would not be prosecuted if they immediately stopped payments, and in 1997 about half those that had been paying off Tei ceased their support. However, MMC among others, continued to pay Tei into 1997. On 28 October 1997 Shimizu admitted initiating payments to Tei. Two days later, MMC President Takemune Kimura and Chairman Hirokazu Nakamura, who had been president from 1989 to 1995, announced that they would resign from their positions to take responsibility for the scandals as soon as successors could be named. They also announced the establishment of an internal inquiry, as well as a department to ensure all *sokaiya* contacts were permanently ended. In fact, however, while Nakamura was replaced as president in November 1997, Kimura was "promoted" to chairman and held the position, which in Japan is largely ceremonial though still highly prestigious, until 1999.

The investigation of the *Umi-no-Ie* affair quickly led to further revelations. On 18 November Noriyoshi Sakamoto, the head of Sakamoto Kigyo Chosakai ("Sakamoto Enterprise Research"), was arrested for allegedly receiving payments of some 1.3 million yen from MMC. On 24 November *sokaiya* Sunao Kakihara, 44, was arrested for allegedly receiving 1.9 million yen in car loan payments between 1995 and 1997 in exchange for staying away from the company's meetings. On 4 February 1998, *sokaiya* Taichiro Otake and his wife were arrested for receiving payoffs from a number of companies, including MMC, under the guise of payment for advertising in a newsletter for would-be stewardesses published by his wife. Half the cost went to Otake himself directly as an "introduction fee."

MMC's June 1998 annual meeting took place under tight security. A police van was parked just around the corner, and numerous security officers and employee "volunteers" were positioned outside to deal with any unwelcome visitors (by first-hand observation of the author).

The trials of those arrested took place during 1998. Due to the statute of limitations, only offences during the last three years could be considered. On 13 February MMC executives Ueba, Ueki and Shimizu pleaded guilty. They were sentenced on 16 April to four months each, suspended for two years in the case of Ueba and Ueki, and three years in the case of Shimizu. Judge Hisaharu Yasui sentenced *sokaiya* Otake to eight months in prison on 15 September and exactly three months later *sokaiya* Tei received eight months (prosecutors had asked for nine months in both cases). Hamada, Tei's accomplice, got four months of prison time.

Press reports seldom mention the exact nature of the information that *sokaiya* were paid not to publicize. In some cases, this information is public knowledge which management would prefer to see forgotten, and in other cases it is insider information, which it hopes will not become public. MMC had an abundance of information of both types.

As a fourth or fifth-ranked firm behind Toyota, Nissan, Honda and (usually) Mazda, MMC had to struggle to stay alive. Its overall domestic market share hovered in the 4–6 percent range, with a strong position only in minicars (vehicles of less than 660 c.c.), which also were sliding in popularity after some of their regulatory advantages had been withdrawn. The company had been listed when it was spun off from its parent, Mitsubishi Heavy Industries, in 1988, just before the Japanese stock market bubble reached its peak and crashed. It was an opportune time to sell shares, but investors who bought them suffered badly: from a peak of 1440 yen in December 1988, shortly after listing, the shares declined to 549 yen in August 1992. They recovered partially, but then plunged again, hitting 208 yen in October 1998, a decline of over 85 percent from the 1988 peak. The firm's interest-bearing debt load, at 36 percent of total assets, was more than seven times industry leader Toyota's ratio (of less than 5 percent). Profitability also languished, with return on sales never exceeding half that of Toyota. Return on sales had sunk to just over one-sixth that of Toyota in the fiscal year ended 31 March 1997, and substantial losses were due to be reported in March 1998. These problems resulted in Moody's downgrading the firm's long-term debt to Baa3 in August 1998, a rating just one notch above junk bond status. By April 2001 the firm's losses would result in Daimler-Chrysler taking a 34 percent stake in the firm, in effect, taking it over.

In addition to these financial indicators, the firm was dogged by reports of corporate misbehavior, including a sexual harassment suit at its US subsidiary in 1996, and revelations in 2001 that since the firm's inception it had hidden more than sixty thousand customer complaints from the Japanese Ministry of Transport in order to avoid costly and embarrassing vehicle recalls.

Clearly, this was a firm that had a lot of things it would rather have not seen brought to the public's attention, and in general it is not clear exactly which problems were related to which *sokaiya* incidents. However, MMC's problems with concealing customer complaints about defective vehicles played a very clear role in an incident which came to light on 18 June 2001 with the re-arrest of *sokaiya* Sunao Kakihara, who had been a minor player in the 1997 series of scandals. Police alleged that he phoned MMC on 14 December 2000 to say that he was going to complain about the firm's defective cars at the 26 June 2001 annual meeting, and that the next day he called the head of general affairs to say that he was going to post material about defective cars on a website. Company officials did not cooperate, but rather brought in the police to deal with the alleged threat.

Conclusions and prognosis

The MMC case suggests several tentative conclusions with respect to why the *sokaiya* exist and how their activities might be eliminated, or at least minimized.

Paying off a *sokaiya* can be regarded as part of an "image management" program. In the case of a very strong firm, such image management may simply spare management some embarrassing moments. Cultural propensity to avoid loss of face and so on may be the dominant factor influencing managerial behavior. In this case stricter enforcement of existing laws and/or improvements in corporate governance through measures such as better financial disclosure and more outside directors may be somewhat effective in reducing illegal behavior. However, in the case of a weaker player such as MMC, such payments could reasonably be argued to be a part of a rational, overall strategy to stay alive in an intensely competitive market. Clearly, even direct police warnings of a crackdown had proven inadequate to persuade management to cut its *sokaiya* ties. The pattern of deception ran deep and was not limited to the use of the *sokaiya*: for decades the firm had been hiding customer complaints and making false reports to the tax and transportation authorities. This pattern of behavior is not uniquely Japanese. Weak and failing firms the world over have tried to stave off the inevitable by keeping the truth of their situations from becoming known. This assessment suggests that the economic and "universalist" explanations of *sokaiya* activity outlined above may be more applicable in the case of weak firms.

If *sokaiya* influence is to be rooted out of the weaker companies as well as from the strong, the economic environment must make it more difficult for firms to maintain the façade that they are doing an acceptable, even if not excellent job. In the past, the whole drift of Japanese economic policy has been to support the weaker players to avoid the disruption of bankruptcies, job losses, and so on. This facilitated the cover-up strategies of weak firms in many ways. For example, near-zero interest rates meant that the burden of unproductive assets was much lighter and hence firms that had incurred heavy losses could limp along for years, or even decades. However, after many years of stalling and avoiding glaring problems, the pace of change in Japan seems to have picked up. The new millennium has seen an increase in reports of rapid unwinding of cross-shareholdings, increased involvement of foreign investors in Japanese companies, new accounting rules forcing firms to account for failed investments and true pension liabilities, and plans by the Koizumi government to press for a more rapid resolution of the long-festering problems in the financial sector. Each of these measures is likely to reduce the business opportunities available for the *sokaiya* by reducing the viability of the overall strategies weak firms have used to stay afloat.

As cross-holding of shares by firms declines, their ability to placate top shareholders through private disclosure of key information lessens.

"Ordinary" investors will demand that information be in the public domain, and once public there will be no premium on its non-dissemination. Foreign firms have now bought large stakes in Japanese firms in many industries including insurance, banking, automobiles and so on. These foreign investors are used to higher levels of disclosure and are less culturally averse to confronting angry shareholders, including the *sokaiya*. They will simply not countenance the level of illegal activity that may have prevailed in their takeover targets. For example, when Renault took over Nissan, Japan's number two automaker, the company refused to pay *sokaiya* and suffered through a turbulent first meeting in June 2000 that lasted several hours. However, the next year the *sokaiya* gave up and the proceedings went smoothly. (We might suggest that given Daimler-Chrysler's expanded role in MMC, it seems unlikely there will be any new incidents there.) New accounting rules will require firms to acknowledge pension liabilities and losses on their investments, thereby minimizing the ability of firms to present questionable financial reports without clearly breaking the law. While some executives might not be deterred by the potential to violate the law, auditing firms, which may have cooperated as long as the practices could be considered as falling into a gray area, are likely to be much less flexible now that they are unambiguously forbidden. The move to have banks accurately report the true quality of their loans will push more marginal firms to the breaking point where no amount of deception can hide their failures. Thus, under a reformed economy, if it actually materializes, there will be less possibility of keeping secrets and fewer firms that see paying the *sokaiya* as a way to survive.

Economic reform can help, but must go beyond adjustments to the Commercial Code to outlaw this or that practice. It must establish an environment where market forces do not allow weak firms who are vulnerable to blackmail to limp along for decades, as Japan has previously done. As long as reform is timid then weak or corrupt companies can stay in business by buying off their critics – but with the stiff wind of deregulation-induced competition, and with positive real interest rates that put pressure on value-destroying corporations, these illicit practices should be less possible. Vigilance in enforcement will still be necessary, as periodic scandals in the West continue to show, but at least such efforts will stand a fighting chance. As the losses of dollars, jobs, and in some cases even lives have shown, tolerance of past patterns of corporate behavior is not a harmless proposition.

However, the *sokaiya* have shown themselves to be highly adaptable. It is likely that rather than disappearing, they will shift to other forms of blackmail outside the highly visible shareholders' meeting arena and will target their activities at sectors where such reforms are lagging, such as regional banks and life insurance companies. In an economy the size of Japan's, there will always be enough managers with things to hide, to keep at least a few enterprising extortionists in business.

References

Asahi Shimbun, paper and online editions, various dates.
Chikudate, N. (2000) A phenomenological approach to inquiring into an ethically-bankrupted organization: A case study of a Japanese company. *Journal of Business Ethics* **28**: 59–72.
The Commercial Code & The Audit Special Exceptions Law of Japan, EHS Law Bulletin Series, Vol. II (1994). Tokyo, Eibun-Horei-Sha Inc.
The Globe and Mail, various dates.
Haley, J. O. (1991) *Authority Without Power: Law and the Japanese Paradox*, New York, NY: Oxford University Press.
Japan Times, paper and online editions, various dates.
Kobayashi, K. (1998) *Rieki Kyoyo no Kinshi to Kaisha Taio no Subete* (everything a company needs to know about coping with the ban on payoffs). Tokyo: Torii Shobo.
Mainichi Shimbun/Mainichi Daily News, paper and online editions, various dates.
Nihon Keizai Shimbun, paper and online editions, various dates.
Nikkei Weekly, various dates.
Sokaiya no Shinso (The Truth about *Sokaiya*), *Shukan Daiyamondo* (The Diamond Weekly), May 10, 1997: 24–33.
Szymkowiak, K. (1994) *Sokaiya*: An examination of the social and legal development of Japan's corporate extortionists. *International Journal of the Sociology of Law* **22**: 123–43.
Ursacki, T. (2000) "Restoring the legitimacy of Japanese business in the post-bubble era: Can good economics make good Ethics easier?" in P. Bowles and L. T. Woods (eds), *Japan After the Economic Miracle: In Search of New Directions*, London: Kluwer Academic.
West, M. D. (1999) Information, institutions and extortion in Japan and the United States: Making sense of *Sokaiya* racketeers. *Northwestern University Law Review* **93**: 767–817.

9
Fighting against Corruption: The Japanese Approach to Reform Corporate Governance

Maiko Miyake, Kathryn Gordon and Iwao Taka

Introduction

The legal framework and enforcement apparatus used in the fight against bribery are being steadily improved in many countries. The public and private sectors in Japan have participated in this trend. This chapter provides an overview of changes in the anti-corruption legal framework and a snapshot of corporate initiatives to fight against corruption in Japan.

The chapter is based on a survey of corporate responsibility conducted by the Asahi Newspaper Foundation.[1] The first section of the chapter discusses the conceptual definition of corruption and the legal implication of such a definition; this section also briefly describes the legal environment surrounding Japanese corporations. The second section analyses the voluntary initiatives on anti-corruption compliance and the third section provides findings from the survey that gives a snapshot of Japanese companies' efforts to achieve a corporate conduct with higher business integrity. In the fourth section, the authors refer to a similar study in order to derive a global perspective. In conclusion, the fifth section introduces initiatives that will aid anti-corruption compliance management in Japan.

Corruption

Definitions and concepts in Japan

The World Bank defines corruption as "the abuse of public office for private gain" (Bottelier, 1998). It is clear from the words – bribery, corruption and abuse – that they refer to transactions that are in some sense "bad." However, the economics literature and studies of anti-bribery commitment (Gordon and Miyake, 2001) show that companies, business associations and civil society groups are having difficulty moving from general characterizations of corruption – such as that proposed by the World Bank – to a more operational definition. It can be difficult to define the frontier between a corrupt transaction and other forms of quid pro quo and networking that are essential to any social intercourse, including the conduct of business relations (Williamson, 1979; Rose-Ackermann, 1999). In addition, difficult questions of responsibility emerge when, as the business community often points out, companies fall victim to the crime of extortion. Finally, defining corrupt transactions is made more difficult by the fact that interpretations of appropriate practice are, to some extent at least, culturally conditioned.

Japan is often said to be a relatively less diverse society in which the population still shares the similar cultural value based on Confucianism, Buddhism and the original religion of Japan (Taka, 1994). Such a heterogeneous society tends to rely less on contractual relationships and more on establishing long-term relationships by reciprocal "favors" (Scott, 1995). This tendency has been further enhanced throughout the development of the political economy in Japan, which emphasizes "co-operation" between the many government agencies and businesses (Wade, 1992). It is thus that close ties have developed between the public and certain businesses in this environment for a number of decades in Japan. This backdrop may help to explain the particular orientation of Japanese legislative strategy, which tends to view the fight against corruption very much through the lens of prohibiting anti-competitive practices.

Following a series of corruption scandals in Japan and the recent ratification of the OECD Bribery Convention, significant revisions were made to the law governing corruption. In response to the OECD Convention, the Japanese government made amendments to the Unfair Competition Prevention Law (*Fusei Kyousou Boushi Hou*) that came into force on February 1999. Domestic bribery offences are regulated under article 198 of the Penal Code. The Japanese treatment of bribery of foreign public officials under the aegis of its domestic unfair competition law, rather than under the law regulating domestic bribery, is not common among adherents to the OECD Bribery Convention.

There are other laws, such as the Code of Criminal Procedure and the Commercial Code that contain provisions relevant to other obligations under the Convention. The seizure of the bribe and its proceeds, especially those subject to money laundering, are governed under the Law Concerning Punishment of Organized Crimes, Control of Crime Proceeds and other Matters (the Anti-Organized Crime Law).

Article 8 of the Bribery Convention requires maintenance of books and records, financial statement disclosures and accounting and auditing standards. It prohibits the making of falsified or fraudulent accounts, statements and records for the purpose of bribing foreign public officials or of hiding such bribery. In Japanese law, under article 32 bis (1) of the Commercial Code, it is found that every "trader" "shall prepare accounting books and balance sheets for making clear the conditions of business properties and profit and loss" (OECD, 2000).

It is also worth observing that an increasing number of companies are trying to control "private to private" corruption – that is, corrupt acts that occur between two or more private actors.[2] Sixty-four per cent of companies refer to private-to-private business relationship in their codes of conduct, often using the words "bribery" to refer to the act. In the Japanese legal framework, it is governed under anti-competition law as it is seen as the intent or the act to obtain undue advantage that is not available in a market place.

Though it takes two partners to undertake a corrupt transaction, countries have different views on who should be punished more severely: this can be manifested in the laws regulating either of the parties, making it harsher for one than the other. In some countries, bribe payers are treated more harshly than recipients. In contrast, some countries do not even criminalize the payment of bribes. In the case of Japan, the recent change in the Code of Civil Servants provides for more severe treatment of the recipients of bribes if they are public officials.

Figure 9.1 depicts the Japanese legal framework on anti-corruption. As seen, a corrupt act often leads to the violation of a number of laws besides "anti-corruption" laws. Lack of accurate record keeping for the purpose of concealing bribery is in violation of the Commercial Laws, while misappropriation of company's asset for personal use is in violation of article 252 and 253 of the Penal Code (*ouryou*). In order to reflect the particular wording of Japanese laws governing corruption, the survey asked whether the following items were mentioned in their codes of conduct. It might be useful to relate "corrupt" acts with applicable laws (Table 9.1).

Figure 9.2 shows anti-corruption related subject mentioned in codes of corporate conduct of Japanese companies.[3] Although the codes started to address a wide range of subjects concerning business integrity, the specific language catering specifically to public–private relationship is still

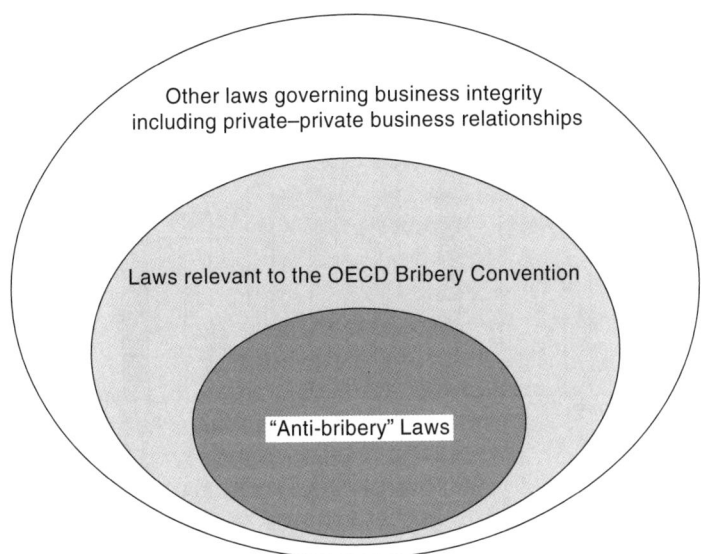

Figure 9.1 Anti-corruption laws in Japan

Table 9.1 Attributes on anti-corruption and governing laws

Attributes	Governing laws
Reference to relationship with foreign government officials	Unfair Competition Prevention Law
Reference to political contributions	Law to Curtail Political Contribution
Reference to relationship with government officials	Article 25 of the Penal Code
Reference to auditing and accounting responsibility	Commercial Code
Reference to the use of company assets for private purposes	Article 252 and 253 of the Penal Code
Reference to reporting obligation of expenses	Article 38 of the Penal Code
Reference to reception and offering of gifts and entertainment	Unfair Competition Prevention Law, Fair Trading Law

under development. "Reception and offering of gifts and entertainment" is quite widespread as an attribute in corporate codes in Japan, with 56 percent of the codes mentioning it. Unfortunately, the language in the Asahi survey questionnaire does not differentiate public–private from private–private relationships.

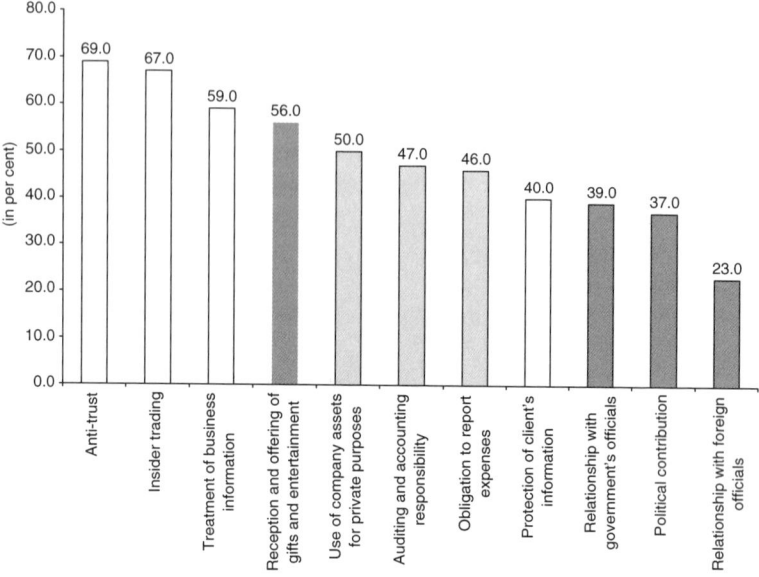

Figure 9.2 Attributes in codes of corporate conduct (percentage of codes mentioning attribute)

Anti-corruption management systems

The emergence of global due diligence in the fight against corruption

From the perspective of legal enforcement, anti-corruption legislation faces formidable challenges. It is becoming more common in enforcement circles to recognize that what companies do in the fight against bribery is as important to the successful outcome of that fight as the actions taken by public enforcement officials. The biggest challenge is to establish patterns of compliance or well-defined expectations so that both internal and external parties can judge a company's compliance efforts. These agreed patterns of management practice in the corporate fight against bribery might be thought of as "due diligence" in the fight against bribery. Precisely because of the difficulty to do so, governments often adopt cooperative enforcement strategies or quasi-voluntary measures to regulate areas where it is hard for outside monitors to determine the degree of corporate compliance (e.g. Haas, 2000 or OECD, 2001).

This has been increasingly the case in anti-corruption enforcement, which often stresses initiatives taken by the private sector.

While the merging and co-ordination of private and public enforcement efforts is located on the cutting edge of regulatory strategy in much of the OECD area, its Japanese equivalent has been around for a long time. The history of economic development in Japan is often identified with the close relationship between the government and large corporations. Companies are often directed by "administrative guidance" which has no enforceability. The companies follow the guidance in order to avoid the adverse effect as a result of non-compliance – for example the loss of discretely preferential treatment. Such practices, as some argue, fostered adoption of semi-voluntary initiatives among Japanese corporate societies (e.g. OECD, 1998). On the other hand, more cynical observers argue that the business sector has been safeguarding the standard by pre-empting the government to enact new regulations (Matthews and Mayes, 1994).

Drawing on an international sample of company codes, Gordon and Miyake (1999) show that a global model of due diligence seems to be emerging. This de facto standard for management practice in the fight against bribery placed heavy emphasis on record keeping, commitment by top management, internal monitoring, and whistle-blowing facilities. Voluntary initiatives to improve corporate conduct are translated into the introduction of a company-wide campaign to improve business integrity. Developing a comprehensive "anticorruption" compliance program as part of a company's standard business practice – and that of its foreign subsidiaries – may limit a company's risk and help avoid potential costs. An anticorruption compliance strategy can also help to protect the company's reputation, minimize its liability, and maintain its long-term viability (adapted from US State Department, 2001: 4).

Formulation of anti-corruption compliance program follows disciplines found in strategic management literature. It involves the following: (1) formulating and articulation of corporate strategy that is in line with internal and external conditions that the firm faces; (2) implementing the strategy with clear and standardized guidance; (3) tracking the strategy, detecting problems and making necessary adjustments (Pearce, 1992; Band and Scanlan, 1995). Their elements are translated into certain actions in the framework of the anti-corruption compliance program that enhances "institutionalization" of anti-corruption culture in a company (see Box 9.1).

Box 9.1 Core elements of anti-corruption compliance program – suggested by the US Department of State

- Full support of senior management
- Establish and adhere to a written corporate code of conduct
- Establish an organizational compliance structure
- Provide anticorruption training and education seminars
- Undertake due diligence: self monitoring, monitoring of suppliers and reports to the BOF
- Auditing and internal accounting controls
- Compliance mechanisms: confidentiality and non retaliation, whistle blowing
- Disciplinary measures

Japanese managerial practice in the fight against corruption

This section provides an overview of anti-corruption compliance programs implemented by Japanese companies as reported in the survey of the Asahi Newspaper Foundation.[4] Here, instead of the total number of companies in the sample, 187, the denominator is 119, the number of companies that responded in the survey that they have an anti-corruption compliance system which specifically deals with one or more of the following subject – reception and offering of gifts and entertainment, political contribution, relationship with foreign officials, and relationship with government officials.

Since the introduction of codes of corporate conduct by Keidanren, the number of companies adopting the codes has increased enormously. In 1990, only 30 percent of large companies had written codes[5] and over 70 percent did not have any monitoring system (Japan Productivity Center, 1991). Below is a snapshot of corporate efforts to implement the anti-corruption compliance program in recent years. In reading the statistics, one needs to keep in mind that the sample is large, of well-known corporations in Japan, but it does not necessarily represent the universe of Japanese companies (see Annex).

Code of conduct: 83.2 percent of companies replied that they distribute a code of corporate conduct to all employees. It is evident that companies adapt various approaches to disseminate policy statement – some employ codes of conduct, while others rely on compliance manuals, or in some cases they have both. 77.1 percent of companies made a compliance manual.

Control of implementation: 87.4 percent of companies responded that they have some units in charge of the implementation; 18.5 percent of them specialized, 23.5 with multiple responsibility and 45.4 percent of companies have several units.

Sensitivity training: 84.8 percent of companies provide some kind of sensitivity training about business integrity to some portion of their employees.[6] 37 percent of companies said they provide seminars for selected members (either certain sections or certain levels). 45.8 percent responded that they provide seminars for everyone in the company.

Resource-bank availability: 68.1 percent of companies responded that they make resources available for employees. 64.7 percent of companies said that they have a place for employees to go and talk about these subjects. 26.1 percent of them widely disseminate telephone numbers or EM addresses. 11.8 percent of respondents mention the protection of inside informers in their codes of conduct, while 65.1 percent refers to disciplinary action. 11.8 percent of companies make records and documents available for reference.

Monitoring mechanisms: 67.8 percent of companies implement monitoring mechanisms. 30.5 percent of companies have a specialized unit to monitor whether policy statement and codes of conduct are complied

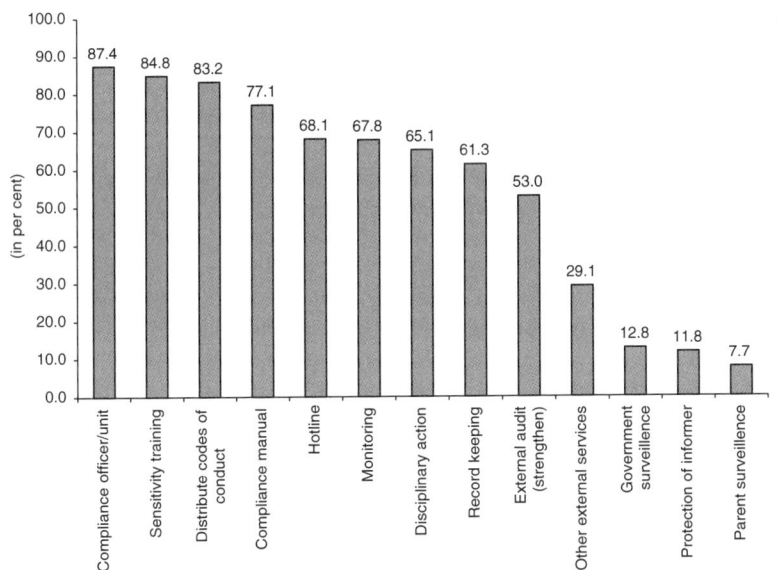

Figure 9.3 Compliance mechanisms

with. 37.3 percent of companies have a unit that has a dual responsibility to carry out compliance monitoring.

Supervisors: 82.2 percent of companies allocate supervisors for compliance program. 8.5 percent assigned a member of the senior management to oversee especially the program. Another 61 percent assigned a senior level manager to oversee the program along with other responsibilities. 5.1 percent have a manager especially in charge of the program, while 7.5 percent of companies have a manager overseeing the program while having other responsibilities.

Record-keeping: 61.3 percent of companies refer to record keeping, 53 percent refer to external audit, 29.1 percent consult with other external services such as lawyers, 12.8 percent use government surveillance, 7.7 percent receive surveillance from parent companies.

Figure 9.3 illustrates these breakdown.

Comparing Japanese and international management practice

This section provides information on how Japanese management practices, as captured in the Asahi survey, compare with international standard practices, as measured in the analysis of corporate codes conducted by Gordon and Miyake (2000). Since sampling and research methodologies are substantially different between the two studies, these comparisons provide only rough indications of differences or similarities.[7] The most robust result that emerges from this comparison of the two studies is that Japanese management practices seem to be similar to global practices. Aside from a stronger emphasis on anti-bribery training, there is no evidence in the Asahi survey of any distinctive "Japanese" managerial approach to the fight against bribery.

Record keeping: 63 percent of companies mentioned record keeping in their codes of conduct. 61.3 percent of Japanese companies responded to the survey that their codes mention the responsibility for good record keeping.

Disciplinary actions: 26.1 percent of codes studied mentioned disciplinary actions. 65.1 percent of Japanese respondents said their codes mention disciplinary actions.

Use of compliance manuals: 32.6 percent of codes studied mention compliance manual, while 77.1 percent of Japanese companies said they have a compliance manual.

Whistle blowing facility: 41.3 percent of companies mention the existence of "hotline" where people can talk in confidence. 68.1 percent of

Japanese companies responded that they provide access to hotlines, although only 11.8 percent clearly state protection for informers.

Compliance offices: 34.8 percent of codes studied said that they have a compliance office/unit/committee, 87.4 percent of Japanese companies responded that they have a compliance office/unit/committee.

Monitoring: 56.5 percent of codes mention internal monitoring, while 67.8 percent of Japanese companies responded that they have internal monitoring.

Training: 13 percent of codes mention training for compliance, 84.8 percent of Japanese companies responded that they have training.

Overall, the frequency of mentioned attributes is higher in the Japanese survey than in OECD survey. However, this is probably largely due to the differences between Asahi's survey-based methodology and Gordon/Miyake's codes-based approach. Nevertheless, a few observations can still be made. First, the extent that the training has been used in Japan is much higher than found in the OECD survey. Second, the extent that record keeping is mentioned in the two surveys came very close. Considering differences recorded in other attributes, this is notable.

Concluding remarks

This study explored the recent changes in Japan's legal framework concerning anti-corruption and the private sector's response to the change. Compared to a decade ago, it seems that Japanese companies are more actively adopting anti-corruption compliance programs. Their effort is comparable to that of other OECD member countries, and may exceed in some areas, such as provision of sensitizing training programs. However, observers in Japan warn that a vast improvement is still required. The effort to mitigate corruption vis-à-vis foreign officials is still in its infancy, for example, it is largely limited to the introduction of anti-corruption programs into their codes of conduct. The few companies that have launched active anti-corruption programs focus on the provision of sensitizing training for their staff before taking up an overseas post. Such an effort should have some impacts to curtail corruption since a majority of Japanese companies still sends expatriates to occupy senior management positions in their subsidiaries. However, the question of how to sensitize local staff still remains.

It is worth noting that there has been an active debate for sensitizing public awareness for ethics management. We note below recent developments.

- In response to the debate, Ethics-Compliance Management Systems Standard 2000 (ECS2000) was introduced in 2000, which provides a detailed guideline on how to implement a management system that was prone to corruption. Many of the elements found in the system are aligned with subjects discussed in this paper.[8]
- The Business Ethics and Compliance Research Center at Reitaku University introduced R-BEC001, a screening framework for selecting social responsible investment last year (2001), in an attempt to raise awareness in the public[9] (*Nikkei*, 18 July 2001).
- A large-scale survey on ethics compliance based on R-BEC001 framework is currently being undertaken by the research firm IntegreX. This covers all the listed companies – over 3500 (*Nikkei*, 10 August 2001). And in December 2001, the Business Ethics and Compliance Research Centre at Reitaku University (R-BEC) published an English version of the ethics-compliance management system standard and its guide. R-BEC will soon publish its Chinese version too.
- Morgan Stanley Dean Witter announced that it would establish a new trust to manage ethical investment funds, to be called Morgan Stanley Asset Management Trust (*Nikkei*, 8 August 2001). The trust will develop an ethical investment fund based on information supplied by IntegreX, and is expected to be launched in spring 2002.

These attempts are intended to involve a wider range of social agents to enforce a company's voluntary initiative, as it is believed that such voluntary initiatives best function when a wider range of monitoring and reporting mechanisms are available.[10]

What this study could not demonstrate, and in fact very little has been published thereon, is the impact of anti-corruption compliance programs on the fight against corruption. Such a study is extremely difficult for two reasons. First of all, it is difficult to establish a causal link between the implementation of the program and the decrease in corruption. Second, which relates to the first difficulty, it is hard to observe the number of potential corrupt acts and corruption that is "deterred" as a result of a compliance program. We also acknowledge that the answer to the question of effectiveness of compliance systems cannot be divorced from the policy and enforcement environment in which the compliance systems are implemented. Nevertheless, it will be useful to introduce further studies on the effectiveness of compliance in order to expand the body of knowledge in this field. Such studies will also help to refine the current understanding as to what type of compliance program works more effectively and what the prerequisites for the successful implementation of compliance programs are.

Acknowledgment

The authors would like to thank Mr Shigeo Inagaki of the Asahi Newspaper Foundation for his generosity to share the data and Ms Mikari Kashima of the Bank of Japan for her valuable inputs.

The data reported in this article are aggregations – made by the authors – of firm-level data supplied by Asahi Newspaper Foundation. The views and data interpretations expressed here are those of the authors and are not necessarily shared by the World Bank, OECD or Reitaku University.

Notes

1 Yuryoku Kigyo no Shakai Kokendo 2000, Asahi Newspaper Foundation (2001) PHP Kenkyusha.
2 See Gordon and Miyake (2000).
3 The survey asked whether the following attributes were mentioned in the company's codes of conduct. For more about research methodology, see Annex.
4 Yuryoku Kigyo no Shakai Kokendo 2000, Asahi Newspaper Foundation (2001) PHP Kenkyusha.
5 Some argue that 30 percent is overstated given the fact that codes of conduct and compliance manual were still foreign concepts in the early 1990s in Japan. Many respondents have probably interpreted policy statement, which is a mere expression of corporate policy, as codes of conduct.
6 Eighteen percent of companies said there was no sensitizing training. Hence the rest is assumed to have some training.
7 The OECD study relies on the results of encoding actual codes of corporate conduct by researchers, while the study by Asahi foundation is based on responses to a questionnaire. See Annex of Gordon and Miyake (2000) and of this chapter for more detail.
8 Documents can be downloaded from http://ecs2000.reitaku-u.ac.jp.
9 Information is fully available to the public. See http://ecs2000.reitaku-u.ac.jp.
10 Brown Weiss (2000) discusses the importance of the "reputation" factor in inducing acceptance of a norm that has not yet been fully internalized by the community or of complying with an established but uncodified norm. For the reputation factor to be important, the author argues, there must be a consensus about the worth of engaging in or abstaining from a specific act, a risk that someone will detect engagement in the act, and that this detection will be publicized throughout the relevant community.
11 *Japan Corporate Governance Forum*.

References

Asahi Newspaper Foundation (2001) *Yuryoku Kigyo no Shakai Kokendo 2000* (Corporate Responsibility of Large Corporations), Tokyo: PHP Kenkyusha.

Band, D. and Scanlan, G. (1995) Strategic control through core competencies. *Long Range Planning* **28**(2): 102–14.
Bottelier, P. (1998) *Corruption and Development*. Remarks for International Symposium on the Prevention and Control of Financial Fraud.
Brown Weiss, E. (2000) "Conclusions: Understanding compliance with soft law," in D. Shelton (ed.), *Commitment and Compliance: The Role of Non-Binding Norms in the International Legal System*, Oxford: Oxford University Press.
Gordon, K. and Miyake, M. (1999) *Deciphering Codes of Corporate Conduct: A Review of their Contents*. Paris, OECD Directorate of Financial, Fiscal and Enterprise Affairs. Working Paper 99/2.
Gordon, K. and Miyake, M. (2000) "Instilling an anti-bribery corporate culture," in *No Longer Business as Usual: Fighting Bribery and Corruption*, OECD: 185–99.
Gordon, K. and Miyake, M. (2001) *Business Approaches to Combating Bribery: A Study of Codes of Conduct*. OECD Working Papers on International Investment Number 2000/1. Forthcoming in the *Journal of Business Ethics*.
Haas, P. (2000) "Choosing to comply: theorizing from international relations and comparative politics," in D. Shelton (ed.), *Commitment and Compliance: The Role of Non-Binding Norms in the International Legal System*, Oxford: Oxford University Press.
Matthews, D. and Mayes, D. G. (1994) *The Role of Soft Law in The Evolution of Rules for a Single European Market: The Case of Retailing*. National Institute of Economic and Social Research, *Discussion Paper* no. 61.
Nikkei Newspaper Morning Edition, 18 July 2001: 19.
Nikkei Newspaper Morning Edition, 8 August 2001: 1.
Nikkei Newspaper Morning Edition, 10 August 2001: 15.
OECD (2001) *Corporate Responsibility: Private Initiatives and Public Goals*, Paris: OECD.
OECD (2000) *Japan: Review of Implementation of the Convention and 1997 Recommendation*, Paris: OECD.
Pearce II, J. (1992) The company mission as a strategic tool. *Sloan Management Review* Spring: 15–24.
Rose-Ackermann, S. (1999) *Corruption and Government: Causes, Consequences, and Reform*, Cambridge: Cambridge University Press.
Scott, W. R. (1995) "Institutions and organizations: Toward a theoretical synthesis," in W. R. Scott and J. W. Meyer (eds), *Institutional Environments and Organizations: Structural Complexity and Individualism*, Thousand Oaks, CA: Sage.
Taka, I. (1994) Business ethics: A Japanese view. *Business Ethics Quarterly* **4**(1): 53–78.
Taka, I. (ed.) (2001) *ECS2000 Konoyouni Rinrihoureijunshu Management System o Kouchiku Suru* (ECS2000 The Way to Establish Legal Compliance Management System). Tokyo, Nikkagirenshuppansha.
Taka, I. Kou, I. and Tadasi, K. (2001) *Yokuwakaru Compliance Keiei* (Compliance Management for Dummys). Tokyo, Nihon Jitsugyo Shuppansha.
United States Department of State (2001) *Fighting Global Corruption: Business Risk Management*. Washington, DC.
Wade, R. (1992) East Asia's economic success: Conflicting perspectives, partial insights, shaky evidence. *World Politics* **44** (January): 270–320.
Williamson, O. (1979) Transaction-Cost economics: The governance of contractual relations. *Journal of Law and Economics* **22**: 233–61.

Annex: Notes on methodology

The data used in this article is a result of the 10th annual survey on corporate responsibility conducted by the Asahi Newspaper Foundation in 2000. For the year 2000 survey, a questionnaire was sent to 187 companies that are well known or have great exposure to consumers in Japan. It should be noted that the purpose of the survey is to draw public attention to corporate social responsibility by providing ranking of these companies and hence the sampling methodology is less vigorous. The sample also includes subsidiaries of non-Japanese multinational enterprises operating in Japan. The secretariat of the foundation sends out a questionnaire and follows up with telephone calls.

The purpose of the survey and the bias towards large companies might have resulted in providing much higher frequency. It is evident when compared to the recent survey on corporate governance, which covers 543 listed companies.[11] The survey demonstrated that only 54.5 percent of companies have codes of conduct and/or compliance manuals. However, the sample might be an adequate comparison to the OECD study mentioned in the text, which also focused on multinational enterprises that tend to be large and relatively well-known.

While the survey addresses a wide range of issues on corporate responsibility, the article concentrated on the data related to corruption extracted under the subject heading *business ethics* (kigyo rinri).

A word of caution is required for non-respondents bias of this survey. Although the total sample size is 187, for some questions, sample size is much smaller. That is to say, there were firms that chose to respond only to selected questions. Among the 187 companies, 2 companies did not respond at all, and further 125 responded to selected questions. The study adopts a conservative assumption – it assumes that all non-respondents do not engage in the activity mentioned.

10
Singapore's Anti-Corruption Strategy: Is this Form of Governance Transferable to Other Asian Countries?
Jon S. T. Quah

Introduction

Corruption refers to "the misuse of public power, office or authority for private benefit – through bribery, extortion, influence peddling, nepotism, fraud, speed money or embezzlement" (UNDP, 1999: 7). Defined thus, corruption is a serious problem afflicting many countries around the world with its own local manifestations (Jacoby *et al.*, 1977: 6–7). In its cover story on "Corruption: The Asian Lubricant" in September 1974, the *Far Eastern Economic Review* (FEER) observed: "With pathetically few exceptions, the countries in this region are so riddled with corruption that the paying of 'tea money' has become almost a way of life." In another cover story on "Corruption: Reform's Dark Side" in the March 20th 1997 issue of the FEER, Aparisim Ghosh *et al.* (1997: 18) wrote:

> Looking back on the Year of the Rat [1996] some time in the future, historians may well marvel at how much Asian newsprint and television time was devoted to reports and discussions on corruption in government. From Pakistan to Japan, corruption was the year's biggest story.

Today, corruption is still a serious problem in many countries in the Asia-Pacific region, judging from the recent annual surveys conducted by the Hong Kong-based Political and Economic Risk Consultancy Ltd (PERC) and the Berlin-based Transparency International (TI). According to TI's Corruption Perceptions Index (CPI), which is a "robust" index that "combines several measures of political corruption for each country"

(Lancaster and Montinola, 1997: 28), Singapore is the least corrupt country in Asia from 1995 to 2001. Table 10.1 indicates the CPI ranking for the 12 Asian countries surveyed by TI during 1995–2001. Similarly, Table 10.2, shows the PERC's ranking for 12 Asian countries from 1998 to 2000, which confirms Singapore's ranking as the least corrupt Asian nation.

However, corruption was rampant during the 140 years of British colonial rule in this island State. It was made an offence in 1871 with

Table 10.1 Ranking of 12 Asian countries on Transparency International's Corruption Perceptions Index, 1995–2001

Country	1995	1996	1997	1998	1999	2000	2001	Average
Singapore	3	7	9	7	7	6	4	6
Hong Kong	17	18	18	16	15	15	14	16
Japan	20	17	21	25	25	23	21	22
Taiwan	25	29	31	29	32	28	27	28
Malaysia	23	26	32	29	32	36	36	31
S. Korea	27	27	34	43	50	48	42	39
Thailand	34	37	39	61	68	60	61	52
China	40	50	41	52	58	63	57	52
Philippines	36	44	40	55	54	69	65	52
India	35	46	45	66	72	69	71	58
Pakistan	39	53	48	71	87	NA	79	63
Indonesia	41	45	46	80	96	85	88	69

Source: Compiled from Transparency International's Corruption Perceptions Index, 1995–2001.

Table 10.2 PERC's ranking of 12 Asian countries, 1998–2000

Country	1998	1999	2000	Average
Singapore	1	1	1	1
Hong Kong	2	2	2	2
Japan	3	3	3	3
Taiwan	4	5	5	4.7
Malaysia	5	6	4	5
Philippines	8	4	8	6.7
Thailand	7	8	7	7.3
South Korea	11	7	6	8
China	6	10	9	8.3
Vietnam	10	9	10	9.7
India	9	11	11	10.3
Indonesia	12	12	12	12

Source: Richardson (2000: 16).

the introduction of the Penal Code of the Straits Settlements. An analysis of the English newspaper, *Straits Times*, from 1845 to 1921 found that bribery was the most common form of police corruption in Singapore then as it constituted nearly two-thirds of the 172 reported cases (Quah, 1979: 17–24). The prevalence of corruption in the police force in Singapore was confirmed by the 1879 and 1886 Commissions of Inquiry (Quah, 1982: 161). During the Japanese occupation (1942–45) rampant inflation contributed to corruption, as civil servants could not survive on their low salaries. The situation deteriorated during the post-war period as "corruption had also become a way of life for many people" to enable them to cope with their low salaries and rising inflation (Yoong, 1973: 55–6). In his 1950 annual report, the Commissioner of Police, J. P. Pennefather-Evans, indicated that "graft was rife" in many government departments (Quah, 1982: 161–2).

How was Singapore able to minimise the problem of corruption? In his doctoral thesis, S. C. Mohan (1987: ii) wrote: "In contrast with most Asian and African nations, the Republic of Singapore has often been cited as a model state where bureaucratic corruption is minimal. What then is the secret of Singapore's success at corruption control?" The purpose of this chapter is two-fold: (1) to explain how Singapore has succeeded in minimising corruption by describing the major features of its comprehensive anti-corruption strategy; and (2) to assess whether Singapore's anti-corruption strategy can be successfully transferred to other Asian countries to assist them in their anti-corruption efforts.

Singapore's anti-corruption strategy

Phase I: Incremental strategy (1871–1959)

As indicated earlier, corruption became an offence in 1871. However, nothing was done for the next 66 years by the British colonial government until it enacted the Prevention of Corruption Ordinance (POCO) on 10 December 1937. However, the POCO was ineffective as the penalty imposed for corruption was a prison term of two years and/or a fine of S$10000. The short prison term of two years for those found guilty of corrupt offences meant that "such offences were not seizable ones, thus limiting the powers of arrest, as warrants for search and investigation were required before arrests by the Police could be made" (Quah, 1978: 9).

The agency responsible for implementing the POCO was the Anti-Corruption Branch (ACB) of the Criminal Investigation Department

(CID). However, the ACB was ineffective for three reasons. First, as a small police unit, it was entrusted with a difficult task to perform, that is, the elimination of corruption in the entire civil service. Second, as part of the CID, the ACB had to compete with the other sections of the CID for limited manpower and other resources. More specifically, anti-corruption activities constituted only one of the 16 duties of the CID's Assistant Commissioner in May 1952. Finally, the ACB was ineffective because it could not curb corruption in the police force. This was illustrated by the discovery that senior police officers were involved in the robbery of S$400 000 worth of opium in October 1951 (Quah, 1978: 14–15).

The involvement of senior police officers in the opium hijacking scandal made the British colonial government realise the importance of establishing an independent anti-corruption agency that was separate from the police. Accordingly, the Corrupt Practices Investigation Bureau (CPIB) was formed in October 1952 to curb corruption in Singapore. In short, Singapore became the first Asian country to establish an independent anti-corruption agency (Quah, 2000: 103).

Phase II: Comprehensive strategy (1960–present)

The People's Action Party's (PAP's) commitment to the elimination of corruption in Singapore contributed significantly to its victory in the May 1959 general election. After winning the December 1957 City Council election on its platform of curbing corruption, the PAP launched its electoral campaign by revealing that the Labour Front's Minister for Education, Chew Swee Kee, had corruptly accepted political funds from the United States government to defeat the PAP in the 1959 general election. The Chief Minister, Lim Yew Hock, appointed a commission of inquiry to investigate the Chew Swee Kee affair. Chew admitted during the investigation that he had received, with his party's knowledge, a total of S$700 000 (about US$233 000 at the time) on two occasions from the United States government. Chew's confession of his corrupt dealings sealed his party's fate and enabled the PAP to win the May 1959 general election (Quah, 1995: 394).

In his memoirs, former Prime Minister Lee Kuan Yew (2000: 182–4) explained his government's commitment to curbing corruption thus:

> When the PAP government took office in 1959, we set out to have a clean administration. We were sickened by the greed, corruption and decadence of many Asian leaders...we had a deep sense of mission

to establish a clean and effective government. When we took the oath of office at the ceremony in the city council chamber in June 1959, we all wore white shirts and white slacks to symbolise purity and honesty in our personal behaviour and our public life ... we made sure from the day we took office in June 1959 that every dollar in revenue would be properly accounted for and would reach the beneficiaries at the grass roots as one dollar, without being siphoned off along the way.

As the British colonial government had not succeeded in curbing corruption, the PAP government decided to replace the incremental anti-corruption strategy with a more comprehensive one. As corruption had become a way of life in Singapore and was perceived by many to be "a low risk, high reward" activity, the PAP government's mission was a challenging one: to minimise corruption and to change the public perception of corruption to "a high risk, low reward" activity. In 1960, the PAP government strengthened the anti-corruption law by introducing the Prevention of Corruption Act (POCA), and gave more powers to the CPIB.

The PAP government's new anti-corruption strategy is based on the "logic of corruption control" (Gardiner and Lyman, 1989: 827) that is, as corruption is caused by both the incentives and the opportunities to be corrupt, "attempts to eradicate corruption must be designed to minimise or remove the conditions of both the incentives and opportunities that make individual corrupt behaviour irresistible" (Quah, 1989: 842). This strategy is comprehensive because of its emphasis on reducing both the opportunities and incentives for corruption.

The Prevention of Corruption Act (POCA)

As Singapore's gross domestic product (GDP) per capita in 1960 was S$1330 or US$443 (Republic of Singapore, 1983: 7), the PAP government was compelled to launch its anti-corruption strategy by strengthening the existing laws to reduce the opportunities for corruption and to increase the penalty for corrupt behaviour as it could not afford to increase the wages of the civil servants.

The Minister for Home Affairs, Ong Pang Boon, clearly stated the PAP government's commitment to curb corruption in the Legislative Assembly on 13 February 1960, when he moved for the second reading of the Prevention of Corruption Bill:

> The Prevention of Corruption Bill is in keeping with the new Government's determination to stamp out bribery and corruption in

the country, especially in the public services. The Government is deeply conscious that a Government cannot survive, no matter how good its aims and instructions are, if corruption exists in its ranks and its public services on which it depends to provide the efficient and effective administrative machinery to translate its policies into action.... Therefore, this Government is determined to take all possible steps to see that all necessary legislative and administrative measures are taken *to reduce the opportunities of corruption*, to make its detection easier, and to deter and punish severely those who are susceptible to it and who engage in it shamelessly (State of Singapore, 1960: cols. 376–7).

The POCA was enacted on 17 June 1960, and it contained the following five features to rectify the POCO's weaknesses and to strengthen the CPIB by giving it additional powers for performing its duties:

1 The POCA's scope is broader than the POCO with 32 sections in contrast to the POCO's 12 sections.
2 Section 2 of the POCA defines corruption in terms of various forms of gratification, and identifies for the first time the CPIB and its Director.
3 The penalty for corrupt behaviour was increased to imprisonment for five years and/or a fine of S$10 000.
4 A person found guilty of accepting an illegal gratification had to pay the amount he had taken as a bribe in addition to any other punishment imposed by a court.
5 The POCA gave the CPIB these powers: its officers could arrest and search arrested persons; its Director and staff could investigate "any bank account, share account, or purchase account" of any person suspected of having committed an offence; and its officers can inspect a civil servant's banker's book and those of his wife, child or agent, if necessary (Quah, 1978: 10–11).

The PAP government ensured the POCA's effectiveness by introducing, whenever necessary, amendments (in 1963, 1966 and 1981) or new legislation (in 1989) to deal with unanticipated problems. In 1963, the POCA was amended to give CPIB officers the power to require the attendance of witnesses and to examine them. The aim of this amendment was to enable the CPIB officers to obtain the co-operation of witnesses to help them in their investigations. Two amendments were introduced in 1966: the first amendment (section 28) stated that a person could be found guilty of corruption even though he did not actually receive the bribe, as the intention on his part to commit the offence would provide sufficient grounds for his conviction. The second amendment (section 35) was directed at those Singaporeans working in embassies and other government agencies abroad as Singaporeans would be prosecuted for corrupt offences committed outside Singapore and would be dealt with as if such offences had occurred in Singapore. In 1981, the POCA was amended to increase its deterrent effect by requiring those convicted of corruption to repay all the money received besides facing the usual court sentence. Those who could not make full restitution would be given heavier court sentences (Quah, 1995: 395–6).

On 14 December 1986, the Minister for National Development, Teh Cheang Wan, committed suicide. This was 12 days after two senior CPIB officers interrogated him for 16 hours regarding two instances of alleged corruption brought against him by a building contractor. Teh was accused of accepting two bribes amounting to S$1 million in 1981 and 1982 from two developers to enable one of them to retain his land, which had been acquired by the government, and to assist the other developer in purchasing State land for private development (Republic of Singapore, 1987: 1 and 36).

One of the consequences of the Commission of Inquiry that followed was the enactment of the Corruption (Confiscation of Benefits) Act 1989, on 3 March 1989. Section 4 of this Act stated that the court should issue "a confiscation order against the defendant in respect of benefits derived from him from corruption if the court is satisfied that such benefits have been so derived." If a defendant has deceased, the court would issue a confiscation order against his estate (Republic of Singapore, 1989: 107 and 110).

The Corrupt Practices Investigation Bureau (CPIB)

The British colonial government entrusted the enforcement of the POCO to the ACB of the CID in the Singapore Police Force. However, the ACB's failure to deal effectively with police corruption as manifested in the October 1951 opium hijacking scandal: this forced the colonial authorities to establish the CPIB as an independent anti-corruption agency.

The CPIB was formed in October 1952 as the *de jure* anti-corruption agency in Singapore. More specifically, it performs the following three functions:

1 to receive and investigate complaints alleging corrupt practices in both the public and private sectors;
2 to investigate malpractices and misconduct by public officers; and

3 to examine the practices and procedures in the public service to minimise opportunities for corrupt practices (CPIB, 1990: 2).

Its size has grown by 15 times, from five officers in 1952 to its present establishment of 77 officers, with a budget of S$10.7 million (Mohan, 1987: 607 and Republic of Singapore, 2001: 489–90). The CPIB is divided into three branches: the Investigation Branch, the Data Management and Support Branch, and the Administration Branch. The Investigation Branch is the largest and most important branch and is responsible for conducting the CPIB's operations. The investigators submit their completed investigation papers to the CPIB's Director, who is required by the POCA to consult the Public Prosecutor and recommend appropriate action on the basis of the available evidence. However, if there is inadequate evidence to prosecute a case in court, the Director will refer the matter to the head of the department concerned for disciplinary action after obtaining the Public Prosecutor's agreement (CPIB, 1990: 3–4).

The CPIB's computer information system comes under the purview of the Data Management and Support Branch, which screens candidates for public appointments and their subsequent promotions, scholarships and training courses, as well as screening applicants for citizenship, and contractors competing for government contracts. The Research Unit analyses the work procedures of corruption-prone government departments and identifies the administrative weaknesses that cause corruption. It also examines completed cases to ascertain the *modus operandi* of corrupt civil servants and recommends the necessary preventive measures. Finally, the Intelligence Unit collects intelligence for the operational needs of the Investigation Branch (CPIB, 1990: 4).

How effective is the CPIB in curbing corruption in Singapore? Mohan (1987: 575–6) contended that the CPIB's "success as a law enforcement body has been almost phenomenal, and it has gained both the respect and confidence of the public." Furthermore, it is also reputed to be "one of the most efficient anti-corruption agencies in the world and regularly helps train officers from many parts of Asia and Africa, including Hong Kong, Malaysia, Brunei, Zambia and Tanzania" (Mohan, 1987: 576). He concluded that the CPIB has been "successful in its work" judging from the nature and extent of its law enforcement activity, the success in its investigations, the conviction rate of those it has prosecuted, its reputation, and the degree of public support and confidence it commands (Mohan, 1987: 631–2).

A more recent analysis by Tan Ah Leak (1999: 64), the CPIB's Deputy Director, contends similarly that the CPIB "has earned the public's confidence and support in its fight against corruption. It is generally regarded as an effective agency and is reputed for its single-minded efficiency." According to Tan (1999: 64), the CPIB's success can be attributed to the following factors: Singapore's cultural climate which is strongly opposed to corruption; a well-paid civil service, which discourages civil servants from being corrupt; such effective administrative measures as "disciplinary proceedings by the Public Service Commission, close scrutiny of government expenditures by the Auditor-General's Department and the Public Accounts Committee of Parliament, and control of public spending by the Ministry of Finance;" a highly literate and sophisticated society, which readily reports corrupt behaviour with no fear of reprisal; and the CPIB's ability to investigate prominent persons has also enhanced its credibility among Singaporeans.

Improving civil service salaries

The PAP government was only able to implement the second prong of its anti-corruption strategy – the reduction of incentives for corruption by improving salaries and working conditions in the civil service. This was in 1972, twelve years after the enactment of the POCA in 1960. When it assumed office in June 1959, the PAP government was forced to reduce expenditure as it inherited "national coffers [which were] seriously depleted." Accordingly, the Cabinet Budget Committee on Expenditure recommended serious cuts in public service expenditures "including the removal of the cost of living allowance payable to civil servants in the middle and upper salary brackets" (Bogaars, 1973: 80). Goh Keng Swee, the then Minister for Finance, said that the government's drastic decision to remove these variable allowances was because of the anticipated budgetary deficit of S$14 million. If the allowances were not removed, the government would be forced to increase taxes or face financial bankruptcy (Seah, 1971: 90).

As the Singapore economy improved in the 1970s, the higher salaries in the private sector contributed to a brain drain from the civil service. Consequently, civil service wages were revised to curb the loss of talent. The National Wages Council (NWC) was created by the PAP government in February 1972 as an advisory body to formulate general guidelines on wage policies, to recommend annual wage adjustments, and to advise on incentive systems for improving efficiency and productivity (Then, 1998: 220–1). The NWC recommended the payment of the Annual Wage Supplement (AWS) [or the 13th month salary] to supplement the employee's annual salary and minimise the gap in salaries in the public and private sectors.

In 1973, the salaries of senior civil servants were increased substantially to reduce the gap with the private sector. However, as the gap between the salaries of the high-flyers in the public and private sectors remained, the salaries in the Administrative Service were further improved in May 1979. Perhaps, the most eloquent justification of the PAP government's approach to combating corruption by reducing or removing the incentives for corruption through the improvement of the salaries of political leaders and senior civil servants was given by the then Prime Minister, Lee Kuan Yew, in Parliament on 22 March 1985, when he explained why the wages of his cabinet ministers deserved to be raised.

Lee contended that political leaders should be paid the top salaries that they deserved in order to ensure a clean and honest government. And, Singapore needed a corruption-free administration and an honest political leadership to preserve its most precious assets. Otherwise, if they were underpaid, they would succumb to temptation and indulge in corrupt behaviour. He concluded that the best way of dealing with corruption was "moving with the market," which is "an honest, open, defensible and workable system" instead of dealing in hypocrisy, which results in duplicity and corruption (*Straits Times*, 1985, 23 March: 14–16).

In March 1989, civil service salaries were substantially revised to increase recruitment to and minimise resignations from the Administrative Service. In October 1994, a White Paper on *Competitive Salaries for Competent and Honest Government* was presented to Parliament to justify the pegging of the salaries of ministers and senior civil servants to the average salaries of the top four earners in six private sector professions: accounting, banking, engineering, law, local manufacturing companies, and multinational corporations. The adoption of the long-term formula suggested in the White Paper not only eliminated the need for justifying the salaries of ministers and senior bureaucrats "from scratch with each salary revision," but also ensured the building of an efficient civil service and a competent and honest political leadership.

During the most recent salary increase in June 2000, the benchmark was extended from the four top earners to the top eight earners in six professions, the variable component of annual salaries was increased from 30 to 40 per cent, and a performance-related component was included in the total wage package of each senior civil servant. Table 10.3 shows that the salaries of the Singaporean ministers and senior civil servants are the highest in the world.

In addition to reducing the incentives for corruption, the PAP government had to improve the salaries and working conditions in the civil service for another reason: to stem the brain drain of competent senior civil

Table 10.3 Salaries of selected ministers and senior civil servants in Singapore, June 2000 (S$)*

Grade	Monthly salary (S$)	Annual salary (S$)	Ranking among top earners**
Prime Minister	85 300	1.94 million	63
Minister	55 700	1.42 million	137
Staff Grade II	49 900	1.27 million	180
	44 600	1.13 million	239
Minister	47 400	1.21 million	206
Staff Grade I	37 900	968 000	367
Superscale B	39 800	1.01 million	318
	28 800	736 000	699
Superscale G	18 800	390 000	> 1000
	17 500	363 000	> 1000

* The exchange rate in August 2001 was US$1 = S$1.75.
** This refers to the ranking among the top earners in Singapore.
Source: Straits Times, 2000, 30 June: 53.

servants to the private sector by offering competitive salaries and fringe benefits to reduce the wage gap between the public and private sectors.

Transferability of Singapore's anti-corruption strategy

Is Singapore's anti-corruption strategy transferable to other Asian countries? And further, what can other Asian countries concerned with minimising corruption learn from Singapore's experience? Writing in 1887, Woodrow Wilson supported "the idea of looking into foreign systems of administration for instruction and suggestion" as "we can borrow the science of administration with safety and profit if only we read all fundamental differences of condition into its essential tenets. We have to filter it through our constitutions, to put it over a slow fire of criticism and distil away its foreign gases" (p. 15). Similarly, Wallace S. Sayre (1967: 354) astutely observed that as "bureaucratic models are not packages ready for export or import; they provide illustrations of options and styles for consideration in their separate parts, and for adaptation before acceptance in a different context."

In addition to the above advice by Wilson and Sayre, two caveats must be noted in discussing the relevance of Singapore's anti-corruption strategy to other Asian countries. First, the extent of transferability of Singapore's experience to other Asian countries depends on the contextual differences between these countries and Singapore. Second, the relevance of Singapore's anti-corruption strategy to other Asian countries depends on whether the governments in these countries have the political will to pay the price required to implement reforms.

Differences in policy context

The extent to which Singapore's anti-corruption strategy is transferable to other Asian countries depends on how similar these countries are to Singapore. Table 10.4 shows the differences in policy context among the twelve Asian countries.

Singapore is the smallest country in terms of land area and population, and the second richest country in Asia after Japan. Of the other eleven countries, Hong Kong is the most similar to Singapore as it is also a city-state, but has a larger territory (by 392.3 sq. km.) and population (by 2.69 million), with a lower GDP per capita (by US$6510). While the

Table 10.4 Policy contexts of 12 Asian countries

Country	Land area (sq. km.)	Population (million)	GDP per capita (US$)	Political system
Singapore	682.7	4.01	30 170	Parliamentary democracy
Hong Kong	1 075	6.70	23 660	Democracy; SAR of China
Japan	377 727	126.3	32 350	Constitutional monarchy
Taiwan	36 179	21.9	12 040	Parliamentary democracy
Malaysia	332 665	21.4	3 670	Constitutional monarchy
South Korea	99 274	46.1	8 600	Parliamentary democracy
Thailand	513 115	60.3	2 160	Constitutional monarchy
China	9 560 900	1 255.7	750	Communist
Philippines	300 000	72.9	1 050	Presidential democracy
India	3 287 263	982.2	440	Parliamentary democracy
Pakistan	803 940	148.2	470	Military regime
Indonesia	1 904 443	206.3	640	Parliamentary democracy

Source: *The Economist* (2000: 120, 140, 144, 146, 158, 162, 176, 180, 192, 200, 208, and 210).

other ten countries are much larger than Singapore in area and population but poorer, except for Japan.

Hence, it is not surprising that Hong Kong has adopted Singapore's anti-corruption strategy by establishing the Independent Commission Against Corruption (ICAC) in February 1974. Though this was nearly six years after a study team visited Singapore and Ceylon (as Sri Lanka was known then) in 1968 to examine how their laws worked in practice. Among other things, the study team was impressed with the independence of the anti-corruption agencies in these countries, and attributed Singapore's success in curbing corruption to the CPIB's independence from the police (Wong, 1981: 47). Furthermore, the knowledge gained from the study tour contributed to the formulation of their Prevention of Bribery Bill on 16 October 1970 and its enactment as an ordinance on 15 May 1971 (Kuan, 1971: 29).

The only other Asian country that has followed Singapore's footsteps in curbing corruption is Malaysia, which established the Anti-Corruption Agency (ACA) in October 1967, fifteen years after the formation of the CPIB. As in the case of Singapore, the task of fighting corruption was the responsibility of the Police before the creation of the ACA (Quah, 1982: 169). Even though Malaysia is larger in area and population than Singapore and Hong Kong, it has adopted a similar anti-corruption strategy possibly because it was also a British colony. However, unlike Singapore and Hong Kong, Malaysia has been less successful in curbing corruption, as reflected in its lower ranking on TI's 2001 CPI: it is ranked 36th compared to Singapore's fourth ranking and Hong Kong's fourteenth ranking. Indeed, Malaysia's lower ranking since 1999 indicates that the ACA is less effective than the CPIB and ICAC. Apart from the growing problem of money politics, the ACA has been criticised for not investigating corruption cases impartially involving "big fish." The 1999 corruption trial of former Deputy Prime Minister Anwar Ibrahim was politically motivated, as other "big fish" were not similarly targeted.

Political will needed to implement reforms

Kpundeh (1998: 92) has defined "political will" as "the demonstrated credible intent of political actors (elected or appointed leaders, civil society watchdogs, stakeholder groups, etc.) to attack perceived causes or effects of corruption at a systemic level." Indeed, without political will, "governments' statements to reform civil service, strengthen transparency and accountability and reinvent the relationship between government and private industry remain mere rhetoric" (Kpundeh, 1998: 92). Similarly, Pope (1999: 115) concluded that "at the end of the day, all anticorruption efforts will be in vain if leaders are not committed, and the public does not have confidence in the reformers' sincerity and ability to effect change."

Indeed, the most important prerequisite for the success of any anti-corruption strategy is political will, which is crucial for minimising corruption in a country. Singapore's experience in curbing corruption shows clearly that the political leaders must be sincerely committed to the eradication of corruption by their exemplary conduct and modest lifestyle. Anyone found guilty of corruption must be punished, regardless of his position or status in society. If the "big fish" (rich and famous) are protected from prosecution for corruption, and only the "small fish" (ordinary people) are caught, the anti-corruption strategy will not be credible – but also doomed to failure.

For example, when Kim Young Sam became the first civilian president in South Korea in February 1993, he launched an intensive anti-corruption campaign, which included, *inter alia*, the voluntary disclosure of his personal and family assets, the introduction of the Real-Name Financial Transaction System to replace the use of anonymous financial accounts, the giving up of golf (as it was a symbol of corporate–government cronyism) and the exchange of corrupt gifts. Kim's anti-corruption drive was hindered by the 17 May 1997 arrest of his son for bribery and tax evasion in the Hanbo loan scandal and his sentencing to three years' imprisonment five months later. Nevertheless Kim has clearly demonstrated his commitment to eliminating corruption by not obstructing the legal arrest and sentencing of his son. However, the Hanbo scandal and his son's arrest and imprisonment have seriously undermined Kim's legitimacy, and jeopardised the continued success of his anti-corruption campaign (Quah, 1999: 181–2).

In contrast, even though the Philippines has the most numerous anti-corruption laws and agencies in Asia, it has failed to curb corruption because its political leaders lack the necessary political will. When Corazon Aquino replaced Ferdinand E. Marcos as president in February 1986, "there was high expectation that the end of the culture of graft and corruption was near" (Varela, 1995: 174). However, according to Carino, "Aquino's honesty has not been matched by the political will to punish the corrupt" (quoted in Timberman, 1991: 235).

In May 1992, Fidel Ramos was elected president of the Philippines and he created the Presidential Commission Against Graft and Corruption (PCAGC) in 1994. However, three years later, PCAGC's chairman,

Eufemio Domingo, lamented that "the system is not working" because the anti-corruption "laws, rules and regulations are not being faithfully implemented" (Balgos, 1998: 267).

Joseph Estrada succeeded Ramos as president in 1998 and in June 2000, the *Financial Times* reported "perceived corruption in the Philippines reached its highest levels for two decades during 1998 and 1999 – the first two years of the Estrada administration" (Lande, 2001: 92). In October 2000, Estrada was accused of receiving large amounts of money from illegal gambling. Impeachment proceedings were initiated against him but ended on 16 January 2001, when the prosecutors walked out and the Senate president resigned. The Senate's failure to act resulted in five days of massive demonstrations (Lande, 2001: 94). On 20 January 2001, Gloria Macapagal-Arroyo was sworn in as president by the chief justice and Estrada agreed to resign when "his" military withdrew its support.

Apart from the critical importance of political will, Singapore's experience in combating corruption also shows that the anti-corruption agency must be incorruptible, and corrupt civil servants and political leaders must be punished to make corruption a high-risk, low-reward activity. Also opportunities for corruption in vulnerable government agencies must be reduced, in part by paying adequate salaries to political leaders and civil servants to reduce their temptation (Quah, 1995: 408–9). Indeed, if political will is absent, none of these requirements can be attained.

Conclusion

Singapore's comprehensive anti-corruption strategy is effective, as Singapore was perceived to be the least corrupt country in Asia during 1995–2001. Its enviable record in curbing corruption can be attributed to the commitment of the political leaders, the periodic review of the POCA to rectify its loopholes, the impartial enforcement of the POCA by the incorruptible CPIB, the reduction of opportunities for corruption in the vulnerable government departments, the punishment of corrupt officials, and the improvement of salaries for civil servants and political leaders to reduce their temptation to be corrupt.

Whether Singapore's effective anti-corruption strategy can be successfully transplanted to other Asian countries depends on two important factors: the nature of their policy context, and whether they possess the political will to implement the required reforms. So far, only Hong Kong and Malaysia have adopted Singapore's anti-corruption strategy, as they are also former British colonies. However, Hong Kong has been more effective than Malaysia in combating corruption, as it is a rich city-state and has the political will to implement the anti-corruption measures impartially. Indeed, Malaysia's experience shows that the ACA's lack of independence from the political leadership in recent years has tarnished its public image and also its effectiveness in curbing corruption.

Otherwise we see that Singapore's effective anti-corruption strategy cannot be successfully transferred to the other nine Asian countries because of their contextual differences and the absence of political will. In this context, Johnston (1999: 225) concluded that while "ICACs (Independent Commissions Against Corruption) are unlikely to be right for every country," they do demonstrate that "permanent, independent agencies addressing corruption as a deep-rooted problem, making society a partner in reform, and developing careful strategies for prevention may be a promising way to confront serious corruption." Nevertheless, these Asian countries can emulate and adapt some features of Singapore's anti-corruption strategy to suit their own needs, provided that their political leaders, civil servants, and the population are prepared to make the required changes.

References

Balgos, C. C. A. (1998) "Ombudsman," in S. S. Coronel (ed.), *Pork and Other Perks: Corruption and Governance in the Philippines*, Metro Manila: Philippine Center for Investigative Journalism, 245–71.
Bogaars, G. E. (1973) "Public services," in *Towards Tomorrow: Essays on Development and Social Transformation in Singapore*. Singapore, National Trades Union Congress, pp. 73–83.
"Corruption: The Asian Lubricant." (1974) *Far Eastern Economic Review*, September 6: 3, 22–31.
CPIB (1990) *The Corrupt Practices Investigation Bureau (An Introduction)*. Singapore.
The Economist (2000) *Pocket World in Figures 2001*. London: Profile Books.
Gardiner, J. A. and Lyman, T. R. (1989) "The logic of corruption control," in A. J. Heidenheimer, M. Johnston and V. T. LeVine (eds.), *Political Corruption: A Handbook*. New Brunswick: Transaction Publishers, 827–40.
Ghosh, Aparisim *et al.* (1997) Corruption: Reform's dark side. *Far Eastern Economic Review* March 20: 18–20.
Jacoby, N. H. *et al.* (1977) *Bribery and Extortion in World Business*, New York: Macmillan.
Johnston, M. (1999) "A brief history of anticorruption agencies," in A. Schedler, L. Diamond and M. F. Plattner (eds.), *The Self-Restraining State: Power and Accountability in New Democracies*, Boulder: Lynne Rienner, 217–26.
Kpundeh, S. J. (1998) "Political will in fighting corruption," in United Nations Development Programme. *Corruption and Integrity Improvement Initiatives in Developing Countries*. New York: UNDP, 91–110.

Kuan, H-C (1971) "Anti-corruption legislation in Hong Kong – A history," in R. P. L. Lee (ed.), *Corruption and Its Control in Hong Kong*, Hong Kong: The Chinese University Press, 15–43.

Lancaster, T. D. and Montinola, G. R. (1997) Towards a Methodology for the Comparative Study of Political Corruption. Unpublished paper.

Lande, C. H. (2001) The return of 'People Power' in the Philippines. *Journal of Democracy* **12**(2): 88–102.

Lee, Kuan Yew (2000) *From Third World to First: The Singapore Story: 1965–2000*. Singapore, Times Media.

Mohan, S. C. (1987) *The Control of Corruption in Singapore*. Ph.D. thesis, School of Oriental and African Studies, University of London, 2 Volumes.

Pope, J. (1999) "Enhancing accountability and ethics in the public sector," in Rick Stapenhurst and Sahr J. Kpundeh (eds.), *Curbing Corruption: Toward a Model for Building National Integrity*. Washington, D.C.: The World Bank, 105–16.

Quah, J. S. T. (1978) *Administrative and Legal Measures for Combatting Bureaucratic Corruption in Singapore*. Singapore, Department of Political Science, University of Singapore, *Occasional Paper* No. 34.

Quah, J. S. T. (1979) Police corruption in Singapore: An analysis of its forms, extent and causes. *Singapore Police Journal* **10**(1) (January): 7–43.

Quah, J. S. T. (1982) Bureaucratic corruption in the ASEAN countries: A comparative analysis of their anti-corruption strategies. *Journal of Southeast Asian Studies* **13**(1) (March): 163–77.

Quah, J. S. T. (1989) "Singapore's experience in curbing corruption," in A. J. Heidenheimer, M. Johnston and V. T. LeVine (eds.), *Political Corruption: A Handbook*, New Brunswick: Transaction Publishers, 841–53.

Quah, J. S. T. (1995) Controlling corruption in city-states: A comparative study of Hong Kong and Singapore. *Crime, Law and Social Change* **22**: 391–414.

Quah, J. S. T. (1999) Singapore's anti-corruption strategy: Some lessons for South Korea. *Korean Corruption Studies Review* **4** (December): 173–93.

Quah, J. S. T. (2000) "Accountability and anti-corruption agencies in the Asia-Pacific Region," in *Combating Corruption in Asian and Pacific Economies*, Manila: Asian Development Bank, 101–24.

Republic of Singapore (1983) *Economic and Social Statistics Singapore 1960–1982*. Singapore, Department of Statistics.

Republic of Singapore (1987) *Report of the Commission of Inquiry on Investigations Concerning the Late Mr Teh Cheang Wan*. Singapore, Singapore National Printers.

Republic of Singapore (1989) *Government Gazette Acts Supplement*. No. 13. Singapore, Singapore National Printers.

Republic of Singapore (2001) *The Budget for the Financial Year 2001/2002*. Cmd. 3 of 2001. Singapore, Ministry of Finance.

Richardson, M. (2000) Fighting graft brings a net advantage, survey says. *International Herald Tribune* March 23: 16.

Sayre, W. S. (1967) "Bureaucracies: Some contrasts in systems," in Nimrod Raphaeli (ed.), *Readings in Comparative Public Administration*, Boston: Allyn and Bacon, 341–54.

Seah, C. M. (1971) *Bureaucratic Evolution and Political Change in an Emerging Nation: A Case Study of Singapore*. Ph.D. thesis, Faculty of Economic and Social Studies, Victoria University of Manchester.

State of Singapore (1960) *Legislative Assembly Debates*. First Session of the First Legislative Assembly. Vol. 12. Singapore: Government Printing Office, 13 February.

Tan, A. L. (1999) "The experience of Singapore in combating corruption," in Rick Stapenhurst and Sahr J. Kpundeh (eds.), *Curbing Corruption: Towards a Model for Building National Integrity*, Washington, D.C.: The World Bank, 59–66.

Then, Y. T. (1998) "The national wages council and the wage system in Singapore," in Lim Chong Yah and Rosalind Chew (eds.), *Wages and Wages Policies: Tripartism in Singapore*. Singapore: World Scientific Publishing Company, 219–29.

Timberman, D. G. (1991) *A Changeless Land: Continuity and Change in Philippine Politics*. Singapore: Institute of Southeast Asian Studies.

United Nations Development Programme (1999) *Fighting Corruption to Improve Governance*, New York: UNDP.

Varela, A. P. (1995) "Different faces of Filipino administrative culture," in D. Proserpina Tapales and N. N. Pilar (eds.), *Public Administration by the Year 2000: Looking Back into the Future*. Quezon City, College of Public Administration: University of the Philippines, 161–77.

Woodrow, W. (1978) "The Study of Administration," in Jay M. Shafritz and Hyde Albert C. (eds.), *Classics of Public Administration*, Oak Park: Moore Publishing Company, 3–17.

Wong, J. K. H. (1981) "The ICAC and its anti-corruption measures," in P. L. Rance, Lee (ed.), *Corruption and Its Control in Hong Kong*, Hong Kong: The Chinese University Press, 45–72.

Yoong, Siew Wah (1973) Some aspects of corruption. *National Youth Leadership Training Institute Journal* January: 54–9.

11
A Human Resource Development Program to Foster Individual Moral Development in Indian Corporations: Aligning Corporate Governance with Natural Law

Dennis Heaton, Thomas Carlisle and Ian Brown

Introduction

The problem of corruption can be approached from each of three sets of factors that influence ethical behavior in organizations – individual characteristics, organizational factors, and opportunity. This paper emphasizes individual characteristics – in particular, development of the consciousness of the individual, including the individual's level of moral development. We review these stages of moral development, as identified by psychological research. At pre-conventional stages individuals are tempted by opportunities for personal gain. In conventional stages, individuals may go along with corruption to fit in with the norms of their social group. At post-conventional stages individuals have the independence of character to resist corruption and to act according to what they hold to be universal principles of right and wrong. We describe a highest state of moral development – a natural law orientation – in which individuals spontaneously act to promote the general good. Natural-Law Based Management is presented as an approach that employs techniques to cultivate individual development in the direction of a natural law orientation. The Maharishi Corporate Development Program has applied this approach in numerous corporate settings in India and around the world to improve the overall effectiveness, well-being, and right action of managers and employees.

Addressing the problem of corruption

Corruption in India takes on five forms:

1. criminal corruption, that which is legally punishable;
2. legalized corruption, laws to benefit those who make and then justify them;
3. market corruption, including the extreme example of the black market;
4. emotional corruption, with the misuse of trust under the defense *of caveat emptor* in the market place; and
5. patronage corruption, the institutionalization or long-term entrenchment of corrupt practices.

Why does corruption, in its various forms, exist? What can be done to curb it? Pride and Ferrell's (2000: 92–5) model of three factors influencing ethical behavior in organizations is one framework for conceptualization of the problem and for possible interventions. The three factors are social influences within the organization, opportunities for unethical behavior, and individual factors (Figure 11.1).

Anti-corruption programs primarily address the issues of opportunities and social influences. For example, new government policies seek to eliminate incentives and opportunities for corruption by increasing financial transparency, ending tax deductibility for bribes, curtailing money laundering, and cleaning up public procurement practices (OECD, 2001).

In our view, a focus on individual factors is fundamental to and essential for substantial progress in reducing and preventing corruption – since behavior is an expression of an individual's inner development.

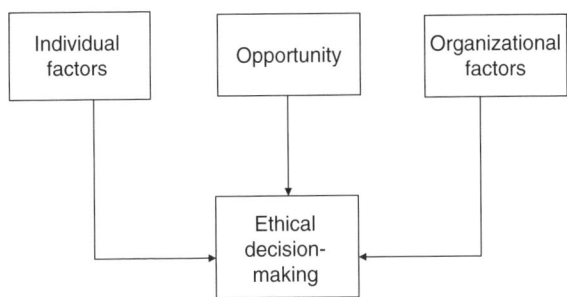

Figure 11.1 Factors that influence ethical decision-making in organizations

To paraphrase the famous axiom on war from the United Nations' Charter, "Corruption begins in the minds of men." Unless there is inner change of individuals, the values and behaviors upheld by the informal organization are not likely to change. The cultivation of high moral development in individuals will be expressed into the social environments through the influence of developed individuals.

Stages of moral development

Developmental psychologists observe that moral development is one aspect of the holistic cognitive and affective maturation that individuals undergo throughout their life span (Alexander and Langer, 1990). Kohlberg and Ryncarz (1990) have identified stages of moral development which progress from morality based on punishment and obedience (pre-conventional level), to morality based on mutual expectations and conformity (conventional level), to principled moral reasoning (post-conventional level). In addition, they theorize about a still more mature stage of human development in which morality is based on a natural law orientation, a stage in which "we identify ourselves with the cosmic or infinite perspective and value life from its standpoint" (Kohlberg and Ryncarz, 1990: 192). One who is developed to the natural law orientation, would spontaneously act to promote the general good. Kohlberg and Ryncarz find evidence of the natural law orientation in Western thinkers including Spinoza, Socrates, Marcus Aurelius, Aquinas, and Martin Luther King, Jr. They associate this orientation with mystical experiences in which the individual identifies with the whole of nature.

Less mature stages of development are generally observed in younger children. Yet, even among adults, a variety of development positions are observed, and very few individuals are found at the highest levels of development. Evidence indicates that most adults do not progress to post-conventional levels. Of the two large surveys of adults of various ages, only 2–3 percent of adults scored at or above the Autonomous level of personality development, as measured by Loevinger's projective test (Loevinger and Wessler, 1970, $N = 1640$; Cook-Greuter, 1990, $N = 1996$). On Kohlberg's interview measure about one-eighth of US males in their thirties scored at Kohlberg's post-conventional stages 5 and 6, or at the transitional stage 4/5 (Colby and Kohlberg, 1987: 101).

This research from developmental psychology is significant to the phenomenon of corruption. To have the independence of character to act according to what one holds to be universal principles of right and wrong, regardless of potentially corrupting influences of their social surroundings, requires post-conventional development. Conventional individuals may go along with corruption to fit in with the norms of their social group; the majority of individuals will go along with what peers and co-workers do or what they perceive the organization wants them to do (Ferrell *et al.*, 2000). Individuals at pre-conventional stages of moral development, by nature, will be tempted toward corruption by opportunities for personal gain.

If it were possible to promote psychological development in individuals, then organizations and society as a whole could intervene to promote ethical behavior by stressing the individual factor. Let us now consider evidence of a human resource development program – the Transcendental Meditation program – that has had success in promoting individual transformation in the direction of higher stages of holistic development, including moral development.

A human resource development program to promote moral development

The Transcendental Meditation® (TM®) is said to be easy to learn and to require no change in life-style or beliefs (Roth, 1987). It is normally practiced for 20 minutes twice daily sitting quietly with the eyes closed. The technique directs attention to experience progressively deeper and finer levels of thinking until thought is completely transcended in the state of Transcendental Consciousness – "a state of inner wakefulness with no object of thought or perception, just pure consciousness aware of its own unbounded nature" (Maharishi Mahesh Yogi, 1976: 123).

Over five hundred prior studies have found evidence of distinct effects during the practice of the TM technique, as well as long-term psychological and physiological benefits from the practice. Research on physiological markers of self-reported episodes of Transcendental Consciousness during the TM practice has found evidence of decreased skin conductance, reduction in volume and rate of respiration, and EEG (brainwave) changes (Farrow and Hebert, 1982; Travis and Wallace, 1997). Further, there is an increased ability to maintain restful alertness during activity (Dillbeck and Orme-Johnson, 1987), reduced anxiety (Eppley *et al.*, 1989), increased creativity (Travis, 1979), improvements on intelligence tests (So and Orme-Johnson, 2001). Even improved cardiovascular health (Schneider *et al.*, 1995; Castillo-Richmond *et al.*, 2000), and reduced health care expenditures (Orme-Johnson, 1987; Orme-Johnson and Herron, 1997; Herron *et al.*, 1996).

The impacts of the Transcendental Meditation technique on people in business settings around the world have been reviewed by Schmidt-Wilk *et al.* (1996). Findings include enhanced employee effectiveness, job satisfaction, and work/personal relationships (Alexander *et al.*, 1993), reduced symptoms of ill health (Haratani and Henmi, 1990), and enhanced vitality, psychological well-being and organizational contribution (DeArmond, 1996), reduced absenteeism and improved company productivity (Schmidt-Wilk *et al.*, 1996).

Executives report that they grow in mental clarity and alertness – the ability to focus on the details and, at the same time maintain broad comprehension. An investigation in Sweden found that a group of meditating managers grew in holistic thinking and became more aware of the important issues facing the company (Gustavsson, 1992: 31). Herriott *et al.* (2001) reported a qualitative study of business people who had practiced the Transcendental Meditation technique for more than 20 years. The subjects reported an increasing inner sense of being anchored to an inner, spiritual core – and experiences of awareness of inner and outer wholeness – expressed in more universal values that embraced the wider interests of the community and environment.

If corruption is an expression of narrow, self-interested awareness, then findings suggest that the Maharishi Corporate Development Program, which teaches the TM technique in business settings, may counter corruption by cultivating a more holistic vision in executives and employees. Specific evidence of the impact of TM on moral development, and other dimension of personality growth, are reviewed next.

Impacts of the TM program on moral development

Why might such a practice be considered a possible intervention to promote moral development toward the post-conventional and natural law orientations? The Transcendental Meditation technique facilitates experience of deeper intrinsic levels of the mind and of Transcendental Consciousness, the "I" or subject of experience. This experience brings about a shift in the frame of reference of the individual to a more inner-directed orientation in which the individual begins to experience ideals and values as coming from "inside," for example, as intuition, instead of orienting to rules and norms that are "outside" of oneself.

Moreover, the TM program is described as leading to the highest levels of human development, at which administrators can achieve "administration as problem-free, ever-progressive, and ever-evolutionary as the administration of the universe through Natural Law" (Maharishi Mahesh

Yogi, 1995: 8). The Transcendental Meditation technique is said to gradually attune individual psychology with the wholeness of "Natural Law" – "that infinite organizing power that sustains the existence of everything in the universe, automatically maintaining the well-coordinated relationship of everything with everything else" (Maharishi Mahesh Yogi, 1995: 8). The application of this approach to human development has been offered as a solution to the problem of corruption in India and other countries (Maharishi Mahesh Yogi Vishwavidyalaya, 1997; Brown, 2000).

A number of research studies provide evidence that the twice-daily practice of this technique does, over time, bring about developmental changes that are not otherwise observed in adult subjects. Alexander and Orme-Johnson (in press) report that prisoners practicing the TM technique underwent a three-stage advancement in moral reasoning, using Kohlberg's instrument. These prisoners basically went from reasoning, "Do what you want to do, but don't get caught," to "I guess I shouldn't do that to him, since I don't want him to do that to me." Regular meditators also decreased significantly in aggression, schizophrenia, and trait-anxiety, compared to controls (Alexander *et al.*, in press). No longitudinal changes were found in other treatment groups or demographically similar controls wait-listed to learn the TM technique. The behavioral consequences of these personality changes are that prisoners who learn the TM technique have 33 to 43 percent lower recidivism rates, or rates of return to prison, than other prisoners (Alexander *et al.*, in press; Rainforth *et al.*, in press).

In a cross-sectional study on the TM program and moral development in college students, Nidich (1975) found that TM practitioners scored higher than students who had not learned the TM program. Also, longer-term meditators scored higher than short-term practitioners, and that there were no differences between non-meditators who were interested in starting the practice and other non-meditating students.

Chandler *et al.* (2001) explored the effects of the Transcendental Meditation (TM) technique on self development as measured by Loevinger's Washington University Sentence Completion Test of ego development, McAdams' measure of intimacy motivation, and Rest's measure of principled moral reasoning. A ten-year longitudinal data indicated that TM subjects increased markedly in ego development in contrast to three control groups matched for gender and age over the same time period ($N = 136$, $p = .0000004$). At post-test 38 percent ($N = 34$) scored at or beyond the post-conventional Autonomous level versus 1 percent of controls ($p < .0001$). TM subjects also increased to very high levels of principled moral reasoning ($p = .002$) and intimacy ($p = .02$).

Nidich *et al.* (forthcoming) have presented evidence associating transcendental experiences during the TM technique with expressions of a natural law moral orientation, as conceived by Kohlberg and Ryncarz (1990). Such findings are consistent with the theory of Natural-Law Based Management, which calls for bringing individuals into alignment with natural law through systematic experience of the transcendental Unified Field of Natural Law (Harung *et al.*, 1999).

The theory of natural-law based management

Corruption is not just the breaking of man-made law; it is even more fundamentally the breaking of natural law. Natural law is commonly understood to be the orderly principles, generally expressed mathematically, which are at the basis of the consistent patterns of behavior observed in the universe (Carlisle, 2001). In philosophy, natural law has been spoken of as eternal and unchanging moral principles common to all people by virtue of their nature as human beings.

Management writer Stephen Covey (1991) has argued that natural laws are not invented by humans, but are the laws of the universe, a part of human consciousness. Other visionary management writers encourage executives to consider the beautiful order and dynamic growth that nature displays – in its management of the universe – as a model for their organizations. Some current management writers also expound a natural law – "a natural law perspective." Ray writes of a new paradigm of business based on "wholeness and connectedness" and "doing business from our most profound inner awareness and in connection with the consciousness of others and the earth" (Ray, 1993: 4–5). Wheatley (1992) has explored the management implications of new scientific theories of the self-evolving order interconnecting everything in nature. Hagelin (1998) presents a quantum physicist's perspective that the unified field and pure consciousness are identical. He further argues that the holistic intelligence of the most basic level of nature can be harnessed in the administration of human institutions by promoting the experience of Transcendental Consciousness. These authors argue that by enlivening the deepest level of consciousness within us, the administration of business and government can be the flow of that natural order through us, rather than an imposition of our dominion over nature. Such writers share an understanding that the laws that structure the universe need to be incorporated into the principles that govern business and public administration (Carlisle, 2001).

Maharishi Mahesh Yogi (1995) defines Natural Law as that invincible force that maintains the existence, integration, and evolution of everything. He articulates the traditional Vedic understanding that by bringing individual awareness to the level of pure, transcendental consciousness, one can become spontaneously aligned with natural law and thereby can achieve the most holistic success:

> When Transcendental Consciousness is fully enlivened in individual awareness and physiology, individual intelligence is spontaneously aligned with Cosmic Intelligence and life is lived in harmony with Natural Law. Individuals cease creating mistakes and violating Natural Law. (Maharishi Mahesh Yogi, Maharishi Mahesh Yogi Vishwavidyalaya, 1997: 40)

Success of administration depends on success of education. For administration to be free from corruption, education must be capable of cultivating wisdom. While modern education has contributed to material progress, the objective approach of knowledge has also led to many shortcomings, including growing stress and health problems, anti-social behavior, and environmental degradation. A subjective approach of awakening to natural law within is required to counterbalance the weaknesses of modern education, and create a foundation for eliminating corruption.

Conclusion

In their analysis of business ethics, Pride and Ferrell (2000: 92–5) posit that ethical or unethical behavior is influenced by three factors: social influences within the organization, opportunities for unethical behavior, and individual characteristics. On the other hand, the anti-corruption programs primarily address the issues of opportunities and social influences. Herein the focus of this paper has been on the individual factor. In our view, the individual approach is fundamental to any attempt to change ethical behavior through social influences because the influence of leaders and peers in one's social environment can only be an expression of the individual development of each of them. If there is no inner change of individuals, then the values and behaviors that they uphold through the informal organization will not change, despite pious policies and resolutions that may be pronounced in their organizations.

Similarly, we feel, enforcement programs to reduce opportunity for corruption can never be fully effective unless the individuals are growing in the ability to spontaneously act in accord with national law and natural law. When discussing reform on the national level, Maharishi Mahesh Yogi commented, "Any number of laws can be enacted, but they will remain on paper and the people in charge will do what they will – corruption and crime all motivated to gain money" (ibid, 1998: 6).

The approach of developing individual consciousness through the TM technique is not about making laws, but it is an approach through which the purpose of law can be achieved by enlivening the full potential of natural law latent in everyone. The findings from studies in psychology and education provide evidence that the Transcendental Meditation program systematically develops individuals toward more autonomous personality, principled moral reasoning, and personal caring. Individuals with pre-conventional moral development may exploit opportunities to obtain personal gain, and conventional individuals may go along with the prevailing practices among their peers. However, post-conventional individuals gain their bearings from an inner sense of right and wrong – from an attunement of their consciousness to the natural law that is lively in their physiologies and in the cosmos.

This notion that spontaneous right behavior is possible by aligning the individual awareness with the Cosmic Intelligence of Natural Law is a central tenet of India's ancient Vedic tradition. Indeed, the key to moral and cultural integrity in India, and effective management in general, may well be found in reestablishing its own spiritual roots. Otherwise, the practice of management in India will be distorted and dominated by foreign management systems (Maharishi's Programmes in India, 2001a).

Evidence suggests that the Transcendental Meditation programs have been well received in Indian companies. The utilization of the TM technique in Indian corporations is mentioned in press articles published in India, such as *Businessworld* (1995) and *Economic Times of India* (Kumar, 1997). The Maharishi Corporate Development Program in India (Maharishi's Programmes in India, 2001b) reports that Transcendental Meditation has been taught to 20 000 managers and employees of Tata Tea and 6000 of Tata Chemicals. Other companies who have implemented programs include Associated Cement, Indian Aluminum, Reckitt & Colman, Oriental Bank of Commerce, SRF, Eveready, Tata Unisys, BHEL, Jindal Polyester, Indian Petro Chemicals Ltd., Anand Group, DCM Shriram, Finolex, Hewlett Packard India, DCM Financial Services, Indian Sugar and General Engineering Corporation, SWIL, Williamson Magor and Co., Kribhco, and South India Research Institute Ltd. This program, which is described as something that "comes naturally to the people of India" (Dr. B. K. Modi, Chairman and President of ModiCorp, quoted in

Maharishi's Programmes in India, 2001c), may provide India with a solution to the problem of corruption from its own tradition of developing higher consciousness.

Note

® Transcendental Meditation, TM, and TM-Sidhi are registered trademarks licensed to Maharishi Vedic Education Development Corporation and used under sublicense.

References

Alexander, C. N., Heaton, D. P. and Chandler, H. M. (1994) "Advanced human development in the Vedic Psychology of Maharishi Mahesh Yogi: Theory and research," in M. Miller and S. Cook-Greuter (eds), *Transcendence and Mature Thought in Adulthood*. Lanham, MD: Rowman and Littlefield.

Alexander, C. N. and Langer, E. J. (eds) (1990) *Higher Stages of Human Development: Perspectives on Adult Growth*, New York: Oxford University Press.

Alexander, C. N. and Orme-Johnson, D. W. (in press) Walpole study of the TM program in maximum security prisoners II: Longitudinal study of development and psychopathology. *Journal of Offender Rehabilitation*.

Alexander, C. N., Rainforth, M. V., Grant, J. D., von Stade, C. and Walton, K. G. (in press) Walpole study of the TM Program in maximum security prisoners III: reduced recidivism. *Journal of Offender Rehabilitation*.

Alexander, C. N., Swanson, G. C., Rainforth, M. V., Carlisle, T. W., Todd, C. C. and Oates, R. (1993) Effects of the Transcendental Meditation program on stress-reduction, health, and employee development: A prospective study in two occupational settings. *Anxiety, Stress, and Coping* 6: 245–62.

Alexander, C. N., Walton, K. G. and Goodman, R. S. (in press) Walpole study of the TM program in maximum security prisoners I: Cross-sectional differences in development and psychopathology. *Journal of Offender Rehabilitation*.

Brown, I. (2000) "Natural law-based corporate governance," in P. Asthana (ed.), *Corporate Excellence through Corporate Governance: Background Papers, Presentations & Proceedings*. ICSI-Centre for Corporate Research and Training, CBD-Belapur: Navi Mumbai, December.

Businessworld (1995) Meditation is the new mantra. October: 4–17.

Carlisle, T. (2001) *Maharishi Corporate Development Program: Natural Law-Based Management*. Mult-media presentation. Fairfield, Iowa: Maharishi University of Management.

Castillo-Richmond, A. B., Schneider, R. H., Alexander, C. N., Cook, R., Myers, H., Nidich, S., Haney, C., Rainforth, M. and Salerno, J. (2000) Effects of stress reduction on carotid atherosclerosis in hypertensive African Americans: A pilot trial. *Stroke* **31**: 568–73.

Colby, A. and Kohlberg, L. (1987) *The Measurement of Moral Judgment*. New York: Cambridge University Press.

Cook-Greuter, S. R. (1990) "Maps for living: Ego development theory from symbiosis to conscious universal embeddedness," in M. L. Commons, C. Armon et al. (eds), *Adult development: Models and methods in the study of adolescent and adult thought* 2: 79–104. New York: Praeger.
Covey, S. R. (1991) *Principle-Centered Leadership*. New York: Summit Books.
DeArmond, D. L. (1996) *Effects of the Transcendental Meditation Program on Psychological, Physiological, Behavioral and Organizational Consequences of Stress in Managers and Executives*. Doctoral Dissertation Maharishi University of Management. Dissertation Abstracts International.
Dillbeck, M. C. and Orme-Johnson, D. W. (1987) Physiological differences between Transcendental Meditation and rest. *American Psychologist* 42: 879–81.
Eppley, K. R., Abrams, A. I. and Shear, J. (1989) Differential effects of relaxation techniques on trait anxiety: A meta-analysis. *Journal of Clinical Psychology* 45: 957–74.
Farrow, J. T. and Hebert, J. R. (1982) Breath suspension during the Transcendental Meditation technique. *Psychosomatic Medicine* 44: 133–53.
Ferrell, O. C., Fraedrich, J. and Ferrell, L. (2000) *Business Ethics*, Boston: Houghton Mifflin.
Gustavsson, B. (1992) *The Transcendent Organization*. Doctoral Dissertation, Stockholm, Sweden: University of Stockholm, Department of Business Administration.
Hagelin, J. S. (1998) *A manual for a perfect government*, Fairfield, Iowa: Maharishi University of Management Press.
Haratani, T. and Henmi, T. (1990) Effects of Transcendental Meditation (TM) on health behavior of industrial workers. *Japanese Journal of Public Health* 37: 729.
Harung, H. S., Alexander, C. N. and Heaton, D. (1999) Evolution of organizations in the new millennium. *Leadership and Organization Development Journal* 20(3): 198–206.
Herriott, E., Schmidt-Wilk, J. and Heaton, D. (2001) *Spiritual dimensions of entrepreneurship in long term practitioners of the Transcendental Meditation and TM-Sidhi Program. Academy of Management Annual Meeting*, Washington, DC.
Herron, R. E., Hillis, S. L., Mandarino, J. V., Orme-Johnson, D. W. and Walton, K. G. (1996) Reducing medical costs: The impact of the Transcendental Meditation program on government payments to physicians in Quebec. *American Journal of Health Promotion* 10(3): 206–16.
Kohlberg, L. and Ryncarz, R. (1990) "Beyond justice reasoning: Moral development and consideration of a seventh stage," in C. N. Alexander and E. J. Langer (eds), *Higher Stages of Human Development*, New York: Oxford University Press.
Kumar, M. (1997) Yogi's corporate mantra *The Economic Times of India*, September 25.
Loevinger, J. and Wessler, R. (1970) *Measuring Ego Development 1: Construction and Use of a Sentence Completion Test*, San Francisco: Jossey-Bass.
Maharishi Mahesh Yogi (1976) *Creating an Ideal Society: A Global Undertaking*, West Germany: MERU Press.
Maharishi Mahesh Yogi (1995) *Maharishi University of Management: Wholeness on the Move*, Vlodrop: Maharishi Vedic University Press.
Maharishi Mahesh Yogi (1998) *Celebrating Perfection in Administration: Creating Invincible India*, India, Age of Enlightenment Publications.
Maharishi Mahesh Yogi Vishwavidyalaya (1997) *Constitution of India Fulfilled through Maharishi's Transcendental Meditation*, India: Age of Enlightenment Publications.

Maharishi's Programmes in India (2001a) Vedic Management. HYPERLINK http://www.maharishi-india.org/programmes/p8/vedic_management.html (September 20, 2001).
Maharishi's Programmes in India (2001b) Case Studies. HYPERLINK http://www.maharishi-india.org/programmes/p8/case_studies.html (September 20, 2001).
Maharishi's Programmes in India (2001c). Reports from Executives. HYPERLINK http://www.maharishi-india.org/programmes/p8/executives.html (September 20, 2001).
Nidich, R. J., Nidich, S. I. and Alexander, C. N. (forthcoming) Moral development and natural law. *Journal of Social Behavior and Personality*.
Nidich, S. I. (1975) *A study of the relationship of the Transcendental Meditation program to Kohlberg's stages of moral reasoning* (Doctoral dissertation, University of Cincinnati). Dissertation Abstracts International, 36: 4361A–4362A.
OECD (2001) No Longer Business As Usual: Fighting Bribery and Corruption. Paris: Organization for Economic Cooperation and Development.
Orme-Johnson, D. W. (1987) Medical care utilization and the Transcendental Meditation program. *Psychosomatic Medicine* **49**: 493–507.
Orme-Johnson, D. W. and Herron, R. (1997) An innovative approach to reducing medical care utilization and expenditures. *American Journal of Managed Care* **3**(1): 135–44.
Pride, W. M. and Ferrell, O. C. (2000) *Marketing: Concepts and Strategies*, Boston: Houghton Mifflin.
Ray, M. L. (1993) "Introduction," in M. Ray and A. Renzler (eds), *The new paradigm in business: Emerging strategies for leadership and organizational change*. Los Angeles. Jeremy P Tarches/Pergee.
Rainforth, M. V., Alexander, C. N. and Cavanaugh, K. L. (in press) Effects of the Transcendental Meditation Program on Recidivism Among Former Inmates of Folsom Prison: Survival Analysis of 15-Year Follow-Up Data. *Journal of Offender Rehabilitation*.
Roth, R. (1987) *Transcendental Meditation*, New York: Donald I. Fine.
Schmidt-Wilk, J., Alexander, C. N. and Swanson, G. C. (1996) Developing consciousness in organizations: The Transcendental Meditation program in business. *Journal of Business and Psychology* **10**(4): 429–44.
Schneider, R. H., Staggers, F., Alexander, C. N., Sheppard, W., Rainforth, M. V., Kondwani, K., Smith, S. and King, C. G. (1995) A randomized controlled trial of stress reduction for hypertension in older African Americans. *Hypertension* **26**(5): 820–7.
So, K.-T. and Orme-Johnson, D. W. (2001) Three randomized experiments on the holistic longitudinal effects of the Transcendental Meditation technique on cognition. *Intelligence* **29**(5): 419–40.
Travis, F. (1979) Creative thinking and the Transcendental Meditation technique. *The Journal of Creative Behavior* **13**(3): 169–80.
Travis, F. and Wallace, R. K. (1997) Autonomic patterns during respiratory suspensions: Possible markers of Transcendental Consciousness. *Psychophysiology* **34**: 39–46.
Wheatley, M. J. (1992) *Leadership and the New Science: Learning About Organization from an Orderly Universe*, San Francisco: Berrett-Koehler.

12
Corruption in Asia – A Bottom-up Approach to its Resolution
Paul Robins

Introduction

It is decided that the moral status of an organization is to be improved. That is to say that management procedures and decisions will be implemented to ensure that corruption and bad practice no longer feature in the organization or are a likely possibility. How is this to be achieved? What guidance is there for making the change? How do you manage the moral development of an organization? These question are not easy to answer and are the focus of this paper.

Traditional moral theory should help but there are problems in applying moral theory to business practice as suggested by Derry and Green (1989) who complained of 'a serious lack of clarity about how to apply the theories to cases and a persistent unwillingness to grapple with tensions between theories of ethical reasoning'. Other critics of a philosophy-dominated approach include Brady and Logsdon (1988) and Taket (1994) who criticize mainstream ethical theory as being too idealistic and pointed to the work of feminist and/or non-Western philosophers who offer useful alternative avenues for exploration. This is one of the reasons for investigating an Eastern tradition, that of Buddhism, in this paper.

In order to overcome the identified shortcomings, some writers have chosen to move away from a single theory by, either combining a number of theories into a single model, or developing a methodology for selecting between different theories according to circumstances. These models, however, have tended to be of limited practical value. In his review of several such models, Howes (1993) concludes that up to now they have either tended to be overly pragmatic and not well founded in theory, or overly descriptive thus unsuited to providing practical guidance.

In an attempt to overcome many of these difficulties the work reported here is based on an analysis of the Buddhist spiritual tradition as an alternative to Western philosophy. Buddhism is an example of an ancient and trusted tradition that places particular emphasis on the practical issues of living a moral life. It provides a source of well-founded guidance for both the individual and the organization wishing to become more moral, without being dependent on the acceptance of a particular theistic or philosophical dogma. It should therefore be possible to extract useful and practical guidelines for organizations of whatever kind. The following analysis seeks to understand the Eastern perspective although escaping from Western thought patterns is hardly complete. It is intended to offer useful guidance for those with a Western background but it may also help to focus the minds of those with an Eastern background whose working environment has come to be influenced, if not dominated, by Western customs and practice.

Pre-requisites for managing moral improvement

There are two basic management requirements of an organization wishing to manage moral development. The first is an ability to determine, at any chosen moment, its moral status, which it will wish to be able to compare with earlier assessments and targets that may have been set. The second is an ability to use status knowledge to select and implement changes that will result in an improved moral status in the future. In practice, this may also involve setting target values which will need to be practical (i.e. they must be demonstrable by measurement) and they must be related to planned actions. Targets by themselves have limited managerial use.

This study examines these two issues and outlines the basis of a practical guide for the assessment of moral status and identifies processes that may be introduced or modified in order to stimulate the moral development of an organization. The analysis is based on an examination of the Buddhist view of moral growth. Moral hierarchies based on an interpretation of the principles of Buddhism are formulated for individuals and organizations or groups. These enable moral assessments to be made and provide guidance on the kinds of actions that may be employed or required for an individual or organization to improve their moral status.

A key design element of this approach is that it should avoid ex-cathedra statements of what is good and what is bad, either as an activity or a status. For any guidance to work in many parts of the world it is essential that it is not merely an expression of a particular culture or school of thought as this could easily lead to conflicts with the basic traditions of minority groups. This is a considerable challenge, but one that it is thought that the characteristics of Buddhism make a practical possibility.

The value of a Buddhist approach

The key aspect of the Buddhist approach to morality that gives rise to the sought-after qualities is the central role that motivation and understanding has in the tradition. The actions of a person are traditionally described as being of two kinds, 'skillful', and 'unskillful'. Unskillful actions are defined as being rooted in the negative mental states of greed, hatred and mental ignorance; and skillful actions as being motivated by the opposite qualities of generosity, compassion and mental clarity. The quality of an action is therefore dependent on the interaction of motivation or intention and knowledge or understanding of the world, or in Buddhist terms, Enlightenment.

Terms such as 'good' and 'bad', 'right' and 'wrong', have no absolute meaning in Buddhism. This highlights the difference between morality based on insight (the Buddhist view) and that based on the Western tradition, which is typically based on rules or power. Morality based on rules or power is determined by those with the power to make the rules, whether founded on the commandments of God, or on the laws of a ruling elite (who in some cases may claim God's authority). Morality based on Insight in the Buddhist sense is based on an understanding that sees everything in the universe as interdependent and recognizes the aspirations and needs of all the inhabitants of the universe.

It is impossible to do full justice to the Buddhist tradition in a short space and the above is a brief outline of some aspects of it. A more detailed treatment of Buddhist cosmology and philosophy can be found in Howes (1993); furthermore one has to say that this chapter is written from the perspective of the authors' western agnostic viewpoint, seeking an understanding of the essential elements of Buddhism.

A hierarchy of individual moral development

Implicit in this view of morality is the existence of a continuum or hierarchy of moral states ranging from the very unskillful to the completely skillful. The notion that a person can move up the hierarchy by developing increasingly skillful mental states is accepted by all schools of

Buddhism although different schools may employ different languages to describe the process.

In earlier works (Howes, 1993; Howes and Robins, 1994) this hierarchy has been formalized into five discrete categories to provide the means of assessing the moral standing of an individual which enables these ideas to be applied to the modern Western individual. These five categories of the moral hierarchy may also be recognized as stages of development. They are

1 Egoistic or pre-moral stage
2 Conventional morality
3 Emerging individuality
4 Genuine altruism
5 Transcendental morality.

They are expressed in terms that are compatible with secular Western psychology and to some extent mirror the work of Maslow and Kohlberg although their theories fall short of the Buddhist view by not taking into account what might be called the transcendental dimension of moral development (Maslow, 1943; Kohlberg, 1981). Each category is viewed as a segment of the pathway to enlightenment and are further described in the following sections.

Stage 1. Egoistic or pre-moral stage
This is hardly a level of morality at all, but is a state where an action will be performed only where a reward is promised, or a punishment threatened. It is perhaps the stage of the infant or of animals where basic need satisfaction for food and shelter are the primary motivators.

Stage 2. Conventional morality
This is the stage of socialization where the norms and values of the group are key. Individual action becomes much less overtly egocentric, and is based much more on what is acceptable to significant others, such as parents, peer groups or teachers.

Stage 3. Emerging individuality
This is a stage of progressive autonomy, where a person starts to emerge from the milieu of (often unconsciously adopted) group norms. It is a stage of 'emerging individuality' where an individual begins to develop his or her own views and values. Increasingly, these may be independent of the need for group approval.

Stage 4. Genuine altruism
There comes a point where a genuine concern for the needs of others becomes at least equal to a concern for the fulfillment of one's own needs (but without denying such needs), and at this point it can be said that one has entered the stage of genuine altruism. As a person develops a stronger sense of self-worth, he or she becomes much less preoccupied with the fulfillment of limited egoistic needs and much more concerned with the greater good. It should be stressed that this stage of moral development is very difficult to reach, and cannot be judged by any propensity to do good acts.

Stage 5. Transcendental morality
This is the highest level of spiritual attainment in which a person has transcended human egoistic limitations altogether. He no longer perceives a difference between subject and object or givers and receivers. According to Buddhism, only rarely in human history has anybody achieved this. However, it is the existence of this possibility in an assessment scale, and having an end point that is important.

The morality of groups

The moral hierarchy or pathway is inevitably defined in terms of an individual's interaction with the world around him and most importantly the significant people or groups that he interacts with. As most of us spend a significant part of our adult lives at work the most significant group influences are provided by our companies and the work environment. It follows that the choice of company to work for is crucial for any individual wishing to live a more moral life. Similarly, where a company aspires to be more moral, its choice of employee has equal importance.

Linking Buddhist ideas about the moral nature of groups with an analysis similar to that described above has enabled a formalization of a moral hierarchy for organizations. It yields a five part typology and is as follows:

1 Egoistic-elite group – the non-group
2 Coercive group
3 Contractual group
4 Co-operative group
5 Spiritual community.

The basis of this hierarchy is described in the following section.

Basis of group morality

As might be expected the Buddhist tradition supports the view that collective moral growth (which presupposes some form of collective moral hierarchy) and individual moral growth go hand in hand. An important aspect in this context is the commitment to the Spiritual Community of individuals who follow the teachings of the Buddha and who have either attained, or aspire to, Enlightenment. This commitment is supported in three principle ways:

1. Material and spiritual support: This is a commitment to collectively provide support to group members to help them to create positive conditions for individual growth.
2. Maintaining a strong altruistic focus: This is viewed as a commitment to anything that stresses the trans-personal nature of spiritual practice and thus counters the tendency towards spiritual individualism. It supports and encourages individuals to develop the ability to transcend their limited selfish needs.
3. Encouraging personal responsibility: As well as encouraging self-transcendence, support is given to less developed members to help them develop their individuality by overcoming significant group conditioning. In practice, this means encouraging individual thought and action to overcome conditioned behavior.

A hierarchy of group moral development

In the best of groups all of these aspects of group morality are assembled together, thereby providing the greatest possible support for the moral development of its individuals. In groups where none of this support is found individuals develop in spite of the group rather than being supported and encouraged by it. A moral hierarchy based on these aspirational ideas is particularly important for providing guidance and advice about how the moral standing of an organization may be assessed and improved. The natures of the five groups in the hierarchy (listed earlier) are elaborated below.

1. Egoistic-Elite Group: the non-group
The Egoistic-Elite Group is the equivalent of the Egoistic or Pre-moral stage in the individual moral hierarchy, and is a group where one or a small number of people (an elite) enjoys absolute power. The concerns and goals of the group are those of the elite. This is not, therefore, truly a group at all. This type of group is (arguably) quite rare in today's fairly

open and democratic Western society, although, in those parts of the world where dictatorship prevails, it may well be the norm.

2. Coercive Group

As in the previous group, the Coercive Group is dominated by a powerful elite, but without absolute power. The elite of this group must, therefore, resort to other means of getting its own way. In extreme cases, actual physical violence may be used or some other form of manipulation. This type of group is not a rare occurrence. For example, it is common among nuclear families to function as a coercive group with the abuse and violent treatment of one family member by another being commonplace. Likewise, in many work groups a coercive mentality prevails as with the Japanese *Sokaiya*, for instance.

3. Contractual Group

In the Contractual Group there is recognition that a degree of formal co-operation may provide the best mechanism for achieving the purposes of the elite. Here a degree of fair play will be evident, with efforts being made to clarify the expectations that the group has towards its individual members and also the benefits that each member might expect in return. Typically, at this level of group morality a legalistic rule-based ethos dominates.

4. Co-operative Group

There is no dominating elite in the Co-operative Group. Instead there is emphasis on a shared (rather than imposed) world-view. Responsibility for decision-making, whilst still tending to be taken by its stronger members is more widely dispersed with every member being encouraged to participate fully in this process. The growth and development of individuals is a primary concern of the group. Its ethos is one of facilitating and encouraging so that everybody develops a sense of responsibility and concern for the welfare of others, whether strong or weak, influential or not.

5. Spiritual Community

In the Spiritual Community individual goals are essentially those of the group. The use of the term 'community' here rather than 'group' is significant. It emphasizes the move away from satisfying the goals or aspirations of an elite to the maintenance of a particular set of group norms. The boundaries of the group have in essence expanded to include those not formally members of the group. Co-operation and collective responsibility are the prime characteristics of this group; and any form of coercion becomes an anathema. At its best the Spiritual Community follows the principle of 'give what you can, take what you need'. While the group in functioning in the real world may require leadership, each group member is encouraged to contribute to that role.

The moral characteristics of business groups

In general terms, moving upwards through the five categories is seen as an increasing tendency to support members developing an ability to act skillfully. The hierarchy is reviewed below in terms of three principle characteristics that can easily be related to the nature of business organizations:

1 the group's aims and objectives;
2 the distribution of power and responsibility;
3 the extent to which the group actively encourages individual growth.

1. The group's aims and objectives
A considerable gulf exists between the way that aims and objectives are determined in groups at each end of the hierarchy. The Egoistic-Elite Group has no interest in the concerns of anyone outside its elite, whereas the Spiritual Community is wholly concerned with the welfare of others. The aims and objectives of the Egoistic-Elite Group are likely to be heavily influenced by

(a) greed, a concern for maximizing group profit (pecuniary or otherwise), selfish pleasure and power,
(b) hatred, a concern for minimizing the influence of all that gets in the way of the group's profit, pleasure and power and
(c) delusion, the belief that such goals are in the best interest of the group as a whole.

The Spiritual Community is more likely to show

(a) generosity, the process that empowers its members and supports their growth,
(b) loving-kindness, providing support for members moving away from their limited selfish concerns, and
(c) insight, encouraging a view of the inter-dependent nature of all things and providing the foundation for general well-being and skillful action.

2. The distribution of power and responsibility

In the Egoistic-Elite Group the power of its significant personalities is absolute and therefore their wishes and needs prevail without question, whereas within the Spiritual Community power and responsibility are shared among its members and common aims pursued. The Spiritual Community is distinguished by the existence of many rather than few significant personalities, all of whom influence its functioning and direction.

3. The extent to which the group actively encourages individual growth

The extent to which a group actively supports the development of its members or creates barriers is a critical distinguishing characteristic. It determines the potential for both individual and group development. Practical categorization depends on, for example, the extent to which the group encourages or discourages the taking of new initiatives among its members, and the proportion of its resources that it devotes to helping individuals develop. The extent to which the conditions exist for new significant personalities to emerge is significant. The Egoistic-Elite Group has no concern for creating such conditions, whereas, they are an integral feature of behavior in a Spiritual Community.

Clearly, there are marked differences between the groups. Adopting slightly different terms, Kennedy has contrasted the two extremes, using the terms positive and negative to indicate the extremes (Kennedy, 1985). In his Buddhist Vision he suggests that, whereas the positive group may encourage healthiness and happiness in its members and is upheld by a higher vision, the negative group holds together only out of the overlapping self-interest of its members and the unwholesome states that predominate within it. He visualizes the transition from greed, hatred and delusion to love, generosity and awareness is the replacement of what has been called the 'power mode' with the 'love mode'. The person in power mode is regarded as immature and sees the world solely in terms of his or her own needs and their ability to dominate and impose, seeing everything, other people included, as objects of gratification. People in the 'love mode' on the other hand would not exploit or manipulate others but try to relate to them as independent, feeling and thinking beings.

Assessing the moral status of an organization in practice

Armed with the two hierarchies described above it is possible to begin to meet the requirements of managers wishing to manage moral development. Each hierarchy may be used as an assessment scale – providing a means for categorizing individuals, organizational units or entire organizations. An organization is treated as an independent entity separate from the individuals that it is composed of (this is the position of the 'methodological individualist' – see, for example, Flew, 1985). Such an entity has aims, objectives and behavioral characteristics, which are determined by its formal and informal structures and procedures, and by the way that these distribute decision-making, responsibility, information and freedom of choice amongst its membership. There are therefore three elements to be assessed, namely:

1. the moral status of the organization as an entity interacting with its environment (especially its aims and objectives);
2. the moral status of an organization based on the quality of its internal processes (particularly the distribution of decision making and responsibility); and
3. the moral quality of the contributions made by individuals within the organization.

In spite of focusing on the organization as an entity there remains a significant concern for individuals and their status. They, of course, are the significant elements of the whole and the channels through which, singly or in groups, organizational improvements flow.

Core qualities in relation to individuals

The starting point of our analysis is the basic Buddhist goal of developing skillful action. The three core qualities of the Buddhist tradition that support this are:

1. a commitment to moral improvement
2. a striving towards skillful moral motivation and
3. an awareness of the moral consequences of actions.

In the following sections theses qualities are examined with a view to providing guidance for making practical use of the hierarchies. The examination begins with the assessment of individuals partly in recognition of the essentially individual focus of Buddhist tradition and partly to ensure that the members of the organization are not overlooked. This is followed by an extension of the ideas to the organization.

1. Commitment to moral improvement
Commitment to moral improvement is central to Buddhist morality, for without it and the constant reaffirmation of such commitment,

Buddhist morality has no practical meaning. Sangharakshita emphasizes this by saying that the development of insight and the eventual attainment of Enlightenment is 'the central preoccupation of Buddhism' (Sangharakshita, 1977: 14). Traditionally, Buddhists speak of Going for Refuge to the Three Jewels, which are three central ideas of Buddhism, namely the Ideal of Enlightenment, the Ideal of the Path to Enlightenment and the Ideal of the Spiritual Community.

Put in more secular terms one could say that a person wishing to become more moral would need to:

- acknowledge, both in him/herself and in others, the possibility of 'something morally higher',
- believe in the possibility of moving towards a higher moral state and be committed to achieving it, and
- recognize the impossibility of 'going it alone' and accepts the guidance, example and friendship of others.

2. Striving towards skillful moral motivation

Establishing the true nature of an individual's motivation is difficult as they are generally poor at making sound judgments about their own motivation; and a judgment by others is notoriously difficult. As pointed out above, good action does not necessarily imply skillful motivation.

A partial resolution of this difficulty is made possible by adopting an indirect approach. The fundamental Buddhist notion that, at root, moral development is concerned with developing a 'way of seeing' which will eventually lead to Enlightenment implies that the way an individual 'sees' the world, his world-view, is at the center of his or her mental processes. Thus, the quality of their 'world view' may be used as an indicator of their moral status. A very similar idea is found in Checkland's approach to Soft System Analysis where the 'World View' or 'Weltanschauung' is posited as a framework for giving meaning to the elements of the systems being analyzed (Checkland, 1981; Checkland and Scholes, 1990).

Here, it is the breadth and quality of the 'world view' that are the crucial features. At the lowest, the pre-moral level on the moral hierarchy, we expect to find a world-view which is typically small, tightly defined and closed, where the individual tends to understand the world in terms of simple cause and effect relationships with the major actors (including the individual his or herself) often being seen in two dimensional, caricaturized forms. The language of this level is the simplistic, polarizing, as with the terminology of low-grade tabloid newspapers, with behavioral responses being largely egotistical and self-seeking, based on a 'what's-in-it-for-me?' attitude.

At higher levels in the hierarchy we expect to find progressively more complex world-views, with an increased openness to views that are different to those of the individual concerned. At the stage of Conventional Morality, individual motivation and behavior is largely conditioned by the values and language of the group and there is a tendency to look to an external authority for guidance and approval. Beyond Conventional Morality the need for external approval becomes much less, and personal choice and responsibility become much more important in determining behavior. Here, laws and rules, whether socially imposed or 'God-given', are only seen as a guide to behavior rather than a fixed edict from 'on high'.

As an individual's motivation moves towards Genuine Altruism his or her behavior will be typified by co-operativeness, by kindly and helpful speech and by an ability to recognize and evaluate alternative viewpoints. At the highest level (Transcendental Morality) we have an all embracing, completely open world-view, which comprehends the real nature of 'things' and their complex and interdependent nature.

So, while motivation may not be assessed or promoted directly the quality of world-view (the model of the world) can both be assessed, and also extended and improved. Further, the dynamic use of the worldview may be considered to create additional approaches to assessment. Thus, the indirect assessment is based on:

- the size and complexity of world-view as assessed directly,
- the quality of interaction and communication skills as a reflection of the world-view in use, and
- the openness to alternative viewpoints as an indication of growth potential.

3. Concern for consequences of actions
Given that it is always difficult to make an objective assessment of one's own (let alone another person's) moral motivation, Buddhism acknowledges another, in many ways more practical, approach. This assesses moral action by evaluating the moral consequences of an action or group of actions. Clearly, this is not completely separate from moral motivation, but rather, a linked aspect of it. It has the advantage of being simple to apply but also has clear limitations. For, according to Buddhism, making judgments on the basis of the moral consequences

of an action has no intrinsic value per se but only insofar as such judgments have a positive effect on a person's moral motivation and future behavior. However, there is a set of five moral precepts which traditionally are seen as reflecting the way an Enlightened person would act and which provide a particular working-out of that most fundamental of all Buddhist (not to say humanistic) injunctions 'not to cause harm of any sort'. These training principles list actions or outcomes to be avoided. They are to refrain from:

- taking life (or more generally, from causing any harm),
- taking the not-given (this is more than stealing, and includes all forms of exploitation),
- sexual misconduct,
- false speech,
- taking substances that intoxicate or cloud the mind.

In addition, to avoid the error of seeing the bare application of these principles as morally sufficient, Buddhists are also encouraged to develop their positive counterparts: loving-kindness, open-handed generosity, contentment, truthfulness and mindfulness.

Core qualities in relation to an organization

It is fortunate that the 'inner life' of an organization is in large measure open to scrutiny. The individuals in an organization are co-ordinated by the rules, procedures and practices of the organization. There may also exist mechanisms for the whole to protect itself against malfunction in the individuals. As with individuals, processes in an organization should show commitment and support for moral development and improvement. Using the principles described above these include:

(1) Collective commitment to moral improvement: The organization is overtly and publicly committed to making moral progress. There will be active encouragement by fostering:

- acknowledgement and search for moral improvement,
- efforts to move towards a higher moral state,
- example guidance and mutual support.

(2) Collective moral motivation: This category uses an indirect assessment of moral motivation similar to that for individuals. The categories

are re-named as:

breadth and complexity of management world-view: was there a single narrow goal guiding decision-making or broader more complex ones?
quality of communication channels: are they mostly one-way, top-down or extensive, two-way communication not significantly limited by organization role or responsibility?
corporate flexibility: is the organization open to growth, responding to imaginative input from any source?

(3) Collective concern for consequences: To be true to the spirit of Buddhist morality attention must be focused on the positive (doing good) aspects as well as on the negative (doing harm) aspects of the actions and the general behavior of the organization. Specific guidance is provided by transforming the precepts identified for an individual into analogous strictures for an organization. Thus, an organization should:

- promote benefit and avoid harming its environment,
- promote benefit for and avoid harming its members,
- give equal respect and consideration to all (individuals and organizations),
- use clearly defined processes and procedures that are open to scrutiny,
- adopt management practices that are guided by information and understanding.

Final words

The above remains a summary analysis but it shows the possibility of linking basic Buddhist ideas to practical management terms and ideas. As mentioned earlier, the details of the analysis is described in Howes (1993). There, an attempt was made to assess the applicability of these ideas in practice by using them as a basis for making an ethical audit of an organization. As a pilot investigation the result was positive, although it brought to light a number of issues needing attention before routine use was thought to be possible. These remain under consideration.

However, the increasing use of computer information systems may mean that much of the administrative burden of the process (which was a significant problem in the pilot study, being a tentative, iterative manual process) is removed, and that creating a system that works for much of the time in the background is possible. While this may be a benefit to those striving to manage the quality of their management systems it may also become the source of difficulties. Such systems may be used as intelligence gathering systems rather than as systems for the broader sharing of data, knowledge and wisdom. This is particularly likely where organizations operate as collaborators where there is a blurring of the boundaries between them. What would pass between them is knowledge of possible problems; weaknesses and motivation that might, as intended, aid understanding but might also inform competitive positioning.

References

Brady and Logsdon (1988) Zimbardo's 'Stanford Prison Experiment' and the Relevance of Social Psychology for Teaching Business Ethics. *Journal of Business Ethics* **7**: 703–10.
Checkland, P. and Scholes, J. (1990) *Soft Systems Methodology in Action*, Chichester: Wiley.
Checkland, P. (1981) *Systems Thinking, Systems Practice*, Chichester: Wiley.
Derry and Green (1989) Ethical theory in business ethics: A critical assessment. *Journal of Business Ethics* **8**: 521–33.
Flew, A. (1985) *Thinking About Social Thinking*, Oxford: Blackwell.
Howes. M. A. (Satyapala) and Robins P. C. (1994) *A Theory of Moral Organization: A Buddhist View of Business Ethics*, Aston Business School Research Institute
Howes, M. A. (Satyapala) (1993) *Changing the Corporate Mind: a Buddhist Perspective on business morality*. Unpublished PhD thesis, University of Aston, Birmingham.
Kennedy, Alex (Dharmachari Subhuti) (1985) *The Buddhist Vision*, London: Rider.
Kohlberg, L. (1981) *The Philosophy of Moral Development*, San Francisco: Harper & Row.
Maslow, A. H. (1943) A theory of human motivation. *Psychological Review* **50**: 370–96.
Sangharakshita, Ven (1977) The origin and development of the Bodhisattva ideal. *Mitrata* **56** Windhorse, Glasgow, October.
Taket, A. (1994) Undercover agency? – Ethics, responsibility and the practice of OR. *Journal of the Operational Research Society* **45**(2): 123–32.

13
Doing the Right Thing: Incorporating the Ethical Imperative into the Sustainable Development Process
Hock-Beng Cheah and Melanie Cheah

> ... the government has promoted stupid development processes which cause disasters both in terms of forest resources and suffering for the generations to come. This catastrophe is the result of both expert consultants and the government apparatus adhering to inherently flawed knowledge which also has resulted in the economic crisis, political crisis, food crisis, forest fires crisis, and moral crisis.
> (Barber and Schweithelm, 2000: 40)

Introduction

For many developing countries, the difficulties with orthodox development strategies lie not just in the relatively slow and uncertain pace of the development process but more significantly, in the very nature of the development model that has been adopted so far. It is a model in which excessive emphasis has been placed on the economic aspects, a model that has generated significant inequities, a model that is not meaningful for a large proportion of the world's population, and a model that may not be sustainable in the longer-term. These concerns have provoked a critical questioning of present forms and processes of development, and have led to a search for better and more viable alternatives.[1]

In 1987, the World Commission on Environment and Development (WCED) promoted a concept of sustainable development that postulated that economic, ecological and social development should be placed on an equal footing.[2] Since then, sustainable development has become an increasingly important concern among researchers, governments, NGOs and development organizations.

At the same time, there has been an increasing concern, fostered most recently by the IMF and the World Bank, about impediments to development caused by corruption in developing countries. However, it is arguable that these problems extend beyond corruption per se, and appropriate concern should also extend to violations of corporate social responsibility, human rights violations and other developments and practices that provide the capacity for individuals or organizations to cause significant harm and suffering to others.

We may categorize these problems and concerns under the rubric of issues related to an ethical imperative in the development process. These problems and concerns should be provided more direct attention. They should be incorporated into the main conceptual framework, and should be monitored as closely as other aspects of the sustainable development framework, because they also exert very significant influence on the overall viability of the development process. In short, an appropriate framework for sustainable development must focus as much attention on issues that relate to the ethical imperative, as on issues related to other kinds of relevant imperatives.

Sustainability: from ecology to the quadruple bottom line

The rising interest in issues relating to sustainable development corresponded with growing concerns that the previous dominant focus on economic growth, in general, and the gross national product, in particular, have been severely inadequate, unbalanced and even deceptive (Cobb et al., 1995, 1999). Initial concerns over sustainability centered on the issues relating to environmental and ecological sustainability, resulting from concerns raised, among others, by Carson (1962), Meadows et al. (1972) and Lovelock (1979).[3]

Subsequently, the WCED helped to expand sustainability concerns to include economic and social aspects. This led to the concept of the "triple bottom line," a significant extension beyond the traditional concerns solely with commercial profitability (the conventional "bottom line") of business enterprise. In this regard, Robinson and Tinker (1998: 14, 22) identified the economy, the ecological system, and human society as three interconnected, overlapping and coequal "prime systems," with corresponding imperatives, namely: the economic imperative is to ensure and maintain adequate material standards of living for all people; the ecological imperative is to remain within planetary biophysical carrying capacity; and the social imperative is to provide social structures, including systems of governance, that effectively propagate and sustain the values that people wish to live by.[4]

Robinson and Tinker (1998) pointed out that these three imperatives are interconnected and mutually reinforcing, with direct and indirect effects on each other, such that "any attempt to address one system in isolation not only runs the risk of intensifying problems in the other systems, but also may give rise to feedback effects from the other systems which overwhelm the effects of the first intervention" (p. 24), and "addressing any of these issues in isolation, without considering their interacting effects, can give rise to unanticipated higher order consequences in other realms, which cause problems of their own or undercut the initial policies" (p. 12).[5] Furthermore, they claimed, "anthropogenic stress generated on a global scale is increasing in all three prime systems" (p. 17), and that "accurately predicting system change in response to stress...requires greater knowledge than we have at present. Such change often goes in counter-intuitive directions" (p. 18).

From this perspective, the crux of sustainable development lies in the fact that satisfying any one imperative without also satisfying the other two is unsustainable; because each is independently crucial to societal functioning, each is urgent in light of the scope and scale of problems currently being faced in the world, and each of the three imperatives are interconnected. Consequently, "addressing any one of the three imperatives in isolation virtually guarantees failure. Nevertheless, this is what current policy-making commonly does" (Robinson and Tinker, 1998: 24).[6] Specifically, "the current tendency is to concentrate on the economic imperative combined with a post hoc attempt to reconcile this with the ecological imperative, while ignoring the social imperative and its questions of North–South and intra-country equity" (p. 35). In contrast, Robinson and Tinker see the necessity for an integrated approach that explicitly and jointly addresses all three prime systems in a complementary manner that can generate positive synergies.[7]

However, whilst Robinson and Tinker have significantly enhanced the analytical foundations of the sustainable development framework, they have not included an explicit recognition and incorporation of an ethical imperative in that analytical framework, and in the sustainable development process. Indeed, recognition of the need to include ethical concerns in sustainable development programs and efforts is, at best, at an early stage. This can be demonstrated by considering three major frameworks or indices that have been introduced in recent years.

First, there is the "comprehensive development framework," being promoted by the World Bank (Wolfensohn, 1999). Among other dimensions, this framework has introduced a focus on corruption, good governance and judicial reform. These aspects have a significant connection to ethical issues. Through them, the CDF has encouraged a broader development focus than the orthodox perspective that was provided for many years principally by its "world development indicators," presented in its annual World Development Reports. The world development indicators have predominantly and traditionally focused on quantifiable macroeconomic aspects of the development process.

Second, there is the 'human development index' introduced by the United Nations Development Program (UNDP), and presented annually in its Human Development Report. The UNDP sought to provide a broader assessment of the development process, by including indicators for levels of income, literacy, and life expectancy, which form the principal components of the index. The annual reports have provided more emphasis on social issues such as poverty. In recent years, the UNDO have added the Human Poverty Index, the Gender-related Development Index, and the Gender Empowerment Measure. The 2000 annual report introduced a focus on human rights. These additions are welcome, and useful in examining significant aspects of the development process in different countries. Moreover, the newer indicators also have a close connection with the ethical dimension in the development process.

However, neither the World Bank's comprehensive development framework, nor the UNDP's human development index is designed specifically to focus on the concept of sustainable development. That task and principal responsibility falls to the United Nations Commission for Sustainable Development, which has oversight of the creation of a "sustainable development index" (SDI). The SDI currently has four principal themes, titled: "social," "environmental," "economic" and "institutional." None of these principal themes has a significant focus on ethics. Within the SDI's "social" theme, there is a sub-theme for "crime" (measured by one indicator: number of recorded crimes per 100000 population), and a sub-theme for "social and ethical values." However, there is no specific indicator designed to directly monitor aspects related to "ethical values" in the SDI. This is a gap that it would be important to close. To do so, it is necessary to note that this lapse may be related directly to the initial failure to include a specific focus on ethics in the sustainable development conceptual framework. This has led to it becoming submerged and, subsequently, neglected and lost within the "social" theme.

Yet, the evidence presented below will demonstrate that unethical practices undermine significantly the efficacy and viability of the overall development process. Such considerations highlight the need to extend the original three-dimension sustainable development analytical framework to include explicitly an ethical dimension focusing on the "value system." Furthermore, the quest for sustainable development at the national and international (macro) level requires a corresponding concept, "sustainable management," at the organizational and enterprise (micro) level; that is, management directly focused on the creation and effective management of economically, ecologically, socially and ethically sustainable enterprises. Where business enterprises had previously focused their concerns and activities largely or completely on competitiveness and the creation of material wealth (measured by various indicators of profitability),[8] in the future, enterprises will need to adopt broader and more balanced foci to include concerns for habitability (measured by various indicators of eco-efficiency), community (measured by various indicators of quality of life), and legitimacy (measured by indicators of corporate reputation, corporate social responsibility, and ethical investment).[9] The specific foci and criteria for these four dimensions are identified in Table 13.1.

Thus, an extended sustainable development framework would incorporate four principal dimensions: (a) the economic imperative, that is, business activities must be economically profitable, (b) the ecological imperative, that is, the activities must also be ecologically friendly and not damaging to the environment, (c) the social imperative, that is, in addition to individual or private gain, the activities must also promote community and societal well-being, for instance by reducing social divisions, inequity and conflict, and (d) the ethical imperative. The ethical imperative may be defined simply and positively as a moral responsibility to "do the right thing," or alternatively as the admonition to "do no harm."[10]

Various aspects of current development efforts have an adverse impact on development outcomes, are harmful to others, or are morally reprehensible. For those reasons, the ethical imperative must be a relevant consideration in the assessment of development efforts. In addition to the economic, ecological and social imperatives currently included in the sustainable development framework, the ethical imperative must be added to this framework to encourage individuals, organizations and governments to incorporate these four imperatives into their planning and operational activities in a more deliberate and integrated manner. Failure to do so, illustrated by the evidence presented below, impairs the viability of development processes in the longer-term.

Table 13.1 The Quadruple Bottom line – dimensions, foci and performance criteria for sustainable management and sustainable development

Dimension	Focus	Corporate performance criterion	Societal performance criterion	Global performance criterion
Economic imperative	Competitiveness	Corporate profitability	Societal wealth[11]	Global wealth
Ecological imperative	Habitability	Corporate eco-efficiency[12]	Societal eco-efficiency	Global eco-efficiency
Social imperative	Community	Corporate reputation[13]	Societal quality of life[14]	Global quality of life
Ethical imperative	Legitimacy	Corporate values	Societal values	Human values
All dimensions	Combined foci	Sustainable management index[15]	Sustainable development index[16]	Sustainable development index

Transgressions of the ethical imperative in Asia and their adverse impact on development

The ethical imperative, defined above as a moral responsibility to "do the right thing," or alternatively as the admonition to "do no harm," may be further defined as the necessity (a) for organizations to observe and practice "corporate social responsibility," (b) for individuals and organizations to avoid corrupt practices, (c) for all peoples and governments to uphold the tenets contained in the Universal Declaration of Human Rights, and (d) for the avoidance of other possible acts of commission or omission that have the likelihood of causing significant harm to others.

Violations of corporate social responsibility

According to Watts and Holme (1999: 3), "Corporate social responsibility is the continuing commitment by business to behave ethically and contribute to economic development while improving the quality of life of the workforce and their families as well as of the local community and society at large."[17] Kenichi Ohmae provided one recent example of disregard for corporate responsibility at the expense of employees. He reported his observations of the accelerating vitality of economic development in China as follows:

> I saw the implications of this recently on a visit to a 3-year-old manufacturing plant in China. This plant had 50 000 workers – all young women, and none wearing eyeglasses.
>
> "Don't you have any employees with bad eyesight?" I asked the manager.
>
> He replied: "We fire them when their eyes go bad. They can find another job – that's not my problem. There are plenty of other people who want to work for us."
>
> From the perspective of industrialized nations, practices like this are brutally cruel and would not exist in any other nation of China's stature due to labor laws. But in Shengzhen, Shanghai, Suzhou, Dalian and many more Chinese cities, where hundreds of millions of people eagerly flock to urban jobs from the hinterlands, such practices are taken for granted (Ohmae, 2001).[18]

Earlier, in Japan, management failings at the Nippon Chisso Company chemical plant at Minamata city caused severe mercury poisoning among the population in that area. Indeed, Ui (1992), noted that "The Chisso Minamata complex, being representative of Japan's chemical industries during the post-war years...achieved the highest economic growth-rate in Japan and at the same time caused the greatest environmental destruction that the country has ever seen." This was compounded by inept government actions, and their efforts to conceal or downplay the problems.

More recently, poor management and unsafe work practices led to an accident at the nuclear material processing plant at Tokaimura in Japan, on 30 September 1999 (Lyman and Dolley, 2000). This was compounded by ineffective regulation by the relevant authorities as well as poor leadership by the government in dealing with the fundamental causes of the problems.

In August 2000, reports revealed that managers and workers at Mitsubishi Motors had knowingly and systematically concealed defects in the design and manufacture of its cars and trucks over a 20-year period. This led to the recall of more than 620 000 vehicles in Japan and abroad, and legal action against the company (Kageyama, 2000; Millett, 2000; Kunii, 2000a). This case raises serious questions about the integrity of this, a major, Japanese corporation.[19] Also see Chapter 8 in this book (eds.).

An example of corporate social irresponsibility by a foreign-owned firm occurred during the massive gas leaks from the Union Carbide factory in Bhopal, India in 3 December 1984. Thousands of people died and, subsequently, many more suffered on-going medical problems and disabilities. Kharbanda and Stallworthy (1986: 50) noted that "the Bhopal disaster was a man-made tragedy. It occurred as a result of faulty design, poor maintenance and faulty plant operation. It could and should have been prevented."[20]

Other more recent instances of alleged exploitative practices by foreign companies, their subsidiaries, subcontractors or franchisees in Asia, include the employment practices of Nike, and other sports wear and clothing manufacturers (Goodman, 1993; Greenhouse, 1997; Connor, 2000; UNITE, 2000; Osborn, 2000; Wong, 2000). These and other examples of corporate social irresponsibility demonstrate that transgressions of the ethical imperative can have serious adverse personal, social, economic and environmental consequences.

Corruption

Corruption may be defined as an effort to obtain private gain through unethical means that causes harm to others.[21] While corruption is not unique to Asia, its burdens are borne by more people in Asia than any other region of the world. However, the great variation in world rankings, based on the corruption perception index (of Transparency International in Berlin), means that further generalizations are difficult because countries in Asia rank among the highest and lowest in the world (see Table 13.2). However, as a group, countries in South Asia (India, Pakistan and Bangladesh) have performed particularly poorly in these rankings.

A recent report portrayed a very bleak picture of the situation in South Asia, suggesting that "corruption has 'floated upwards' – from petty corruption in the 1950s, to mid-level corruption in the 1960s and 1970s, to corruption at the very highest levels of the state in the 1980s and 1990s" (Haq, 1999: 96). Its distinctive characteristics are: it occurs "upstream" and distorts strategic decisions on development priorities, policies and projects; it has "wings" and leads to substantial capital flight abroad; it leads to "promotion, not prison" as the powerful are seldom called to account; and it occurs in a context of widespread poverty, and so it compounds the massive human deprivation and the extreme income inequalities (Haq, 1999: 99; Gill, 1998).

Other Asian countries also encounter serious problems with corruption. For instance, reports have indicated that poverty combined with corruption led to the sale of body parts or blood by impoverished

Table 13.2 Corruption Perception Index, 2000 and 2001

Country	2000			2001		
	CPI score	World rank	Regional rank	CPI score	World rank	Regional rank
Singapore	9.1	6	1	9.2	4	1
Hong Kong	7.7	15	2	7.9	14	2
Japan	6.4	23	3	7.1	21	3
Taiwan	5.5	28	4	5.9	27	4
Malaysia	4.8	36	5	5.0	36	5
South Korea	4.0	48	6	4.2	42	6
China	3.1	63	8	3.5	57	7
Thailand	3.2	60	7	3.2	61	8
Philippines	2.8	69	9	2.9	65	9
India	2.8	69	9	2.7	71	10
Vietnam	2.5	76	11	2.6	75	11
Pakistan	na	—	—	2.3	79	12
Indonesia	1.7	85	12	1.9	88	13
Bangladesh	na	—	—	0.4	91	14

Notes: The Corruption Perception Index (CPI) ranges from 10 (highly clean) to 0 (highly corrupt). World rank is based on 90 countries in 2000, and 91 countries in 2001. Regional rank in Asia is based on 12 countries in 2000, and 14 countries in 2001. na: not available (also —).

Source: Transparency International.

people – and the use of infected instruments has resulted in a massive AIDS epidemic in Henan province in China (Rosenthal, 2001).

The problems also extend deeply into government agencies. In 2000, state auditors in China discovered from an extensive investigation of government and Communist Party officials and managers of state-owned companies that $11 billion of public funds had been embezzled or seriously misused in the last two years (Wingfield-Hayes, 2000). While China has episodically conducted anti-corruption campaigns and sought to curb excesses, some fundamental causes may be traced to the inadequate accountability of the government itself (Havely, 2000).

In this regard, the recent strong efforts to promote privatization and deregulation, emanating from the World Bank, the IMF, Western governments and mainstream economists, have led to mixed and even questionable outcomes, such as an increase in the opportunities for and the incidence of corruption (Haq, 1999). Specifically, it has been contended that:

> If corruption is growing throughout the world, it is largely a result of the rapid privatization (and associated practices of contracting-out and concessions) of public enterprises worldwide. This process has been pushed by Western creditors and governments and carried out in such a way as to allow multinational companies to operate with increased impunity. Thus multinationals, supported by western governments and their agencies such as the World Bank and the International Monetary Fund frequently put forward anti-poverty and 'good governance' agendas, but their other actions send a different signal about where their priorities lie (Hawley, 2000).

Such processes also run counter to the expressed objectives of the 1977 Foreign Corrupt Practices Act in America, and the 1997 OECD-sponsored Convention on Combating Bribery of Foreign Public Officials in International Business Transactions.[22] At the macro level, it has also been suggested that similar pressures from the same sources, quoted above, urging Asian governments to promote rapid economic liberalization, contributed to the economic crisis in several Asian countries during 1997–98; which was subsequently blamed on domestic deficiencies, such as weak financial and regulatory institutions and "crony capitalism."[23]

These problems and controversies illustrate the close connections between corruption and the viability of the development process.

Human rights violations

The Universal Declaration of Human Rights provides the principal statement of major rights that have been internationally recognized (UNDP, 2000: 14–18). They represent a very significant aspect of the moral standards that should guide human activities, and the authors of the Human Development Report 2000 also contended "the divide between the human development agenda and the human rights agenda is narrowing" (UNDP, 2000: 2).

Recognition of human rights provides support to the development agenda by conveying moral legitimacy to the objectives of human development, and by incorporating civil and political rights as integral parts of the development process. Numerous agencies have emerged to monitor, report and sometimes protest against human rights violations.[24] However, these have not prevented some of the worst human rights violations from being committed in Asia.

Diplomacy and adherence to the principle of non-interference in the internal affairs of another sovereign country have led to a reluctance among many governments to take a firm stand against ethically questionable or unconscionable practices elsewhere. On the contrary, it has been argued that the adoption of more accommodative policies would achieve better results. This was the approach adopted by the ASEAN countries towards the despotic ruling regime in Burma [Myanmar] (Bello, 1997; Inbaraj, 1997).

An appeal to "Asian values" also helped to provide an argument for a greater emphasis on pragmatism, and reduced emphasis on human rights.[25] Despite the fact that prominent contributors to the basic tenets of values upheld by Asians (and non-Asians), such as Confucius, Buddha and others, placed great emphasis on moral virtues, and ethical behavior, the principal proponents of Asian values placed less emphasis on such aspects and more emphasis on other aspects that directly and indirectly support wealth creation, authoritarian rule and realpolitik. In this respect, the Asian values debate has also functioned as an attempt to define, maintain and protect the legitimacy of current authorities and their adopted policies.

However, Asian values did not prevent the economic crisis of the 1990s from befalling all the Asian countries, from Japan to Indonesia. They did not prevent the occurrence and continuation of widespread corruption within Indonesia, the Philippines, and other Asian countries. Indeed, the persistence of gross violations of the ethical imperative in various Asian countries has undermined significantly the legitimacy of their governing regimes and the (peculiar) values that they espoused.[26]

To summarize, the phenomena associated with transgressions of corporate social responsibility, corruption, human rights violations, as well as other events that have the capacity to cause significant harm and suffering may, in many instances, be intertwined in both their causes and their effects. In addition to their ethical consequences, they may also have economic, environmental and social ramifications. For instance, corruption, leading to illegal logging in tropical rain forests may cause significant environmental damage, and disrupt the livelihoods of indigenous communities residing in those locations, so leading to their impoverishment, and an increased competition and conflict over the remaining resources. These kinds of dynamics and interactions further justify the adoption of a more comprehensive and integrated approach to the pursuit of sustainable development.

Unsustainable development: the case of Indonesia

An illustration of the interrelated dynamics in the development process, mentioned above, may be observed in the case of Indonesia under the rule of past President Suharto. An assessment based on the four imperatives for sustainable development provides the following perspective on Indonesia's development experience from 1965–98:

Ethical imperative

General Suharto came to power in 1967, following murky circumstances beginning in October 1965, in which an estimated 500 000 (even up to one million) people were killed, with American involvement, during a wave of anti-communist hysteria (Scott, 1985). With Suharto's ascendancy, the Indonesian military came to play a major political role in the country, in a manner that undermined genuine democratic practices. The human rights record of Indonesia during the period of Suharto's rule was far from exemplary.[27] Corruption was also a significant feature in Indonesia during this period, and vested business interests linked to members of the political leadership, to the military and, specifically, to members of Suharto's family, thrived in a situation appropriately described as "crony capitalism." These and other transgressions of the ethical imperative were associated with major economic, ecological and social developments in the country.

Economic imperative

Suharto's "strong-man rule" was viewed positively in various domestic and international circles as providing the security and stability necessary for "investor confidence" that would lay the foundations for sustained economic development. Indeed, Indonesia experienced a period of rising economic growth from 1967–96. It benefited from its exports of petroleum and natural gas, as well as primary commodities such as coffee, tea, timber, and palm oil, the growth in tourism, and its promotion of low-labor-cost manufacturing industries such as textiles, garments, plywood, and electrical appliances with support from foreign multinational companies. It was widely regarded as a "second-generation" newly industrializing country.[28] These positive developments encouraged the conviction and the rationalization that concerns over human rights and other ethical lapses should not be pressed or should be postponed, as economic development would lay the foundations for such transgressions to be diminished or to be eliminated in the future.

Such support helped Suharto to entrench his control and to dominate the Indonesian political scene for three decades. His family members gained substantial financial benefits from this situation, through the many business ventures that they initiated, were co-opted into, or were associated with, directly and indirectly. These numerous business activities ranged from the domestic arena to international ventures, with a web of connections among them (Aditjondro, 1998; Celarier, 1998, Head, 1998; Root, 2000: 230–3).

Selected local and foreign business interests benefited from, and directly and indirectly supported, the consolidation of this structure. As a consequence, a group of wealthy Indonesian businessmen emerged, with close connections to Suharto and his family. Foreign business interests also established links with Suharto's family, and foreign governments provided economic and political support, as well as other links, such as military supplies and training (Inbaraj, 1997).

The extreme fragility of this structure was only widely recognized ex post, during the so-called "Asian crisis," when foreign investors took fright and withdrew financial investments from Indonesia in 1997. As a consequence, the currency lost 80 percent of its value relative to the US dollar, the stock market crashed, and per capita income dived from $1300 to $340 per annum (Root, 2000: 228). Many business ventures failed and the country's banks were left with high levels of bad debts. Several decades of development progress had been reversed within two years.

In this situation, the government was compelled to turn to the IMF for assistance. Following its normal practice, the IMF imposed stringent conditions that required policies of economic and financial tightening, involving reductions in government expenditure, cuts in subsidies for essential goods, as well as public assumption of responsibility for bad debts incurred by the private sector. These efforts compounded the economic distress in the country, and impacted most severely on the poorer groups in the population (Oxfam International, 1998). However, even after his resignation from the presidency under public pressure in May 1998, significant portions of the Suharto family business empire have survived (Shari, 1999; Delaney, 2000).

Ecological imperative

The most glaring illustration of the harm caused to the environment by policies and practices traceable to Suharto and his government was the forest fires that blighted substantial areas in Sumatra and Kalimantan, and blanketed vast areas of Southeast Asia with haze and smog (Glover and Jessup, 1999; Aditjondro, 2000; Barber and Schweithelm, 2000). In relation to Indonesia's environment and ecology, the connections between the Suharto administration's policies, his family's business ventures, other local and foreign vested interests, and a variety of corrupt practices, paralleled the situation depicted for the economy. Specifically,

> In the forest and natural resources sector, the New Order political economy was characterized by a heavily centralized bureaucracy and industry, effectively dominated by a small number of corporate conglomerates with close connections to top politicians. These business groups and their bureaucratic cronies were essentially above the law for three decades, seeking short-term profits at the expense of the environment and local communities while enjoying the protection of a legal and political system in which neither industry nor the bureaucracy could be held accountable.
>
> Indonesian forest policies have provided powerful legal incentives for 'cut-and-run' resource extraction and have failed to create effective mechanisms for enforcing even minimum standards of forest resource stewardship (Barber and Schweithelm, 2000: 1).

Thus, in this arena too, the ethical failures of the regime caused substantial harm to its people and to the country (Sari, 1999). Among those most severely afflicted were the indigenous groups who resided in areas where logging concessions, new timber and oil palm plantations, and other development projects were located. They lost land and livelihoods, with little or no compensation in return.[29]

Social imperative

In concert with the rise in economic growth rates following Suharto's ascendancy to power, living standards also improved generally in Indonesia from the 1960s to the 1990s, before the economic crisis. Poverty levels declined from estimates of 60 percent in 1970, to 28 percent in 1980, to between 15 to 17 percent in 1996. However, following the crisis, they rose to 27 percent in February 1999 (Root, 2000: 229; Suryahadi *et al.*, 2000: 23).

Furthermore, beneath the appearance of rising social well-being, there were increasingly serious and intense social divisions and resentments in many parts of Indonesia. These were being fueled by discrimination against minorities, official and unofficial expropriation of property and resources especially in the regions, from Aceh to Kalimantan to Irian Jaya to East Timor; as well as by poorly formulated and badly implemented transmigration and other development programs. The tensions led to outbreaks of conflict in which the massacres that occurred in East Timor, conducted by militia with direct and indirect support from the military, were only the most publicized of a host of extra-judicial attacks, retaliations, and rebellions that occurred and that continue in the country.[30]

Thus, the moral lapses of the regime in power, eventually infected the whole country, and created a contagion that preceded the economic crisis, and undermined its capacity to respond correctly and effectively to the crisis. While that crisis had larger causes beyond Indonesia (Dieter, 1998; Cheah, 2000), the foundations of Indonesian economy, society, polity and, in particular, its value system, had been significantly eroded such that, arguably, some trigger would eventually have sparked an unraveling of the situation (see Clad, 1996). In short, that form of development in Indonesia was not sustainable.

Other factors that contributed to transgressions of the ethical imperative

Why has the ethical imperative not been more explicitly incorporated as an integral element in the promotion of sustainable development?

There has been an overwhelming pre-occupation with commercial concerns at the expense of moral principles in the development process. In business organizations, this resulted in active pursuit or tacit condoning of corrupt practices, exploitation of employees, neglect of safety provisions and other activities, justified by a narrow definition of "the bottom line." At the national level, similar pre-occupations with economic growth resulted in priorities being downgraded for non-economic concerns. Some consequences included the suppression of workers rights, disregard for employee health and safety, political repression, and torture of alleged dissidents and subversive elements. Two major reasons may be offered here for these practices.

First, perceptions of national interests led rulers in various countries to adopt policies aligned with the "realist" theory of politics. This preoccupation with national economic, political and security interests was often at the expense of moral principles.[31] For instance, after World War II, the onset of the Cold War against the Communist Bloc led American politicians to support dictatorships such as that in the Dominican Republic, led by General Rafael Molino Trujillo, a leading Latin American anticommunist. The US Secretary of State, Cordell Hull, summed up this attitude when he said of Trujillo, "He may be a son-of-a-bitch, but he is our son-of-a-bitch."

In Asia, this attitude and practice led to CIA collaboration in the massacres of alleged PKI supporters in Indonesia (National Security Archive, 2001: 386–7), as well as their support for corrupt and dictatorial rulers, such as Suharto in Indonesia and Marcos in the Philippines. It also led to occasions of US indifference or acquiescence to human rights violations in Asia (Chomsky and Herman, 1979; Chomsky, 2000). Within Asia itself, leaders from Mao Zedong to Suharto and others engaged in ruthless politics for their proclaimed national causes (see Mirsky, 1999; Tanter, 1998; Templer, 1998). The reality of such gross transgressions of the ethical imperative span the political spectrum, from the political right to the political left, from the East to the West, despite the grand pronouncements to the contrary by national leaders and prominent statesmen (see Bryce, 2000). Realpolitik has often been the norm, and this has undermined the practice of principled politics and, consequently, the integrity of development efforts in the past decades.

Second, we may also relate the neglect of the ethical imperative to the nature of the evolution of Economics, which now dominates so much of governmental policy formulation and business decision-making. When the followers of Adam Smith (1776) lauded *The Wealth of Nations* and championed the practice of laissez faire, that promotes private interests over common interests, purportedly guided by an "invisible hand,"[32] they neglected or ignored the restraints and the balance that Adam Smith (1759) had himself emphasized earlier in *The Theory of Moral Sentiments* (Bronk, 1998). From that point, Economics was increasingly divorced from Moral Philosophy and, arguably, lost its soul. The loss of this moral ballast; specifically, the failure to temper self-interest with sympathy for others, that Adam Smith felt to be necessary, contributed to many economic practices that may be regarded as extremely self-interested and selfish, exploitative and, increasingly, destructive.[33] This has led to growing public opprobrium towards, and loss of legitimacy for many private corporations (Bernstein, 2000; Kunii, 2000b; Dawson, 2001), national agencies and even international organizations.[34]

Recently, there have been a growing number of efforts to re-emphasize various aspects of what has been termed here as the ethical imperative (see Goulet, 1995; Fukuyama, 1995; Galbraith, 1996; Sen, 1987 and 1999). We may view these as attempts to assist Capitalism to find or regain the soul it lost. Similar efforts have been directed at corporations as well as governmental agencies.[35]

Towards sustainability: the twenty-first-century challenge

Increasingly, governments and business organizations must participate in efforts to incorporate sustainability issues into their planning and operational activities. Sustainability, or the concern for long-term viability, must include at least four main dimensions: economic sustainability, that is, business activities must be economically profitable; ecological sustainability, that is, the activities must also be ecologically friendly and not damaging to the environment; social sustainability, that is, in addition to individual or private gain, the activities must also promote community and societal well-being, for instance by reducing social divisions, inequity and conflict; and ethical sustainability, that is, the necessity to act responsibly, and to avoid causing significant harm to ourselves, to others and to the environment.[36]

While there has been growing concern over corporate social responsibility, corruption and human rights, these heightened concerns need to be more explicitly incorporated as an integral aspect of the analytical framework so that, by this means, sustainable management and sustainable development can provide the more integrated, holistic and balanced approach necessary for creating genuinely sustainable enterprises and societies. Finally, while Goulet (1971) had characterized the development process as involving unavoidably a "cruel choice," the ethical imperative has the power to confer the wisdom needed to "do the right thing" in making such choices.

Notes

1 See, among others, Myrdal (1968), Illich (1973), Schumacher (1974), Brandt Commission (1983). Mollison (1990), Meadows *et al.* (1992), Brookfield and Byron (1993), Khandker (1998), Kaul *et al.* (1999), UNRISD (2000) and Social Development Department (2000).
2 The concept of sustainable development has been broadly defined as development that "meets the needs of the present without compromising the ability of future generations to meet their own needs... Sustainable development is not a fixed state of harmony, but rather a process of change in which the exploitation of resources, the direction of investments, the orientation of technological development, and institutional change are made consistent with the future as well as present needs" (WCED, 1987). See also UNCED (1992) and Wheeler *et al.* (2000).

However, Barraclough (2001: 1–2) pointed out that the concept had earlier origins and applications. He offers a serious critique of the concept, noting various conceptual flaws, methodological difficulties and operational problems associated with it. He argues that "Any interpretation of 'sustainable development' implies dealing both with profound non-commensurabilities and great uncertainties. Conflicts of interest resulting from such divergent perceptions can only be resolved politically, usually through some combination of compromise and compulsion" (Barraclough, 2001: 6). However, while such "realist" practices may apply successfully a "might is right" solution in many conflicts, such resolutions based on the current power relationships can and do raise serious questions about the ethical foundations of the outcomes, and may lead to moral challenges to those outcomes (see Goulet, 1971: 335–41). This brings into sharper focus the role of the ethical imperative in the development process.

3   These concerns have continued with more recent work by Leakey and Lewin (1995), Colborn et al. (1996), and others.

4   It may be suggested that specific concerns for morality and the ethical imperative could receive appropriate attention in this sphere. However, in practice they have not, and other social concerns relating to poverty, inequality, and other matters have dominated this space, to the exclusion of specific attention to values and ethics.

5   They provide the example that "raising energy prices significantly to reduce energy emissions will disproportionately affect poorer citizens, thus increasing income disparities and contributing to social unsustainability" (Robinson and Tinker, 1998: 12).

6   In this regard, Oxfam International (1998: 8) emphasized that "it is crucial that the artificial separation of social and economic policy be ended. Human development and poverty considerations should be integral parts of the macroeconomic policy framework, which is currently dominated by narrow – and deeply flawed – financial targets. Second, an institutional framework must be created within which the IMF and the World Bank can provide a more integrated response to financial crisis. The alternative is for the World Bank to continue its present policy of arriving after the event in a largely futile effort to counteract the negative consequences of IMF prescriptions."

7   They suggest that this integrated approach should incorporate two sets of policy measures that aim to promote "dematerialization" of the economy and "resocialization" of the society. The former involves the uncoupling of (a) economic growth and improvements in living standards (consumption of goods and services) from (b) increased consumption of energy and materials (for instance, by further development and greater utilization of more environmentally benign technologies). The latter involves the uncoupling of (c) human well being from (a), for instance, by greater participation in the informal economy.

8   In this regard, the maxim that "greed is good," pronounced by the fictional Wall Street financier, Gordon Gecko, is matched by China's former Premier, Deng Xiao Ping's exhortation, "to get rich is glorious."

9   From this perspective, there has been an excessive dominance of Economics and the profession of economists in the public policy arena, as well as the excessive emphasis on competitiveness by Business Schools and the management profession in the corporate arena.

10 Confucius expressed it as follows: "Do not do unto others what you would not have them do unto you" (Analects 15:23); while the Judeo-Christian tradition advised followers to "Do unto others as you would have them do unto you." More recently, Immanual Kant's Categorical Imperative advised that "we should act in such a way that we could wish the maxim of our action to become a universal law."

11 An improved version of, or an alternative to, the orthodox gross national product (GNP) should be formulated for the societal (global) wealth indicator (SWI). At the very least, the *gross* national product should be converted

to a *net* national product, after appropriate offsets of the associated costs and disbenefits imposed on people and society by certain aspects of wealth creation and related activities.
12 See WBCSD (1999).
13 See Fombrun (1986); Kahn *et al.* (1999).
14 This should take into account the "human poverty index" (UNDP, 2000). Another relevant concept is the "index of social progress" (Estes, 1992). See also Hirschhorn (2000).
15 See the sustainability reporting guidelines presented by GRI (2000).
16 Existing relevant concepts include the "human development index" (UNDP, 2000) and the "genuine progress indicator" (Cobb *et al.*, 1999). Another intriguing concept in this regard is the "gross national happiness," used in Bhutan.
17 See also Holme and Watts (2000).
18 Ohmae, himself, excused such practices by referring to precedents in Dickensian England and the "robber baron" era in America.
19 The case is reminiscent of an earlier crisis associated with the Ford Pinto, that brought Ralph Nader into public prominence in America. See Nader (1965) and Dowie (1977).
20 See also Cohen (1999) and Sen (2000).
21 It ranges from bribery, extortion, fraud, trafficking, embezzlement, to nepotism and cronyism. "Even...advantages, such as membership of an exclusive club or promises of scholarships for children, have been used as 'sweeteners' to clinch deals" (Quiñones, 2000). See Bowles (2000) for a recent survey of the relevant literature.
22 However, Hines (1995) contended that the Foreign Corrupt Practices Act of 1977 weakened the competitive positions of American firms, without significantly reducing the importance of bribery to foreign business transactions.
23 For non-orthodox perspectives on these issues, see Johnson (1999) and Henderson (1999).
24 The agencies range from NGOs such as Amnesty International and Human Rights Watch, to various United Nations agencies, to governmental agencies such as the US Department of State, and the British Foreign and Commonwealth Office. These organizations have regularly issued reports on the human rights situation in various countries and regions.
25 See the rebuttals by Fukuyama (1999) and Sen (1997). Indeed, Sen (1999) goes further, and advances the thesis of "development as freedom."
26 Fukuyama (1999) noted that "legitimacy was built on economic success and the view that authoritarian government was better at producing growth than democracy. The Asian crisis has...demonstrated the weakness of this position." See also Habermas (1976).
27 See various reports by Amnesty International, Human Rights Watch, US Department of State, United Nations Commission on Human Rights, and others.
28 One account noted that "This populous, resource-rich country was the flagship model of assisted development.... The World Bank endorsed the Indonesian model with $25 billion over three decades. International investors interpreted the World Bank's enthusiasm to lend as a sign that Indonesia was a prime investment environment. Foreign investment peaked at $18 billion in 1996" (Root, 2000: 228).

29 For descriptions of the gross outcomes of some megaprojects undertaken in Kalimantan and Irian Jaya, see Barber and Schweithelm (2000: 33–7).
30 "At the root of instability in Indonesia are not the insurgent movements but rather the impunity of the Indonesian armed forces which fuels these movements." This observation was made by Hendardi, the founder and director of Legal Aid Indonesia, at the inaugural conference for the Indonesian Human Rights Network, in Washington, DC on 28 February 2001.
31 "Political realism is a theory of political philosophy that ... takes as its assumption that power is (or ought to be) the primary end of political action .... Political realism in essence reduces to the political–ethical principle that might is right" (Moseley, 2001).
32 Specifically, two of Smith's often-cited passages proclaimed that:

> "It is not from the benevolence of the butcher, the brewer, or the baker, that we expect our dinner, but from their regard to their own interest. We address ourselves, not to their humanity but to their self-love, and never talk to them of our own necessities but of their advantages" *Wealth of Nations*, Book I, Chapter 2, paragraph 3; and

> "[The individual] generally, indeed, neither intends to promote the public interest, nor knows how much he is promoting it. ... he intends only his own security; and ... he intends only his own gain, and he is in this, as in many other cases, led by an invisible hand to promote an end which was no part of his intention. Nor is it always the worse for the society that it was no part of it. By pursuing his own interest he frequently promotes that of the society more effectually than when he really intends to promote it" *Wealth of Nations*, Book IV, Chapter 2, paragraph 9.

33 See, among others, Galbraith (1958), Harrington (1962), Strange (1986), Blumberg (1989), Omerod (1994), Herman (1995), Korten (1996), Harrison (1997), Lappe *et al.* (1998), Vidal (1998), Forrester (1999), Douthwaite (1999), Hayward (2000).
34 See Bello *et al.* (1982), Danaher (1994), Chossudovsky (1997), Krugman (1998), Tobin and Ranis (1998), Hellinger (2000), Woodroffe and Ellis-Jones (2000), Stiglitz (2000), and Bello (2001).
35 See Fombrun (1986), Robin and Reidenbach (1989), Chappell (1993), Anderson (1997), Harmon and Porter (1997), UNDP (1998), Kahn *et al.* (1999), Watts and Holme (1999), Cottrell and Rankin (2000) and Utting (2000).
36 In this regard, the ethical imperative is also 'the imperative of responsibility' emphasized by Jonas (1984). According to Jonas, the vast expansion of human powers creates the necessity for a new ethic, one that takes into consideration not just the present, but also the needs of future generations.

References

Aditjondro, G. (1998) Suharto & sons (and daughters, in-laws & cronies). *The Washington Post*, 25 January: C01.
Aditjondro, G. (2000) Indonesian forest fires. *Ecopolitics: Thought and Action* 1(1).

Anderson, C. (1997) Values-based management. *Academy of Management Executive* **11**(4): 25–46.

Barber, C. and Schweithelm, J. (2000) *Trial by Fire: Forest fires and forestry policy in Indonesia's era of crisis and reform*, Washington, DC: World Resources Institute.

Barraclough, S. (2001) Toward integrated and sustainable development? *UNRISD Overarching Concerns* Paper no. 1.

Bello, W. (1997) ASEAN's fateful choice: to 'enlarge' or to 'deepen'? *Focus on Trade*, July, **16**.

Bello, W. (2001) 2000: the year of global protest against globalization. *Focus on Trade*, January, **58**.

Bello, W., Kinley, D. and Elinson, E. (1982) *Development Debacle: The World Bank in the Philippines*, San Francisco, Institute for Food and Development Policy.

Bernstein, A. (2000) Too much corporate power? *BusinessWeek*, 11 September.

Blumberg, P. (1989) *The Predatory Society: Deception in the American Marketplace*, Oxford: OUP.

Bowles, R. (2000) "Corruption," in B. Bouckaert and G. De Geest (eds), *Encyclopedia of Law and Economics*, **5**, Cheltenham: Edward Elgar.

Brandt Commission (1983) *Common Crisis North–South: Co-operation for world recovery*, London: Pan.

Bronk, R. (1998) *Progress and the Invisible Hand: The Philosophy and Economics of Human Advance*, London: Little Brown.

Brookfield, H. and Byron, Y. (1993) *Southeast Asia's Environmental Future: The Search for Sustainability*, New York: United Nations University Press.

Bryce, R. (2000) Realpolitik. *The Austin Chronicle*, 19 May.

Carson, R. (1962) *Silent Spring*, Boston: Houghton Mifflin.

Celarier, M. (1998) The road to excess. *CFO Magazine*, 1 November.

Chappell, T. (1993) *The Soul of a Business: Managing for Profit and the Common Good*, Bantam Press.

Cheah, H. B. (2000) "The Asian Economic Crisis: Three perspectives on the unfolding problems in the global economy," in F. Richter (ed.), *The East Asian Development Model: Economic Growth, Institutional Failure and the Aftermath of the Crisis*, London: Macmillan.

Chomsky, N. (2000) *Rogue States: The Role of Force in World Affairs*, Cambridge, MA: South End Press.

Chomsky, N. and Herman, E. (1979) *The Washington Connection and Third World Fascism*, Cambridge, MA: South End Press.

Chossudovsky, M. (1997) *The Globalisation of Poverty: Impacts of IMF and World Bank Reforms*, London: Zed Books.

Clad, J. (1996) The end of Indonesia's New Order. *Wilson Quarterly*, Autumn.

Cobb, C., Goodman, G. and Wackernagel, M. (1999) *Why Bigger isn't Better: The Genuine Progress Indicator – 1999 Update*, San Francisco: Redefining Progress.

Cobb, C., Halstead, T. and Rowe, J. (1995) If the GDP is up, why is America down? *Atlantic Monthly*, October.

Cohen, G. (1999) *Bhopal and the Age of Globalisation*, Global Policy Forum, November.

Colborn, T., Dumanoski, D. and Myers, J. P. (1996) *Our Stolen Future: Are We Threatening Our Fertility, Intelligence, and Survival? A Scientific Detective Story*, New York: Dutton.

Connor, T. (2000) *Like Cutting Bamboo: Nike and Indonesian Workers' Right to Freedom of Association*, Community Aid Abroad – Oxfam Australia Briefing Paper no. 27.

Cottrell, G. and Rankin, L. (2000) *Creating Business Value through Corporate Sustainability*, Sydney: PricewaterhouseCoopers.

Danaher, K. (ed.) (1994) *50 Years is Enough: The Case Against the World Bank and the International Monetary Fund*, Cambridge: South End Press.

Dawson, C. (2001) At long last, lawsuits. *BusinessWeek* (International edition) 5, February.

Delaney, R. (2000) Business almost as usual for the Soeharto clan. *Sydney Morning Herald*, 19 May.

Dieter, H. (1998) Crises in Asia or crisis of globalisation? *Center for the Study of Globalisation and Regionalisation, Working Paper* no. 15/98, Coventry: CSGR.

Douthwaite, R. (1999) *The Growth Illusion: How Economic Growth has Enriched the Few, Impoverished the Many and Endangered the Planet*, Gabriola Island: New Society Publishers.

Dowie, M. (1977) Pinto madness. *Mother Jones*, September–October: 18–32.

Estes, R. (1992) *At the Crossroads: Dilemmas in Social Development Toward the Year 2000 and Beyond*, New York: Praeger.

Fombrun, C. (1986) *Realising Value from the Corporate Image*, Boston: Harvard University Press.

Forrester, V. (ed.) (1999) *The Economic Horror*, Cambridge: Polity Press.

Fukuyama, F. (1995) *Trust: The Social Virtues and the Creation of Prosperity*, London: Hamish Hamilton.

Fukuyama, F. (1999) *Asian Values in the Wake of the Current Crisis*. A paper presented at the *Conference on Democracy, Market Economy and Development*, at Seoul, Korea in February 1999.

Galbraith, J. K. (1958) *The Affluent Society*, London: Hamilton.

Galbraith, J. K. (1996) *The Good Society: The Humane Agenda*, Boston: Houghton Mifflin.

Gill, S. (1998) *The Pathology of Corruption*, New Delhi: Harper Collins.

Glover, D. and Jessup, T. (eds.) (1999) *Indonesia's Fires and Haze: The Cost of Catastrophe*, Ottawa: International Development Research Centre.

Goodman, P. (1993) Reebok, Nike and Levi Strauss on the prowl for cheap labour in Indonesia. *The Progressive*, 26 June.

Goulet, D. (1971) *The Cruel Choice: A New Concept in the Theory of Development*, New York: Atheneum.

Goulet, D. (1995) *Development Ethics: A Guide to Theory and Practice*, London: Zed Press.

Greenhouse, S. (1997) Nike shoe plant in Vietnam is called unsafe for workers. *New York Times*, 8 November.

GRI (2000) *Sustainability Reporting Guidelines on Economic, Environmental and Social Performance*, Boston: Global Reporting Initiative.

Habermas, J. (1976) *Legitimation Crisis*, London: Heinemann.

Haq, K. (1999) *Human Development in South Asia 1999*, Oxford: OUP.

Harman, W. and Porter, M. (eds.) (1997) *The New Business of Business: Sharing Responsibility for a Positive Global Future*, London: Berrett-Koehler Pub.

Harrington, M. (1962) *The Other America: Poverty in the United States*, New York: Macmillan.

Harrison, D. (1997) Greed fuels disaster of world-wide proportions. *The Observer*, 7 October.
Havely, J. (2000) Corruption: End of China's party? *BBC News Online*, 13 September.
Hawley, S. (2000) Exporting corruption: privatisation, multinationals and bribery. *The Corner House*, June.
Hayward, H. (2000) *Costing the Casino: The Real Impact of Currency Speculation in the 1990s*, London, War on Want.
Hazlitt, (1964) *The Foundations of Morality* (1972 edition), Los Angeles: Nash Pub.
Head, M. (1998) Australian business and the Indonesian regime. *World Social Web Site*, 26 May.
Hellinger, S. (2000) World Bank ignores own failure. *The Financial Times*, 23 June.
Henderson, C. (1999) Cronies and booty capitalism, *Asia Pacific Management Forum*, September.
Herman, E. (1995) *Triumph of the Market*, Cambridge, MA: South End Press.
Hines, J. (1995) Forbidden payment: Foreign bribery and American business after 1977. *NBER Working Paper* no. 5266.
Hirschhorn, J. (2000) *Growing Pains: Quality of Life in the New Economy*, Washington, DC: National Governors Association.
Holme, L. and Watts, P. (2000) *Corporate Social Responsibility: Making Good Business Sense*, Geneva: World Business Council for Sustainable Development.
Illich, I. (1973) "Outwitting the 'developed' countries," in H. Bernstein (ed.), *Underdevelopment and Development*, Harmondsworth: Penguin.
Inbaraj, S. (1997) *The Geopolitics of East Timor: A Media Perspective*. A paper presented at the *Conference on Alternative Security Systems in the Asia-Pacific*, Bangkok, 27–30 March.
Johnson, C. (1999) Let's revisit Asia's 'crony capitalism'. *Los Angeles Times*, 25 June.
Jonas, H. (1984) *The Imperative of Responsibility: In Search of an Ethics for the Technological Age*, Chicago: University of Chicago Press.
Kageyama, Y. (2000) Mitsubishi admits defect cover-up. *Columbus Dispatch*, 23 August.
Kahn, H., Peters, G. and Ponemon, L. (1999) *Reputation Assurance: The Value of a Good Name, re: Business*, PricewaterhouseCoopers, February.
Kaul, I., Grunberg, I. and Stern, M. (1999) *Global Public Goods: International Cooperation in the 21st Century*, Oxford: OUP.
Khandker, S. (1998) *Fighting Poverty with Microcredit: Experience in Bangladesh*, Oxford: OUP.
Kharbanda, O. and Stallworthy, E. A. (1986) *Management Disasters and How to Prevent Them*, Aldershot: Gower.
Korten, D. (1996) *When Corporations Rule the World*, West Hartford, CT: Kumarian Press.
Krugman, P. (1998) The confidence game: How Washington worsened Asia's crash. *The New Republic*, 5 October.
Kunii, I. (2000a) A cover-up at Mitsubishi? *BusinessWeek* (International edition), 9 October.
Kunii, I. (2000b) Can Japanese consumers stand up and fight. *BusinessWeek*, 11 September.
Lappe, F., Collins, J. and Rosset, P. (1998) *World Hunger: Twelve Myths* (2nd ed.), Oakland, CA: Grove Press.

Leaky, R. and Lewin, R. (1995) *The Sixth Extinction: Biodiversity and its Survival*, New York: Doubleday.
Lovelock, J. (1979) *Gaia: A New Look at Life on Earth*, Oxford: OUP.
Lyman, E. and Dolley, S. (2000) Accident-prone: The trouble at Tokaimura. *Bulletin of the Atomic Scientists* 56(2): 42–6.
Meadows, D. H., et al. (1972) *The Limits to Growth: A Report for the Club of Rome's Project on the Predicament of Mankind*, New York: Universe Books.
Meadows, D. H., Meadows, D. L. and Randers, J. (1992) *Beyond the Limits: Confronting Global Collapse, Envisioning a Sustainable Future*, Post Mills: Chelsea Green.
Millett, M. (2000) Police prepare case against car makers. *The Age*, 29 August.
Mirsky, J. (1999) Nothing to celebrate: China's wasted half century. *The New Republic*, October.
Mollison, B. (1990) *Permaculture: A Practical Guide for a Sustainable Future*, Washington, DC: Island Press.
Moseley, A. (2001) *Political Realism*, The Internet Encyclopedia of Philosophy.
Myrdal, G. (1968) *Asian Drama: An Inquiry into the Poverty of Nations*, Harmondsworth: Penguin.
Nader, R. (1965) *Unsafe at Any Speed: The Designed-in Dangers of the American Automobile*, New York: Grossman.
National Security Archive (2001) *Foreign Relations of the United States, 1964–68*, vol. XXVI, Washington, DC: George Washington University.
Ohmae, K. (2001) Asia's next crisis: 'Made in China', *Japan Times*, 30 July.
Omerod, P. (1994) *The Death of Economics*, London: Faber and Faber.
Osborn, A. (2000) Adidas attacked for Asian 'sweatshops'. *Guardian Unlimited*, 23 November.
Oxfam International (1998) *East Asian 'recovery' Leaves the Poor Sinking*, Oxfam International Briefing, October.
Quiñones, E. (2000) What is corruption? *OECD Observer*, 12 May.
Robin, D. and Reidenbach, R. (1989) *Business Ethics: Where Profits Meet Value Systems*, New Jersey: Prentice Hall.
Robinson, J. and Tinker, J. (1998) "Reconciling ecological, economic and social imperatives: Towards an analytical framework," in J. Schurr and S. Holtz (eds), *The Cornerstone of Development: Integrating Environmental, Social and Economic Policies*, London: Lewis Publishers.
Root, H. (2000) "Suharto's tax on Indonesia's future," in F. Richter (ed.), *The East Asian Development Model: Economic Growth, Institutional Failure and the Aftermath of the Crisis*, London: Macmillan.
Rosenthal, E. (2001) China's dark secret: AIDS and corruption in a poor province. *International Herald Tribune*, 31 May.
Sari, A. (1999) Environmental policy and crisis in Indonesia. *NIPA Review*, Summer.
Schumacher, E. F. (1974) *Small is Beautiful: A Study of Economics as if People Mattered*, London: Abacus.
Scott, P. (1985) The United States and the overthrow of Sukarno, 1965–1967. *Pacific Affairs*, Summer, **58**, 239–64.
Sen, A. (1987) *On Ethics and Economics*, Oxford: Blackwell.
Sen, A. (1997) Human rights and Asian values. *The New Republic*, 217(2–3).

Sen, A. (1999) *Development as Freedom*, New York: Knopf.
Sen, A. K. (2000) 120,000 survivors are in desperate need of medical attention. *The Asian Age*, 29 May.
Shari, M. (1999) Suharto billions may be sneaking back. *BusinessWeek* (International edition), 26 July.
Smith, Adam (1759) *The Theory of Moral Sentiments* (1982 edition), Indianapolis: Liberty Classics.
Smith, Adam (1776) *The Wealth of Nations* (1937 edition), New York: Modern Library.
Social Development Department (2000) *New Paths to Social Development: Community and Global Networks in Action*, Washington, DC: World Bank.
Stiglitz, J. (2000) The insider: What I learned at the world economic crisis. *The New Republic*, 17 April.
Strange, S. (1986) *Casino Capitalism*, Oxford: Blackwell.
Suryahadi, A., Sumarto, S., Suharso, Y. and Pritchett, L. (2000) *The Evolution of Poverty during the Crisis in Indonesia, 1996 to 1999*. World Bank *Working Paper* no. 2435, Washington, DC: World Bank.
Tanter, R. (1998) Suharto, war criminal. *Inside Indonesia*, no. 55.
Templer, R. (1998) *Shadows and Wind: A View of Modern Vietnam*, London: Little Brown.
Tobin, J. and Ranis, G. (1998) Flawed fund: the IMF's misplaced priorities. *The New Republic*, 9 March.
Ui, J. (1992) *Industrial Pollution in Japan*, Tokyo: United Nations University Press.
UNCED (1992) *Agenda 21: Report of the United Nations Conference on Environment and Development*, Rio de Janeiro, 3–14 June 1992, New York: United Nations.
UNDP (1998) *Corruption and Integrity Improvement in Developing Countries*, New York: UNDP.
UNDP (2000) *Human Development Report 2000*, New York: Oxford University Press.
UNITE (2000) *Sweatshops Behind the Swoosh*, New York: Union of Needletrades, Industrial and Textile Employees.
UNRISD (2000) *Visible Hands: Taking Responsibility for Social Development*, Geneva: UNRISD.
Utting, P. (2000) *Business Responsibility for Sustainable Development*. Geneva 2000 *Occasional Paper* no. 2, Geneva: UNRISD.
Vidal, J. (1998) *McLibel: Burger Culture on Trial*, New York: New Press.
Watts, P. and Holme, L. (1999) *Corporate Social Responsibility: Meeting Changing Expectations*, Geneva: World Business Council for Sustainable Development.
WBCSD (1996) *Environmental Assessment: A Business Perspective*, Geneva: WBCSD.
WBCSD (1999) *Eco-efficiency Indicators and Reporting*, Geneva: WBCSD.
Wheeler, D. et al. (2000) *Greening Industry: New Roles for Communities, Markets and Governments*, Washington, DC, World Bank.
Wingfield-Hayes, R. (2000) China audit finds billions stolen. *BBC News Online*, 27 October.
Wolfensohn, James (1999) *A Proposal for a Comprehensive Development Framework*. A statement to the Board, Management and staff of the World Bank group, 21 January.

Wong, M. (2000) Children toil in sweatshop. *South China Morning Post*, 27 August.
Woodroffe, J. and Ellis-Jones, M. (2000) States of unrest: resistance to IMF policies in poor countries. *World Development Movement Report*, September.
World Commission on Environment and Development (1987) *Our Common Future: From One Earth to One World*, Oxford: Oxford University Press.

Index

accountability, 49, 51, 54, 58, 99
accounting transparency, 39
Annual Wage Supplement (AWS), 188
anomie, 11–12, 14
anti-bribery commitment, 167
anti-competition law, 168
anti-corruption
　activities, 183
　compliance programs, 171–2, 175–6
　laws, 168–9
　management systems, 170
　programs, 199
　strategy, 22, 180, 182, 184, 188, 190, 193–5
Anti-Corruption Agency (ACA), 192
Anti-Corruption Branch (ACB), 182
'armament gifts', 117–19, 122, 126, 128
Art of War, 92–4, 102, 104
　ideological system of strategy, 94
Asahi Newspaper Foundation, 166, 172
'Asian crisis', 237
'Asian values', 235
asymmetric learning, 9, 11, 15
audit trails, 18

balance sheets
　cleaning up, 56
banqueting, 123
Barraclough, S., 241
Becker, G. S., 133
benevolence, 95–6
'black economy', 30
'blue collar workers', 7
Boryokudan (violent groups), 158
Bottelier, P., 166
Bourdieu, P., 108–9, 114, 126–7
bowing (*jugong*), 113
brain drain, 188–9
　from the civil service, 188
bribery, 33, 39, 98, 180, 184
bribery offences
　domestic, 167
bribes
　tax deductibility of, 40
bribe takers, 139, 141–2

bribing (*xinghui*), 107, 109
buddhist approach, 212
　to morality, 212–14
Burton, J., 8
business gift, 116
business groups
　moral characteristics of, 217–18
business interaction, 89

"4 Cs", 62
capital mobility, 45
Carlisle, T., 204
Chabal, P., 108
chaebols, 62
Chang, H. C., 67
Chan, W. T., 91
Cheo, R. K. S., 57
Cheung, S. N. S., 140
the Chinese business world, 114
　gifts in, 114–26
the Chinese mind
　understanding, 102
chin-shins (confidantes), 77
chit-chat (*liaotiaor*), 118
Chomsky, N., 240
Chu, C. N., 101
civil service salaries, 188
　improving, 188–90
Clifford, M. L., 44
"cliques", 64
code of conduct, 172
'cognitive dissonance', 6
Cohen, W. M., 3
Cold War, 239
collective responsibility, 88
collectivism, 19, 61, 71, 76
collusion, 62
competence (*chaineng*), 74
competition, 164
competitive advantage
　analysis of, 2
complacency, 62
compliance manuals, 174
compliance offices, 175
composure, 96
comprehensive strategy, 183
　anti-corruption strategy, 183–4

Confucianism, 19, 61, 92, 167
  the Confucian philosophy, 87–90
Confucian values, 66–8
Confucius, 20, 87
consensus-orientation equity, 51
control of implementation, 173
conventional morality, 213, 221
'co-opetition', 9
  mode, 11, 15
corporate extortionists, 149
corporate fraud, 58
corporate governance, 15, 18, 43,
  46–8, 50, 166
  poor, 1
corporate governance practices, 53
corporate–government cronyism, 193
corporate restructuring, 43, 47, 53, 57
  in the East Asian economie, 53
corporate social responsibility, 230
  violations of, 230–2
corporations
  value destroying, 164
corruption, 28–9, 44, 49, 62, 107,
  109, 131–3, 137, 139, 143–5, 166,
  172, 180, 184–5, 199, 210, 232
  addressing the problem of, 199
  in Asia, 210
  economic analysis of, 132
  economic impact of, 29
  fight against, 172–4
  in India, 199
  nature of, 28–30
  network of, 144
  as a problem of morality, 133
  various forms of gratification, 185
Corruption Perceptions Index (CPI),
  180–1
corrupt practices, 40
Corrupt Practices Investigation
  Bureau (CPIB), 183, 186–8
courage, 96
Covey, S. R., 204
Cragg, W., 52
criminal corruption, 199
'crony capitalism', 62, 234, 236
cronyism, 12, 18–19, 43–4, 49, 54,
  61–4, 66, 73, 79, 131–5, 137,
  142–5
  in Chinese societies, 79
  cultural antecedents of, 66–73
  immediate antecedents of, 73–8
  as a labour market problem, 135
  as a network for discrimination,
    142, 144
  origin of, 63–4

as a problem of morality, 133
  in work organizations, 19, 61–2
  two-stage model of, 61
  cultural factors, 154–5
  for sokaiya existence, 154
cultural literacy
  lack of, 10

Daloz, J. P., 108
dark-side strategies, 21
debt restructuring, 56
'dematerialization'
  of the economy, 242
deregulation, 233
Dey, P., 52
Dirou, P., 55–6
disciplinary actions, 174
dispassion, 100
"due diligence", 170–1
  global model of, 171
Dunning, J. H., 11
dynamism, 89

Earley, P. C., 71, 80
East Asian economies, 48–50, 57
  corporate governance problems,
    48–50
ecological imperative, 229, 237–8
economic factors
  for sokaiya existence, 155
economic imperative, 229, 236–7
economic reform
  deregulation-induced, 164
economic sustainability, 241
Edwards, J. S., 2
embezzlement, 47, 139, 151, 180
emerging individuality, 213
emotional corruption, 199
emptiness, 98
endurance
  power of, 100
Engardio, P., 44
the Enron debacle, 16
the ethical imperative, 226, 229–30,
  236
  transgressions of, 230, 239–40
equitable risk sharing, 51
equity markets, 49
ethical behavior
  in organizations, 198
ethical decision-making, 199
ethical failure, 238
ethics compliance, 176
ethics management, 175
the European Union, 32–5

Index 253

exploitative practices, 232
extortion, 180

face (*mianzi*), 111
'facilitation payments', 31, 39
Fairholm, G. W., 72
favoritism, 63, 65
feeling (*ganqing*), 124
Fei Xiatong, 111
Ferrell, O. C., 199
Financial Action Task Force (FATF), 35
financial institution
    customer-oriented, 54
Financial Stability Forum (FSF), 37
financial transparency, 199
flattery, 98
Flew, A., 219
Foreign Direct Investment (FDI), 11
foreign investors, 38, 54, 164
    in Japanese companies, 163
    withholding tax, 38
fraud, 47
'friendship' relationship, 119
Fruin, W. M., 8

GAPP (Generally Acceptable
    Accounting Principles), 5
Gender Empowerment Measure, 228
Gender-related Development Index,
    228
genuine altruism, 213–14, 221
Ghani, R. A., 3
gift (*songli*), 124
gift-giver
    skilled, 119
gift-giving, 4, 20, 107–8, 114, 122,
    126–8, 154
    in Chinese businesses, 107
    complexities of, 126
    notion of time in, 108, 126–8
    sophisticated choreography of, 107
global economy, 1, 18
Goman, C. K., 78
Goodwin, R., 65
Gordon, K., 167, 174
governance
    'corporate' aspect of, 4
    cultural view of, 61
    oppression of, 1
government 'interventionism', 30
Graham, G. 64
grand corruption, 28
Granitas, A., 58
Granovetter, M. S., 13
Grant, R. M., 2

'grenades' (*shouliudan*), 116
group moral development
    hierarchy of, 215–16
group-oriented culture, 155
guanxi, 4, 65, 67, 70, 89, 107, 110–11
    and gifts, 110–14
    networks, 12, 113–14, 122
    in a relationship-based society, 70
    "*guanxi* capitalism", 49
'guided missiles', 107, 109, 122,
    125–6, 128
    as gifts, 122–5

Hagelin, J. S., 204
Haley, J. O., 156
'hand-grenades', 107, 116
    new categories of gifts, 116
'hand-grenades and machine
    guns', 109
Haq, K., 233
Hayek, F. A. V., 12
Heider, J., 91
Helfer, R. T., 50
Hendrischke, H., 135
He, Q., 121
Herman, E., 240
high Power Distance, 80
Hill, C. W. L., 12
Hofstede, G., 13, 71
Holland, L., 50
Holme, L., 230
Holt, G. R., 67
Howes, M. A., 212
Huang, G., 111–12
Huber, G. P., 7
'human development index', 228
'human poverty index', 228, 243
human rights violations, 234
Husted, B. W., 72
Hwang, K. K., 67

illegal gratification, 185
"image management" program, 163
incremental strategy, 182
    anti-corruption strategy, 182–3
Independent Commission Against
    Corruption (ICAC), 192
influence peddling, 180
information and communications
    technology (ICT), 3
information elicitation, 7
ingroup members, 73
    selection of, 73–4
Inkpen, A., 8
insider (*neiburen*), 117

institutional barriers, 155
institutional investors, 49
"institutionalization", 171
'integrity pacts', 39
intellectual capital
  role of, 2
internalization, 104
International Accounting Standards Committee, IASC, 5
international management practice, 174

Japanese management practices, 174
Japanese stock market bubble, 162
Jayasankaran, S., 50
Jen, 88
Kali, R., 112
Kanda, M., 3
Kautz, K., 12
Kawai, M., 44
keiretsu, 62
Kidd, J. B., 2–3, 5, 89–90
Kim, U., 71
Kipnis, A. B., 113
knowledge imitability, 2
knowledge management (KM), 2
Knutt, E., 88
Koh, P. T., 46
Korean First Bank (KFB), 54
kowtowing (*ketou*), 113
Kpundeh, S. J., 192
Krackhardt, D., 70
Krugman, 45

Lachica, E., 49
lack of transparency, 76
  contributing factor to corruption, 76
Lao Tzu, 20, 86–7, 90–2
  founder of Taoism, 90
Lau, D. C., 90
learning in alliances
  dynamics of, 8, 11–14
Lee, C. S., 48, 54
Lee Zhong Wu, 97
legalized corruption, 199
leninist state-party system, 132
Leung, T. K. P., 89
Leventhal, D. A., 3
Levi-Strauss, C., 109–10
li (profit), 90
Liang, S. M., 111
Linstone, H., 6
Longstaff, S., 52

Lovett, S., 112
Low, S. P., 94, 97, 102
loyalty (*zhongcheng*), 74, 77
  overemphasis on, 77–8
loyalty upwards, 78

'machine guns' (*Jiguangqiang*), 107, 116
  new categories of gifts, 116
Maharishi Mahesh Yogi, 201, 205
mainstream ethical theory, 210
management, 204
  natural-law based, 204–5
market corruption, 199
market discipline, 43, 50
market liberalization, 145
Mauro, P., 30
Merry, P., 10
'methodological individualist', 219
the mind of the Chinese
  understanding, 86
  sokaiya, 158
Mitsubishi Motors Corporation, 21, 150, 231
Miyake, M., 167, 174
Mohan, S. C., 187
money laundering, 18, 27, 35, 41, 58, 168, 199
  curtailing, 199
monitoring mechanisms, 173
monopolistic rent, 139
Moore, C. A., 113
moral development, 200, 202–3, 211
  impact of TM on, 202–4
  stages of, 200–1
moral hazard, 49
moral hierarchy, 213–14
moral improvement
  collective commitment to, 222
morality
  based on mutual expectations, 200
moral reasoning
  principled, 200, 203
Morgan Stanley Asset Management Trust, 176
Mushkat, M., 45

National Wages Council (NWC), 188
natural law, 204
Neilson, W. S., 134
nepotism, 12, 65, 132, 134, 180
'network capitalism', 111
"newsletters"
  sokaiya-run, 154
North, D., 133

OECD Bribery Convention, 167
Off-Shore Financial Centres (OFC), 27, 36–8
open governance, 53
  within knowledge-based companies, 53
opportunism, 89
'ordinary business gift', 126–7
'ordinary gifts', 116
organizational learning (OL), 2
Ott, J. S., 64
out-of-court settlement, 57

Pan, A., 121
"pangloss value", 45
participation in governance, 51
passivity, 92
paternalism, 19, 61, 77, 80
patronage corruption, 199
patronage downwards, 78
'patron–client relationship', 121
payoffs, 161
Pepper, G. L., 64
personal connections (*guanxi*), 20
personal relationships
  over emphasis on, 76
personalism, 77
Petronas, 50
petty corruption, 28
Pinto, J. K., 64
political cronyism, 61
"political will", 192
poor governance, 44
Posner, R. A., 144
Power Distance, 76
  'the power-economy', 121
pre-moral stage, 213
Prevention of Corruption Act (POCA), 184–6
Prevention of Corruption Ordinance (POCO), 22, 182
Pride, W. M., 199
principal–agent problem, 28
principal–agent relations, 136, 140, 145
private sector, 38
  role of the, 38–9
"private to private" corruption, 168
privatization, 233
protectionism, 89
Proton, 50
Prowse, S., 47, 49, 52
public procurement practices, 199

Quah, J. S. T., 182–3

Rape of Nanjin, 87
Ray, M. L., 204
reciprocal "favors", 125, 127–8, 167
reciprocity, 88
record-keeping, 174
Redding, S. G., 68, 73, 77, 111
reformed economy, 164
reform of governance
  an institutional approach, 131
"relational personalism", 67–8
relationship (*guanxi*), 74
renqing (to give a gift), 67–8, 112, 117–18, 121, 127
renqing debt, 122
renqing favour, 120
'resocialization'
  of the society, 242
resource-bank availability, 173
respect (*jingyi*), 113
return on sales, 162
Richter, F.-J., 8
Rickett, W. A., 16
Ring, P. S., 6
ritual gifts
  'traditional', 113
ritual of gift-giving, 122
Rose-Ackermann, S., 167
Roth, R., 201

Sangharakshita, Ven, 220
Sari, A., 238
Scott, K., 46
Scott, P., 236
Scott, W. R., 167
Securities Commission (SC), 55
self-praise, 98
sempai–kohai (senior–junior) relationships, 154
sensitivity training
  about business integrity, 173
shengwuxüe, 108
Shleifer, A., 141
Simmons, L. C., 112
Simonin, B. L., 8
sincerity, 95
small and medium sized firms (SMEs), 3
the social imperative, 229
sokaiya, 21, 151–2, 158, 160–1, 163, 216
  modus operandi, 151–4
  paying off a, 163

sokaiya activities, 149, 156, 163
  attempts to control, 156
sokaiya "general meeting handlers", 149
sokaiya payoffs, 155
sokaiya phenomenon, 21
sokaiya-related infraction, 150
sokaiya scandals, 156, 158
Spender, J.-C., 2
state of anomie, 14
strictness, 96
Sun Tzu, 20, 86–7, 92
supervisors, 174
sustainable development, 225–6, 229, 235, 241
  a process of change, 241
  'sustainable development index' (SDI), 228
  'swapping of identical gifts', 127
Szulanski, G., 7
Szymkowiak, K., 150

Taka, I., 167
Tang, C. S. K., 65
Taoism, 91–2, 104
Tao Te Ching, 90–2, 102
Teramoto, Y., 5
'the art' of networking–*guanxixüe*, 108
The Wealth of Nations, 240
the Thick Black Theory, 87, 97, 99, 101–2, 104
Thick Face, Black Heart, 100–1
  doctrine of, 100
  state of the mind, 101
"*tokushu kabunushi*" (special shareholders), 151
training
  for compliance, 175
transcendental consciousness, 201, 204–5
transcendental meditation programs, 201, 206
transcendental meditation technique, 202, 203
transcendental morality, 213–14, 221
transitional economies, 29, 31
transparency, 49, 51, 54, 58
Transparency International (TI), 180, 232
Triandis, H. C., 71
trust, 5
  between individual, 5–6

Tsai, C. C., 91
Tsang, D., 52
Tsang, E. W. K., 65

Umi-no-Ie affair, 161
Umi-no-Ie case, 160
uncertainty avoidance, 76
United Nations Development Program (UNDP), 228
universalist argument, 155–6
  for *sokaiya* existence, 155
unsustainable development, 235
Ursacki, T., 154

Van de Ven, A. H., 6
Vendelø, M. T., 12
Vishny, R. W., 141
Vogl, F., 62
voluntary Codes of Conduct, 39
"voluntary contributions", 141
Wade, R., 167
Walder, A. G., 64
Watts, P., 230
'Weltanschauung,' 220
West, M. D., 152–3
'whistleblowers', 32
'whistleblowing', 41
whistle blowing facility, 174
white-collar criminals, 58
Wie, S., 30
Williamson, O., 167
'win–win' situation, 8, 11, 15
Wisdom, 95
Wong, Y. H., 89
'working on *guanxi*', 120, 121
World Commission on Environment and Development (WCED), 225
'world view', 220
wu-lun, 67, 89

yakuza (Japanese mafia), 53
Yan, Y., 113, 124
Yang, M., 118, 123, 134
Yap, P. P. Y., 55
"*yato sokaiya*" ("incumbent party *sokaiya*"), 152
Yeo, K. K., 94
yi (justice), 90

Zhu, Z., 6